Johannes Lischka

Semantic-based E-Learning Framework

Johannes Lischka

Semantic-based E-Learning Framework

E-Learning Shift: from a Technology Driven to an Organizationally Driven Discipline that is Supported by ICT with the Help of an Engineering Approach

VDM Verlag Dr. Müller

Imprint

Bibliographic information by the German National Library: The German National Library lists this publication at the German National Bibliography; detailed bibliographic information is available on the Internet at http://dnb.d-nb.de.

Cover image: www.purestockx.com

Publisher:
VDM Verlag Dr. Müller Aktiengesellschaft & Co. KG, Dudweiler Landstr. 125 a, 66123 Saarbrücken, Germany,
Phone +49 681 9100-698, Fax +49 681 9100-988,
Email: info@vdm-verlag.de

Produced in USA and UK by:
Lightning Source Inc., La Vergne, Tennessee, USA
Lightning Source UK Ltd., Milton Keynes, UK
BookSurge LLC, 5341 Dorchester Road, Suite 16, North Charleston, SC 29418, USA

ISBN: 978-3-8364-9697-1

Contents

List of Figures

List of Code-Examples

List of Tables

List of Abbreviations

ADL	ADONIS Definition Language
AI	Artificial Intelligence
AICC	Aviation Industry CBT Committee
API	Application Programming Interface
ARIADNE	Alliance of Remote Instructional Authoring and Distribution Networks for Europe
B2B	Business-to-Business
BM:BWK	Austrian Federal Ministry for Education, Science and Culture
BPEL4WS	Business Process Execution Language for Web-Services
BPM	Business Process Management
BPSS	Business Process Specification Schema
BSC	Balanced Scorecard
CBT	Computer based Training
CEN/CENELEC	Comité Européen de Normalisation/European Committee for Electrotechnical Standardization
CMI	Computer Managed Instruction
CMS	Content Management System
CORBA	Common Object Request Broker Architecture
DARPA	U.S. Defense Advanced Research Project Agency
DCMI	Dublin Core Meta-data Initiative
DCOM	Distributed Component Object Model
DKE	Department of Knowledge Engineering
EAI	Enterprise Application Integration
EDI	Electronic Data Interchange
EML	Educational Modeling Language
FDL	MQSeries Workflow Definition Language
GXA	Global XML Web Services Architecture
HDM	Hypertext Design Model

HTTP	Hypertext Transfer Protocol
ICT	Information (and Communication) Technology
IEEE	Institute of Electrical and Electronics Engineers
IIOP	Internet Inter-ORB Protocol
IMS	Instructional Management Systems
INRIA	l'Institut National de Recherche en Informatique et en Automatique
ISO	International Organization for Standardization
ISSS	Information Society Standardization System
J2ME	Java 2 Platform, Micro Edition
KIF	Knowledge Interchange Format
KM	Knowledge Management
KMP	KM Process
KMR	KM Research
L(C)MS	Learning (Content) Management System
LMML	Learning Material Markup Language
LO	Learning Object
LOM	Learning Object Meta-data
LP	Learner Profile
LTSA	Learning Technology Systems Architecture
LTSC	Learning Technologies Standard Committee
LTWS	Learning Technologies Workshop
MBI	Master of Business Informatics
MOF	Meta Object Facility
NADA	Numerical analysis and computer science
OASIS	Organization for the Advancement of Structured Information Standards
OHDM	Object-oriented Hypermedia Design Model
OM	Organizational Memory
PAPI	Public and Private Information
PROLOG	PROgramming in Logic
RDF	Resource Description Framework
RDF-QEL-i	RDF Query Exchange Language
RMI	Remote Method Invocation
RMM	Relationship Management Methodology
ROI	Return on Investment
RQL	RDF Query Language
RSS	RDF Site Summary

SCORM	Sharable Content Object Reference Model
SGML	Standard Generalized Markup Language
SHOE	Simple HTML Ontology Extensions
SOA	Service-oriented Architecture
SOAP	Simple Object Access Protocol
SWOT	Strengths, Weaknesses, Opportunities, Threats
UDDI	Universal Description, Discovery and Integration of Web-Services
UML	Unified Modeling Language
URI	Uniform Resource Identifiers
VGU	Virtual Global University
W3C	World Wide Web Consortium
WBT	Web-Based Training
WFM	Workflow Management
WfMS	Workflow Management System
WG	Working Group
WS	Web-Service
WSBPEL	Web Services Business Process Execution Language
WSCL	Web-Services Conversation Language
WSDL	Web-Services Description Language
WSFL	Web-Services Flow Language
WSRP	Web Services Remote Portlets
WWW	World-wide Web
XML	Extensible Markup Language
XMLS	XML Schema
XTM	XML Topic Maps
XTMP	XTM Processing Model

Abstract

The discipline of E-Learning emerged among many others on the verge of the 21st century as a technological answer to new forms of online education.

Since its advent due to an often seen hype-phenomenon, experts and analysts tend to state that the term "E-Learning" will soon disappear, as learning itself is a main focus and ingredient of human life per se. Nowadays, termini like learning enhanced with Educational Technologies, life-long learning and knowledge society coin the fact that electronic means have to be used to reach and connect individuals anywhere, anytime and anyplace in order to integrate them into an educational lifecycle.

The structure of this PhD thesis is aligned to the following ideas: first, it puts the scope of learning into a scientific setting of the business informatics domain, a blended field trying to bridge the gap between organizational requirements and technological implementation; second, using these scientific findings, a survey and State-of-the-Art report marks contemporary solutions and technologies when talking about E-Learning; third and fourth, taking today's technology centered situation into account, an E-Learning Framework together with the conceptual approach for E-Learning Engineering is introduced in order to structure and identify learning scenarios; fifth and sixth, all theoretical and conceptual research is put into action with two test-beds.

Speaking of the actual content, this thesis highlights a small segment of E-Learning scrutinizing the topic from several angles. On the one hand, a historical evolution on the basis of an E-Learning Framework is sketched, spanning E-Learning according to four dimensions, namely Management, Didactics, Content and Technology. Focusing on the Technology dimension, two different scenarios are presented in order to reflect the paradigm shift in contemporary learning situations, namely the transition from stand-alone proprietary solutions to globally distributed and inter-weaved learning resources. On the other hand, a learning scenario is examined from an instructor's point of view; depending on the learning requirements and an actual situation, an instructor either has his learning sequences already in mind building mainly in existing material, or he is still not aware of the actual learning structure, because the application field is too heterogeneous from his domain point of view.

Both viewpoints of the regarded E-Learning segment are then shown with actual test-beds or prototypes: the first - called Document-centric Learning approach - using mainly XML technologies for exchanging and engineering learning resources, and the second - called Resource-driven Learning approach - making use of new software application frameworks based on the service-oriented architecture and Semantic Web techniques.

In a nutshell, instructors are provided with two different mechanisms to structure and organize their content, depending on the problem scenario. This approach enables a degree of flexibility depending on the instructor's organizational and technical setting as well as his personal interests and preferred application surroundings.

Chapter 1

Introduction

E-Learning has become one of the most dominant technologies in computer sciences[1]. The term life-long learning has diffused into various disciplines like Knowledge Management (KM), Business Process Management (BPM) and of course E-Learning itself, to name but a few.

1.1 Exposition

The term E-Learning was coined somewhere in the mid 1990-ies to express the urgent need for Information and Communication Technology (ICT) to do something about the learning and training of computer and system users on the one hand and to introduce ICT to educational institutions on all levels on the other hand.

Yet another E-Term was invented, lacking a distinct and specific definition for itself, with no connection to other E-Terms (is E-Learning a part of E-Business or vice versa) and therefore facing the problem of getting a proprietary solution. Fortunately, standardization in E-Learning is a big topic and the fact, that the Institute of Electrical and Electronics Engineers (IEEE) has already passed the Learning Objects Meta-data (LOM) standard shows great potential for interoperability and scalability in E-Learning. Unfortunately, State-of-the-Art applications lack interfaces to these standards or only produce poor command-line tools.

Almost at the same time with these developments in E-Learning, new areas are evolving: Semantic Web, ontologies, Web-Services, etc., that have also been adopted by the E-Learning community. But together with the ill-implemented standard interfaces and the early dispute with these new developments leave E-Learning in a difficult position,

---

[1] The discipline or term 'computer science(s)' is used as a representative or subsumption term for all fields concerning ICT, information systems, (business) informatics, etc.

because it has to make a quantum leap from monolithic application to heavily distributed Peer-to-Peer architectures on top of a service-oriented architecture. These facts endanger E-Learning to end up as technology-driven discipline, neglecting top-level business strategies.

Compared to other - non ICT-driven disciplines - the accordance between domain requirements and technical requirements is reached by introducing engineering methods and visual modeling (plans) that bring together both worlds. Visual modeling is one of the primary means of reducing the complexity and cognitive load during the design of a system. With the help of visual models the understanding of a problem can be made easily accessible to different people by defining a shared language. Take Architecture: an architect models a building defining its dimensions, the type of material that is to be used, the electrical wiring, etc. The models/plans that are sketched employ a common language that can be used to convey the ideas to the builders and stakeholders, making up the requirements for mechanical engineers, electricians, etc. Via visual models, domain requirements and technical solution are aligned. E.g. in Software Engineering the Unified Modeling Language (UML)[2] has emerged as the common conceptual, visual language for systems design. Despite the claims of some authors[3], there are at this time no commonly used visual languages for instructional design and E-Learning. While the design and development of E-Learning activities surely has a high degree of structural and communication complexity[4], instructors, instructional designers, and educational technology staff do not have plans or blueprints for their E-Learning environments.

Exactly this hiatus is the motivation for the thesis at hand that tries to tackle this problem with the following propositions which can be seen as requirements for the Roadmap towards life-long learning:

- Presentation of an E-Learning Framework to categorize learning scenarios according to different dimensions

- Linking E-Learning to strategic issues, methodologies and domain requirements according to this Framework

- The Framework has to be instantiated with the help of E-Learning Engineering and visual modeling methods either aligned to the Document-centric or a Resource-driven approach

---

[2]See [209]
[3]See [99] and [100]
[4]See [1]

- Using State-of-the-Art ICT (Educational Technologies) to reflect a new learning paradigm

  - Defining learning specific Modeling Methods (Skills, Learning Objects, Exams, Tests, etc.)
  - Defining resources according to Semantic Web technologies
  - Executing business and learning logic with Web-Services

According to these enumerated visions, the structure of the thesis first copes with E-Learning itself and step-by-step adds pieces to form a holistic puzzle. Chapter 1.2 goes into more detail about the outline of topics. But before stepping in medias res an excursion into scientific methods and the deployed scientific instance in computer science for this thesis is presented.

1.1.1 Scientific research methods and philosophy of science

Scientific research methods in philosophy, in natural sciences like mathematics or physics and in social sciences are long established ones. A science may be defined as a *"procedure for answering questions, solving problems and developing more effective procedures for answering questions and solving problems"*[5]. Science uses scientific methods and methodologies.

But what about economical sciences and computer sciences? Literature about scientific methods[6] and philosophy of science is rare, especially when coming towards application oriented business informatics. The debate on questions in philosophy of science and methodological approaches is sometimes related to *"nonsense chattering"* and lacking of factual and relevant treatment of research[7]. This especially holds true with the use of methodologies. In the following, the focus lies on methods applied in economical science and computer sciences, especially the branch Business Informatics.

Having discussed these methods, a conjoint subsumption will set grounds for the method that this thesis is based on.

---

[5][2], p. 1 and p. 6

[6]A scientific method needs to be appropriate for communication and teaching, normative and prescriptive and inter-subjectively manageable (see [262], p. 2)

[7]See [51], p. 5, and [333], p. 5

1.1.1.1 Economical sciences

Philosophy of science in economical sciences has to be strictly separated from any theological ideas of philosophy: the aim is to evaluate and check theories[8] on the basis of rational assertions in order to conclude with socio-critical and "enlightening" assumptions; the use of a methodology to align the scientific process is hereby essential[9].

A generic methodology - with no claim to being complete and ordered - in economical sciences based on empirical studies may look as follows[10]:

- Searching for topic and definitive description of the problem area

- Definition of terms

- Preparing and execute empirical research (operationalization/implementation)

- Evaluation

- Creating hypothesis and theory

- Creating an evaluation report

Important differences in comparison to other disciplines can be seen in the handling of technology[11] in economical sciences; whereas other disciplines seek for solutions in terms of cause and effect, economical science is target-driven, seeking for the means to reach the goal[12]. In this context, theories may be clustered into two different characteristics[13]:

1. Scientific theory: concerned with cause-and-effect (pure science)

2. Technological theory: related to the output of scientific theories (applied science)

Speaking of theories, an often used concept or tool to support them is to use the concept of modeling. A model is a picture of reality[14] representing states, objects and events[15]. With the help of modeling, complex situations can be abstracted. Normally, modeling is

---

[8]Theories can be defined as general assertions or laws with special properties and contents. Theories serve for subsumption, coordination, reproduction, explanation and prediction of phenomena (see [258], p. 636). The complementary discipline is practical proof of the theory.

[9]See [51], p. 5

[10]Composed from [38] or [262]

[11]The concept "technology" is not restricted to engineering but has also the dimension of target-aimed design (see [51], p. 169).

[12]See [51], p. 169

[13]See [38], p. 105; for pure and applied science see [2], p. 7

[14]See [333], p. 1

[15]See [2], p. 108

based on a trial-and-error process[16].

Modeling is only one tool in economical sciences. Philosophy of science also supports a variety of scientific methods, from which some are mentioned in the following enumeration[17]:

- Modeling

- Quantitative methods

  - Judging

  - Testing

  - Questioning

  - Monitoring

  - Physiological measuring

- Qualitative methods

1.1.1.2 Computer sciences

Computer sciences until today are lacking a pure definition and distinction of its scientific methods: some people see computer sciences as a branch of mathematics, as an engineering discipline or as a social science; some people even deny the scientific character to computer sciences[18].

Computer sciences include mainly four disciplines:

- Theoretical computer sciences

- Applied computer sciences

- Technical computer sciences

- Practical computer sciences.

Philosophy of science especially fits into theoretical computer sciences[19]. The "science" in computer sciences tries to explain processes within a computer including explanations for computers themselves; besides these explanation efforts, the discipline of programming has emerged to be a key method within computer sciences purely representing the need

---

[16]See [333], p. 2

[17]See general literature on research methods such as [38] or [262]

[18]See statements from different literature in [110], p. 13 and 14, and [42], p. 91

[19]See [237], p. 1

to implement subjective and non-scientific requirements[20].

Computer sciences therefore are a purely technical discipline that sometimes lacks scientific methods and use of methodologies due to its applied character. Computer sciences do not long for explicit theories but are searching for techniques to solve problems without the need for theoretical explanation[21].

Referring to computer sciences as a science, the following scientific methods can be used[22]:

- Formal methods (Boolean algebra, predicative programming languages, etc.)

- Axiomatic methods

- Empirical methods

- Constructivist methods (arising from practical scenarios in everyday life)

1.1.1.3 Conjoint method for Business Informatics

The philosophy of Business Informatics:

> *"Do not look for fundamental truths or universal explanations - search for pragmatic solutions!"* (Referring to a discussion with Dimitris Karagiannis)
> *"Search for orderliness in technically supported experiences and the 'nature' of support."* (Referring to a discussion with Renate Motschnig)

Business Informatics is a hybrid science, taking the best parts from computer sciences and economical sciences. Especially the criticism on computer sciences on being only technically-driven, Business Informatics is an interface between human and economical requirements and technical implementation.

Business Informatics can be seen as a subsumption of a number of theories, e.g. Business Process Management, Knowledge Management, Semantic Web, Business Intelligence, etc., with the problem to lack of central definitions and being outdated soon after their invention: there is no conjoint taxonomy of Business Informatics and its related theories; furthermore, Business Informatics is an applied science, that is taken seriously when reaching a certain level of economical success again lacking theoretical foundation[23].

The core task of Business Informatics - and this should be the scientific claim - is to explore the connections between organizational structures, technological implementation

---

[20]See [110], p. 18
[21]See [110], p. 25
[22]See [42], pp. 102
[23]See [173], p. 8

and the resulting social changes. This holistic demand raises the need for modeling many parts of the complex reality together with relationships among certain objects within models in a process-oriented manner, so that success can be measured along value-chains. Widespread in Business Informatics is the introduction of several levels of abstraction to structure the high complexity and the inter-relation of organizational and technical aspects. Most architectures, also referred to as modeling frameworks[24] , therefore propose at least four levels:

- Strategy level

- Business modeling and technical modeling level

- Technical platforms

- Execution

Like in computer sciences[25], the main task is to at least document static and dynamic interdependencies in the form of models. The need for these tasks creates the discipline Business Engineering[26]. Business Engineering can be compared to the task of an architect, who is building a house. In order to plan, manage and co-ordinate all actors involved, the architect designs a variety of different models, ranging from high-level plans like ground plans to detailed description for electrical installations. In Business Informatics, these models range from strategic information in the form of business models or process models to technical flow models that document detailed technical information how to implement the business processes. Unlike the architect, who needs plans to document everything, Business Engineering provides further advantages[27]:

- Basis for documentation and communication (e.g. teaching complex business scenarios)

- Evaluation

- Support for technical implementation

- Control and execution of the modeled environment in an enactment engine

The answer to the question *"Is Business Informatics a scientific field?"* therefore has to be *"Yes!"*, because with the help of Business Engineering the discipline Business Informatics

---

[24]See [150], pp. 35
[25]See Chapter 1.1.1.2
[26]See [210]
[27]See [150], p. 43

is able to fulfill the scientific requirements mentioned in the beginning of Chapter 1.1.1[28].
Especially:

- Enforcment the idea of Business Engineering by visualizing real-world problems with models to provide help and communication through modeled abstraction between organizational and technical staff

- Creation or invention of new modeling methods for an existing business area to enable better support for management decision making, e.g. support the management concept Balanced Scorecard (BSC)[29] technically

- Integration of existing modeling methods (E-Learning, KM, Web-Services, ERP, etc.)

- New findings and technologies to combine business scenarios with technical implementations for fully automated Web-Services workflows representing the State-of-the-Art[30]

are some examples of new scientific approaches.

1.1.1.4   ICT-supported Management

The term ICT-supported Management has been coined by the Department of Knowledge Engineering (DKE) at the University of Vienna's Institute of Computer Sciences and Business Informatics (http://www.dke.univie.ac.at). According to the scientific requirements of Business Informatics to show cause and effects of the relationship between organizational processes and technical implementation, a methodology has to align the E-Business on all business and technical levels[31].

For the DKE, Figure 1.1 shows the relevant ICT research areas. Referring to the term Business Engineering[32], ICT supported Management needs to provide modeling mechanisms. The DKE's core competency therefore to enable ICT supported Management is meta-modeling[33], that provides the possibility to create own modeling methods in an

---

[28]Sometimes, especially "applied-scientists", trade in the scientific proof of concept (technical feasibility) of theory with financial efficiency (return on investment). Interesting enrichment to Business Engineering's proof of concept would be laying statistical grounds with empirical studies, especially with quantitative or qualitative methods.

[29]See [152] and [153]

[30]See Chapter 2

[31]See [171]

[32]See Chapter 1.1.1.3

[33]For details see Chapter 6

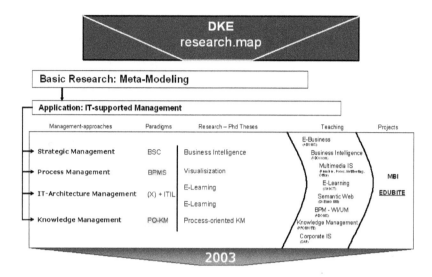

Figure 1.1: DKE research map

online and non-programming way. For meta-modeling, the concept of modeling has to be abstracted. Meta-modeling in the DKE-sense has the following properties:

- Everything that has following features in common can be meta-modeled:

  - Descriptive character

  - Classes have relations among each other

  - Classes have properties

  - The modeled information can be transformed and set the basis for implementation at run-time

  - Meta-modeling needs to be strongly coupled with methodology[34].

- Each aspect of the real world may be instantiated from a meta-model

For this thesis, the following scientific methods according to an E-Learning framework[35] have been chosen[36]:

- Literature survey

---

[34]See [156]
[35]See [179], p. 13
[36]not ordered in any way

- – Relying on existing literature, particularly books for the theoretical foundation and scientific thesis (IEEE, ACM, etc.) for new and quickly evolving technologies

- Definition of methodology[37]

- Hypothesis (theory)

  - – Creating a generic E-Learning Engineering framework that is able to cope with strategic as well as with technological issues
  - – Awareness of the fact that the generic framework is conceptually compliant with contemporary technologies coming from the Semantic Web (ontologies) to enable E-Learning

- Proof

  - – Creation a modeling method for E-Learning
  - – Proof of theory of interconnection and reasoning among several ontologies
  - – Proof of technical feasibility
  - – Empirical studies are not part of this thesis

- Modeling as an inter-subjective checkable method of the constructivist paradigm: *"if you can sell it"*, then it is relevant (Induction). In theory, the model may be falsified (critique by Sir Karl Popper's critical rationalism), but if still there is the need of the market so that the model further exists, this is ok, too.

1.2 Motivation: The deficiencies of State-of-the-Art in E-Learning and a resolution-strategy

State-of-the-Art E-Learning is a technology driven discipline. As always in application development, computer programmers design according to organizational requirements and implement the product in a bottom-up way within a certain software paradigm that is en vogue at the moment. Most of the E-Learning tools that facilitate learning with electronic means at the moment are the product of such an ad-hoc programming process. Depending on the level of sophistication the money invested into the development process

---

[37]Not based on scientific findings; defining the methodology was not part of the research efforts of this thesis.

and the programmers' expertise and ability to render organizational requirements into technical solutions, contemporary learning with computers is difficult to handle, manage and integrate into other (legacy) systems or enterprise software.

The so created isolated E-Learning solutions enable learners and tutors to produce and use online courses with the help and support of groupware technologies after training and learning the E-Learning itself. The success of these isolated solutions was evident in the late 1990-ies and early 2000-s and market leaders of so called Learning (Content) Management Systems L(C)MS could be identified. But the more sophisticated the technical implementations became the more it became evident, that strategic alignment of the learning effort and moreover the inability towards global business goals and integration into Enterprise Resource Planning (ERP) systems could not be established. Globalization, different cultures and languages and the distributed character of information systems were the adversaries. The task to resolve this present situation is to enable the integration of E-Learning tools into organizational value chains and business processes[38] so that evaluation of the learning strategy can be measured against company goals.

This thesis changes E-Learning from a technology driven discipline into an organizationally-driven discipline that is supported by ICT (Educational Technologies) with the help of a top-down engineering approach[39].

As already pointed out, the hiatus between organizational and technical requirements is derived from the inability and inexistence of structured visual modeling methods that define a problem scenario so that both organizational and technical experts are able to produce a satisfactory E-Learning solution. Especially in the field of learning where experts from many different domains come together and different technical roles have to decide about the ICT-supported applications such a common language in form of visual Modeling Methods that defines the semantics is indispensable.

As one scenario that can be derived from the E-Learning Framework, the so called E-Learning Engineering Framework introduces such a visual modeling method. It takes most its wit from existing Business Engineering[40] ideas transferring them into the domain of E-Learning. With the help of E-Learning Engineering it should be possible to

---

[38] [214] identifies a business process as an imperative matter in an organization linking business flows with product-processes and organizational structures. The need for ICT to round up the re-engineered landscape is also already considered.

[39] [76] addresses the need for organizational Re-Engineering to be supported by ICT; a business process is the main method to depict the organizational flows that have to be augmented with an ICT strategy and Client-Server technologies (Client-Server has been the State-of-the-Art architecture solution at the time the books was written).

[40] [98], pp. 2-4, introduces the basic ideas of Business Engineering and provides references to renowned scientists like Hammer, Champy and Davenport.

fit learning management into the framework of an educational institution. Depending on the setting - corporate or university - different transformations can be customized from the visually modeled E-Learning scenario[41]. Like many disciplines in the usual business - procurement, supply-chain management, accounting, etc. - E-Learning also needs to fit into a global strategy in order to measure and increase general efficiency[42]. Life-long learning can only be reached in this described way. Besides fitting into the global strategy it would be helpful not only to achieve a documented business and training landscape but also to map the engineered models into an ERP system[43] or into another run-time environment. Engineering ideas or even integration into ERP systems is relatively new and unproven in E-Learning[44].

E-Learning Engineering itself increasingly arises on the E-Learning horizon getting support from rapidly evolving E-Learning specifications and standards to provide input for the engineering methods[45]. Still, E-Learning Engineering[46] or Course Engineering is limited to the learning domain neglecting the link to integration into the whole business.

This thesis takes these definitions into a larger scope introducing a generic E-Learning Engineering Framework providing methodologies and engineering methods that are able to produce the instances Document-centric and Resource-driven Learning. Therefore it combines traditional Business Engineering with engineering E-Learning environments.

The following enumeration lists the overall complexity of an E-Learning project[47] and clearly points out the deficiencies of the State-of-the-Art situation and the missing link to a common strategy and methodology in the special focus of an E-Learning application:

- The degree of virtuality is high. In case of a virtual university to deliver E-Learning, the actors taking part never even get the chance to see each other. The only means of communication is a portal in the internet.

- The organizational structure is complex. Many different entities formulate different requirements based on different interpretations of learning contents, didactical

---

[41]Later to be called document-centric and resource-driven approaches; see Chapter 3.5

[42][8], p. 13, states that Supply-Chain Management includes holistic optimization of material- and information-flows across all offices of a company aligned towards the organizational processes. The same as for supply-Chain Management has to be said and done for all other ingredients of disciplines within a company including E-Learning.

[43][236] elaborates success factors for ERP integration of business models.

[44][315] introduced the use of ERP systems in education.

[45]Global conferences like the ACM SAC 2004 conference, http://www.acm.org./conferences/sac2004, gradually apply the research area "E-Learning Engineering" on their agendas.

[46]E-Learning Engineering can be defined as applying Software Engineering to instructional design - "Blended" definition by [80] combining instructional design and Software Engineering - or as *methods and techniques that deal with the creation of E-Learning applications*", see [207].

[47]The scenario has been taken from three years (2001-2003) of experience at the Virtual Global University, http://www.vg-u.de, and its Master of Business Informatics (MBI) project.

issues, etc.

- The learning domains show great diversity and therefore include a set of disjoint ideas of roles.

- The underlying existing technical infrastructure is diverse and based on several operating systems and programming architectures.

- The aim is to present a portal with a unified corporate identity that is able to bring the highest level of flexibility and benefit to students and tutors.

The most reasonable way to address all these requirements and restrictions in order to find the best ICT solution would be to first bring all participating entities to the negotiating table and discuss project structure and organizational dependencies. All results based on the discussions lead into a legally binding contract that in turn defines a system specification to serve as input for an invitation to a bid. Until now, all this information is condensed in piles of paperwork where process flows are not included.

Stage one of E-Learning Engineering steps in at the top-level supporting the E-Learning project management with a structured methodology and engineering methods on an organizational and technical level describing the E-Learning environment meaning that the organizational and the knowledge environment has to be acquired and modeled within a re-engineering phase. Stage one can be said to be a combination of BPM and KM tasks. Stage two addresses the already mentioned integration into ERP systems of other runtime environments, in this case especially into E-Learning specific ones.

The following Chapter outlines the structure of this thesis and explains the interdependencies of the techniques and methods to reach the generic E-Learning Engineering framework.

1.3 Outline of Chapters

According to the scientific methods defined for Business Informatics, the composition of this thesis consists of one plus three main parts (plus conclusion) depicted in Figure 1.2. Chapter 1 starts out with an outline of scientific methods and philosophy of science. Due to the fact, that research in Business Informatics is quite new and often argued as non-scientific, this Chapter subsumes methods for this new scientific branch by aggregating from existing economical science and computer sciences. Chapter 1.1.1.3 distills the information into the scientific methods that are used in this thesis calling them ICT-supported Management.

Chapter 2 clearly points out the main focus on the discipline E-Learning. With the help of the method "literature survey", the topic E-Learning is scrutinized historically and with definitions. Besides general issues, the focus lies on standardization issues, because they lay grounds to integration and interoperability and the connection to the remaining chapters, and the common technical architecture for an L(C)MS. Following up to the technical architecture, newly established technology Web-Services (Appendix A) enter the E-Learning arena. Web-Services will change the two- or three-tier architecture with proprietary applications to n-tier service-oriented architectures.

Chapters 4 together with 5 and 6 make up the scientific antagonists theory and practical proof. The theory - as a first step in Chapter 4 - has to evaluate several technological aspects concerning Knowledge Representation Formalisms. This topic is discussed in Appendix B showing historical developments and focuses especially on technologies related to the Semantic Web. On top of that, a generic approach is presented theoretically; main topics will be the presentation of an E-Learning Engineering Framework together with a methodology that places the approach into a Business-to-Business (B2B) context and a theoretical model of different ontologies that are queried to get an ideal learning object (LO) for a specific person. Chapters 5 and 6 take the theory as input and evaluate it. The evaluation is performed on two levels:

- Level 1 is to present a modeling method called eduWeaver and DKElearn that holistically aligns a methodology to representing E-Learning ontologies.

- Level 2 is concerned with snapshot applications that try to prove particular parts with practical test-beds.

Finally, Chapter 7 concludes with remarks and future potential of E-Learning.

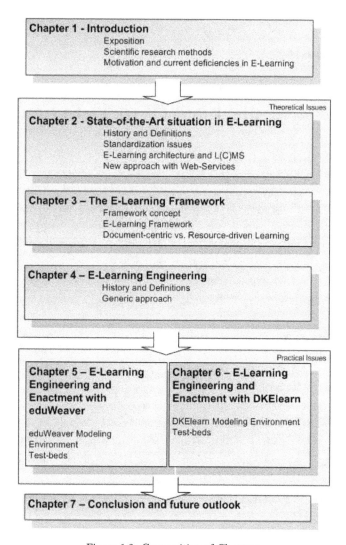

Figure 1.2: Composition of Chapters

Chapter 2

The State-of-the-Art in E-Learning

This Chapter outlines and motivates general ideas about E-Learning, how it has evolved over history and what future concepts and how E-Learning will tackle in the near future. A special emphasis lies on standardization issues and technology integration efforts.

The thorough examination of the historical development and interrelations in the field of E-Learning have been the foundation for the proposed E-Learning Framework[1].

Therefore, existing methodologies, specifications, standards and implementations shall be scrutinized and compared, as many commercial vendors present their own view on integrated E-Learning and thus offer proprietary solutions.

2.1 Chapter Outline

Generally speaking, the terms mentioned above correlate in the following way (simplified view):

The overview, as shown in Figure 2.1, also reflects the structure of this Chapter.

It symbolizes a generic and simplified E-Learning lifecycle. Central issue is the use of a methodology that sets basic milestones and phases within an E-Learning project. This methodology comprises strategic decisions, creating LOs, modeling a meta-model that is input for a Run-Time Implementation within an L(C)MS.

Chapter 2.2 and 2.3 will deal with historical issues, general terms, and definitions and will especially focus on E-Learning methodologies, as methodologies set the basis for a successful E-Learning implementation.

Chapter 2.4 sets its emphasis on E-Learning standard bodies and affiliated organizations, specifications, standards and technologies and will try to point out the State-of-the-Art

---

[1]In fact, all technologies and solutions discussed in this Chapter can all be aligned to the E-Learning Framework. E.g. WBTs and CBTs all focus on the Technology Dimension; see Chapter 3.4.

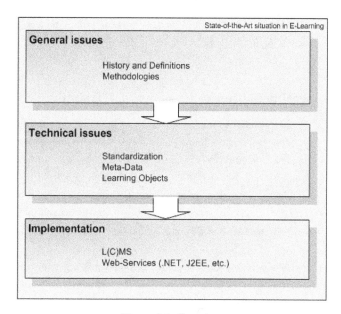

Figure 2.1: Overview

situation today.

Chapter 2.5.1 focuses on practical implementations and solution based on concepts from Chapters 2.4 and 2.5.1. There are major differences in functionality as well as in the methodological support. To point out these differences and potentials will be the target of this Chapter.

Finally, Chapter 2.6 will try to depict a future outlook concerning the discussed E-Learning topics.

2.2 History and Definitions

This Chapter deals with two different topics:

- Basic definitions and brief history of E-Learning

- E-Learning methodologies

Topic 1 shall only be mentioned briefly, because it builds the non-technical foundation of modern E-Learning. It focuses on aspects that influence the methodology and the Run-Time Implementation deeply.

Topic 2 will be discussed in detail, as it plays a key role concerning the technical foundation of an E-Learning platform.

2.2.1 General definition of Learning and Training

In order to understand and define the term E-Learning it can be quite helpful to explore both roots of the term itself. This Chapter is dedicated to the term "Learning".

According to Gagné[2] *"Learning is a change in human disposition or capabilities, which can be retained, and which is not simply attributed to the process of growth"*.

This definition originated in psychology and relates very much to neural processes. In a more technical view, learning, according to Rosenberg[3], can be defined as *"the process, by which people acquire new skills and knowledge for the purpose of enhancing their performance"*.

Bringing the two definitions together, learning can be seen as a mental transition from one state of mind to another, implying a greater knowledge in the learning individual and thus bringing him a competitive advantage.

In order to keep the new skills and knowledge, the individual has to be trained. Rosenberg[4] calls training a necessity *"to shape learning in a specific direction - to support learners in acquiring a new skill or to utilize new knowledge"*. Theoretically speaking, several approaches or paradigms to learning in general exist. They are[5]:

- **Behaviorism**:
  Learning behaviorally describes a habit, namely responding to external stimuli. If the wanted reaction is achieved, the individual is granted a reward (Pawlow´s dog).

- **Cognitivism**:
  Learning is based on cognitive structures, which imply adaptive processes of an individual to an environment in order to reach a new equilibrium.

- **Constructivism**:
  Learning is part of a genesis of knowledge. Each individual constructs his own reality dynamically. According to Clement[6], *"... this means that the learning of*

---

[2][96]
[3][229], p. 4
[4]See [229]
[5]See [244], pp. 65
[6][53], p 377 in [244], p. 68

complex, unfamiliar or counterintuitive models in science requires a kind of learning by doing and by construction ...".

2.2.2 Computer-based Training (CBT)

With the emergence of computers, Learning and Training as described in Chapter 2.2.1, gains new potential. Dittler[7] calls CBT the oldest form of E-Learning. Training in CBT is computer-based and supported with one medium (floppy disk, CD-ROM, DVD-ROM, etc.) supplying automated courses. Courses first present the facts and in order to confirm the newly learned contents, tests and exams are held[8].

One big advantage of CBT is its *"possibility of automated supplementary education ... , where the requirements of an individual are considered properly"*[9].

CBT therefore has the following characteristics[10]:

- The user is not bound to a location

- Contents are not teacher-centered but media-centered

- Learning is done asynchronously

- A certain degree of interactivity exists

2.2.3 Web-based Training (WBT)

WBT takes CBT a step further. Klein and Kretzschmar[11] state that WBT is CBT´s transformation into a distance learning approach using web-based applications together with multimedia.

There are two causes for this development:

1. The extensive use of the internet, as means for communication and data exchange.

2. The emergence of "New Content"[12] that implies new structures in hypermedia-documents. This development can easily be compared to the emergence of letter-press printing in the 15th century when talking about content publishing.

Implicitly, this brings up two other issues:

---

[7]See [75], p. 27
[8][245], p. 311
[9][75], p. 27 (translation)
[10][75], p. 31
[11]See [164]
[12]See [259], p. 289

1. The possibility to present up-to-date contents, which makes learning-on-demand a lot easier.

2. The need for standardization of this content in order to be able to supply mass-audiences.

Jechle[13] mentions following advantages of WBT: *"Dynamic media ... as well as the possibility of supervision ... make learning solutions much more attractive. ... . Through the use of the internet the contents remain within the access of the producer and can be easily adapted and updated. Furthermore, distribution from the producer to consumer is much shorter"*.

2.2.4 E-Learning

E-Learning is - historically as well as functionally - the most recent and holistic approach in online learning.

2.2.4.1 General terms and definitions

E-Learning includes methodologies, a technical architecture, content supply and dissemination and evaluation of online learning materials. Whereas CBT and WBT can be seen as learning tools, E-Learning is more than just a tool; it is a concept for providing learning contents together with administering the contents and students. Figure 2.2 shows the correlation between the terms used so far: CBT, WBT and E-Learning.

In Chapter 2.2.1 the term learning was explained. In order to define E-Learning, both terms "Electronic" and "Learning" have to be combined.

Excursion into "E-Business":
The definitions of E-Business and E-Learning have some features in common. A look at E-Business therefore will help to better understand the terminus technicus "E-Learning".
One of the first definition efforts were coined by IBM: *"E-Business is defined as the support of all internal or external corporate business processes with the help of communication networks, especially the internet"*[14]. Schubert defines E-Business quite similar as the *"support of processes and relationships between business entities, employees and customers via electronic media"*[15].

---

[13][149], p. 265 (translation)
[14]See http://www.ibm.com
[15][242], p. 3 (translation)

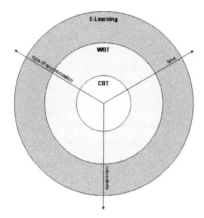

Figure 2.2: Dependencies E-Learning-WBT-CBT

To put it in a nut-shell, E-Business is the support or combination - either partially or fully - of the "normal business"[16] with electronic means, especially with the use of the internet.

According to the information taken from the "Excursion into E-Business", E-Learning is the support or combination of "normal learning" as defined in Chapter 2.2.1 with the help of electronic means, especially with the use of internet technologies. As already mentioned, E-Learning also implies administering contents and persons involved, therefore all these features are integrated into a platform.

Excursion into "Knowledge Management":
Knowledge Management refers to the new resource "knowledge" that must be paid attention to in modern entities, besides common factors as human resources, raw materials, etc. It is not only the common factors that make up success, but also the knowledge of employees and managers. Moreover, a strong interrelation to E-Learning can be drawn, as the resource "knowledge" has to be taught to employees and managers.

"Knowledge Management takes organizational learning a step further. A central issue is increasing organizational skills at all organizational levels with the help of a better use of the resource knowledge"[17]. Probst/Romhardt[18] also

---

[16]"Normal business" is defined as a trade, in which a person or entity is engaged. This includes a strategy that implies products to be sold with the target of maximizing profits. To take a "business-informatics" approach, business is, any internal or external business process within a company.
[17][219] (translation)
[18]See [219]

define a kind of methodology with so called components as elements (knowledge identification, knowledge acquisition, knowledge production, knowledge distribution, use, knowledge preservation).

The following enumeration shall give an additional overview of definitions mentioned in contemporary literature, as there exist many different views:

- E-Learning is networked, which makes it capable of instant updating, storage and retrieval, distribution and sharing ... It is delivered to the end-user via a computer using standard Internet technology ... It focuses on the broadest view of learning-learning solutions that go beyond the traditional paradigms of training[19].

- E-Learning is learning with the help of electronic media. Methods are CBT, WBT and Online Learning. ... An E-Learning Platform is a system implementing a corporate knowledge center[20].

- E-Learning takes place, when learning processes interact within scenarios, where multi-medial and (tele-)communicational technologies are integrated[21].

- E-Learning comprises learning supported with information- and communication technologies ... . But E-Learning is not inhibited by these technological aspects, furthermore E-Learning also embraces ... process management and strategy definition and includes management aspects[22].

Blending these different definitions and also taking the information from the excursions, interrelations between E-Learning and other technologies can best be visualized with Figure 2.3.

It is obvious that these three technologies have strong interconnections. Briefly, the relationships between them point out, how:

- **E-Business**:
  E-Business is either corporate or educational, depending on the business (i.e. company XY or university YZ). Depending on the type of business, business plans focus on different aspects (i.e. making profit or educating students).
  E-Business has two outgoing relationships, "supported via" and "increased skills". Both relationships add value to E-Business.

---

[19][229], p. 28
[20][326], pp. 205 (translation)
[21][249], p. 45 (translation)
[22][20], p. 28 (translation)

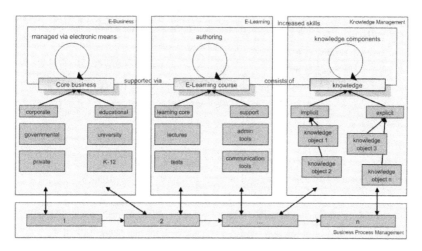

Figure 2.3: E-Learning interrelations

- **E-Learning**:
  E-Learning provides courses and thus supports E-Business. On the other hand, E-Learning consists of knowledge objects coming from Knowledge Management. E-Learning assembles these objects into reasonable courses.

- **Knowledge Management**:
  Knowledge Management takes care of all knowledge objects, assembled in an organizational memory. This organizational memory is input for E-Business and E-Learning and enhances them via structured data and information.

- **Special issue: Relationship E-Learning-Knowledge Management**:
  Depending on the view, each of the two technologies serves as input for the other. On the one hand, knowledge objects could refer to learning processes coming from E-Learning, augmenting the organizational memory, and on the other hand, E-Learning courses consist of knowledge objects. Back et al.[23] list mutual contributions:

  - E-Learning to Knowledge Management: knowledge apprehension, knowledge transfer and sharing as a core target of E-Learning, knowledge creation.

  - Knowledge Management to E-Learning: human resource management and skill management, knowledge processes as basis for training, knowledge sharing

---

[23]See [20], pp. 62

	CBT	WBT	E-Learning
Behaviorism	X		
Cognitivism	X	X	
Constructivism	X	X	X

Table 2.1: Psychological Theories and Learning Technologies

through communities.

BPM tops and integrates the other three technologies, because it gives contextual information and hence provides technological and organizational integration.

Figure 2.3 shows a fully integrated approach to the mentioned E-Terms and Knowledge Management. Thus, it should still be possible, to use "old-fashioned" ways. These blended solutions[24] can also be integrated and referenced by including them into BPM.

2.2.4.2 Psychological aspects of E-Learning

As already mentioned, psychology gives three different approaches concerning the type of learning, namely behaviorism, cognitivism and constructivism. Depending on the scenario, E-Learning has to provide certain instances according to these theories.

It should also be kept in mind, that the three classical approaches come from traditional learning, meaning that all scenarios include human beings: students on the one hand and teachers on the other hand. Adopting these approaches to computer-aided learning[25] sets major changes to these scenarios, because a new entity centers the stage: a computer system. Applying behavioristic elements into a computer-aided course for instance means to implement the right tools and interfaces to "simulate" a teacher.

Table 2.1 shows the connection between learning technologies and the psychological theories.

CBT as the oldest form of computer supported learning only consists of behavioral aspects. CBT starts with serving contents, which then is checked with tests afterwards[26]. WBT adds the capability to distribute contents via the internet, which implies a hypertext-structure. The user can learn individually with having the possibility to assemble the contents cognitively, taking advantage of thinking-processes reflected in the human brain (i.e. via Mind Maps)[27].

---

[24]i.e. Blended Learning: refers to the combination of E-Learning with traditional forms of learning.

[25]Computer-aided learning in this context does not refer to CBT, WBT or E-Learning, it just means "learning with the help of computers"

[26]See [245], p. 311

[27]See [248], p. 47

E-Learning merges all aspects and is able to combine all three psychological approaches, depending on the scenario and the underlying model.

2.3 Methodologies

Introduction and implementation of a new Software product alone still misses strategic support and logical structure, which makes the use of a holistic methodology an important matter for successful E-Learning.

Figure 2.1 already showed the fact that a methodology gives coherence to all other elements involved in E-Learning. This Chapter deals with definition issues and evaluates methodologies coming from other disciplines and again depicts the connections between them and introduces an E-Learning methodology.

2.3.1 What is a methodology?

The term "methodology" is defined as *"doctrine of systematic approaches that yield into a predefined target"*[28] and is a very general term for describing a method of actions to fulfill a certain aim, including strategic decision making, tactical and operational execution and improvement through evaluation. Depending on the branch of industry, methodologies can differ. To avoid misunderstandings this Chapter will focus on methodologies in the context of Project-Management[29] and Software-Engineering. E-Learning itself is embedded into such a greater picture defined by a methodology; depending on the application scenario, an E-Learning methodology has to be aligned with the one used in this scenario (e.g. Business Engineering, Software Engineering, etc.).

The following definitions of methodology are available in contemporary literature:

- A methodology describes the coordination and organization of a designing process. Projects typically underlie different steps. These steps are finished with a document called milestone[30].

- The term methodology is derived from the term phase-model as follows: a phase-model is a systematic arrangement of tasks within an ICT-project into sequential processes ... with a certain target. These processes require methods and tools. ...

---

[28]See [333], p. 5

[29]"Project-Management concentrates on a project. A project is an undertaking that has a beginning and an end and is carried out to meet established goals within cost, schedule and quality objectives. Project-Management brings together and optimizes the resources necessary to complete the project successfully", from [109], p. 10.

[30][85], p. 152 (translation)

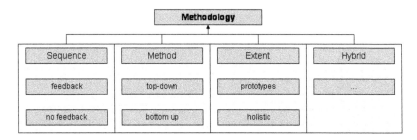

Figure 2.4: Classification of methodologies

> Via process-descriptions ... the phase-model is transformed into a methodology. ...
> A methodology is not monolithic and therefore can be made up out of sub-models
> ...[31]

2.3.2 A classification of methodologies

Methodologies can be classified as shown in Figure 2.4:

The purpose of this classification is to give an overview in order to classify BPM-, E-Business-, KM- and E-Learning methodologies only. Therefore, only the top level of the classification will be defined:

- **Sequence**:
  Each step is processed sequentially. A sequence can be processed only once without feedback (i.e. waterfall-model) or with feedback.

- **Method**:
  A methodology can originate in the strategic management, where strategies are generated and processed top-down, or in the operative working area, where new products are designed and serve as input for strategic management.

- **Extent**:
  The target (i.e. a piece of software) can be engineered prototypical, because the area of implementation is quite new and testing is required, resulting in a prototype, or holistic (or evolutionary), where the working field is defined well, resulting in a fully functional product.

- **Hybrid**:
  Advantages of one or more methodologies are merged.

---

[31][111], p. 2 (translation)

2.3.3 The big picture: Correlation between BPM, KM and E-Learning methodologies

In the context of E-Learning, what are the requirements towards a methodology? There are two aspects in this regard, namely a more global one and the requirements towards an E-Learning methodology itself:

- Global requirements

  - Fitting into other technologies, like BPM or KM

  - Finding out the added-value components between these methodologies

- E-Learning methodology requirements

  - Hybrid structure, according to Figure 2.4

  - Openness towards scalability and Change Management

  - Inclusion of strategic view

  - Evaluation

The global requirements will be further scrutinized in Chapter 2.5.4 and E-Learning methodology requirements will be discussed according to present implementations in Chapter 2.3.3.1.

2.3.3.1 Present E-Learning methodologies

The following section gives a State-of-the-Art overview of existing E-Learning methodologies.

The Plato-Cookbook[32]: The Plato-Cookbook approaches the E-Learning area with an analogy to a normal cookbook with corresponding steps in each recipe. Figure 2.5[33] shows the Plato-Cookbook methodology:

The steps in detail, reflecting the questions posed:

1. **Orientation**:

   Orientation decides upon which teaching method is best for the course design, whether declarative or procedural knowledge underlies the E-Learning intentions. It also tries to decide about the students´ situations in order to find out what to teach.

---

[32]for this Chapter, see [248], pp. 60
[33]See Figure [248], p. 60

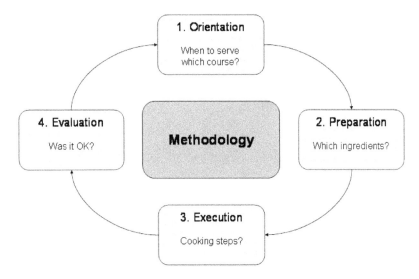

Figure 2.5: The Plato-Cookbook methodology

2. **Preparation**:

Preparation deals with the questions, which technological means and methods to pick in the selected scenario, in order to fulfill the requirements.

3. **Execution**:

Execution includes the recipe for cooking and interactions between student and E-Learning system. Recommendations on how to "E-Learn" are given and tests and exams give feedback.

4. **Evaluation**:

Evaluation extracts operational data from the courses and gives answer on how successful the course was.

E-Learning strategy by Rosenberg[34]: Marc J. Rosenberg´s book is a must in Anglo-Saxon regions. Although no methodology is mentioned explicitly, there is a need to include his thoughts about E-Learning strategies, which can be seen as first part when adding them up to a sequence of steps. They are:

- Who should participate?

  Stakeholders for strategy deployment are elected and gather in an all-day workshop

---

[34]for this Chapter see [229], pp. 291

to discuss primary matters.

- Analyze your current situation
  Determine the current status concerning overall learning and development efforts
  and the state of current E-Learning initiatives to find out, how well E-Learning is
  aligned with the direction of present business.

- Describe your desired situation
  Create a detailed description of E-Learning development efforts together with senior
  stakeholders.

- Set your vision
  Formulate vision of the desired situation in the future: visions *"reflect the future,
  ideal state"*.

- State your mission
  After having agreed on the vision, the development of a mission statement is the
  next step. A mission statement expresses the steps of how to accomplish the vision.

- Gap Analysis
  To find disparities between the current and the desired situation is the aim of a gap
  analysis.

- Conduct Force-Field and SWOT Analyses
  To help underline your strategic thoughts, two analytical techniques can be used:
  the force-field analysis (for each statement in the gap analysis detects factors that inhibit or aid closing the gap) and the Strengths, Weaknesses, Opportunities, Threats
  (SWOT) analysis (the entire organization is source for analyses concerning strengths,
  weaknesses, opportunities and threats at this point or in the future).

- Strategy recommendations
  Up to this point within the methodology, recommendations about closing gaps,
  implementing the mission and achieving the vision can be made.

- Build an Action Plan
  *"Implement your E-Learning strategy recommendations through a comprehensive
  action plan"*.

- Be Wary
  An E-Learning strategy is essential to give general directions. Still, besides giving

directions, current situations have to be evaluated and future developments have to be anticipated.

Six Steps by Brandon Hall[35]: Brandon Hall´s approach to an E-Learning methodology includes the following six steps:

1. Preparation for E-Learning
   Before business benefits can be achieved via E-Learning, careful strategic planning and assessment to determine major barriers is necessary. This includes selecting relevant dimensions (stakeholders, content, technology, etc.), identifying major assets and barriers for each dimension and considering implementation strategies.

2. Developing a Strategy
   In this step, developing a *"strategy securing executive sponsorship is the first critical steps"*. Depending on the level of E-Learning experience, three different strategies are suggested.

3. Selecting Technology and Content
   The two fundamental parts of E-Learning have to be chosen, a Learning Management System (LMS)[36] and the content. The LMS should apply to certain standards, features and requirements. Concerning the content, the decision mostly is, whether to build or to buy it. This decision is driven by cost issues.

4. Selling E-Learning to Everyone in the Organization
   Successful E-Learning implementations need a leading team or steering committee to promote the idea. Several sub-strategies to form teams or to market E-Learning internally are imposed.

5. Implementation Enterprise-Wide
   A *"significant, system-wide implementation of E-Learning"* should aim at *"making significant business impact"*.

6. Measurement of the Business Benefit
   This step proposes choosing *"measures on growth in performance, competencies and intellectual capital. These critical measures are naturally linked to business impact and help to maintain the case for the E-Learning initiative"*.

---

[35]for this Chapter see [108], pp. 234
[36]according to [108], p. 241, an LMS *"automates the administration of training events"*

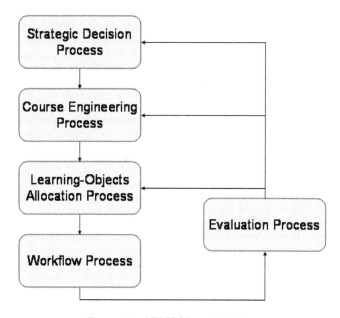

Figure 2.6: ADVISOR methodology

ADVISOR: The ADVISOR methodology[37] historically derives from the Business Process Management Systems (BPMS)[38] methodology, a holistic framework for BPM that integrates organizational, analytical as well as ICT aspects of business processes[39]. ADVISOR was first introduced as an add-on to this BPM-methodology, leveraging the existing business process models with a new dimension towards learning and training of these processes. This combination enables companies to train employees to quickly adapt to new scenarios.

Deriving from this status, ADVISOR´s development in the future is set to serve as stand-alone E-Learning methodology with close relationships to BPMS as well as to KM. Figure 2.3 has already pointed out these close interrelations.

The ADVISOR methodology is depicted in Figure 2.6:

The five sub-processes in detail:

1. **Strategic Decision Process**:

   The Strategic Decision Process detects top-level and long-term issues that are deter-

---

[37]See [34]
[38]See Chapter 2.5.4
[39]See [156], p. 5

mined by top-level executives. Targets are the fitting into the company strategy[40], setting evaluation criteria, aiming and implementation of E-Learning, choosing didactical concepts, etc.

2. **Course Engineering Process**:

   Depending on the current situation, existing learning and training activities and process have to be modeled. After the determination of this current situation, the future-to-be activities and processes are modeled. This includes overview snapshots and detailed course scenarios as well as people involved. Target is the structure of people's courses and all related process information.

3. **Learning-Objects Allocation Process**:

   In this process, the models engineered are enriched with references to resources, human as well as ICT and LOs. This process targets in an integrated model building the foundation of a technical implementation instanced through this model in the following step.

4. **Workflow Process**:

   The Workflow Process is the instance of the model generated in the Learning-Objects Allocation Process. This includes application, administration, application and actual studying by students, teachers and administrative personnel. During use, all transactions and movements are recorded and logged in order to serve as input in the Evaluation Process.

5. **Evaluation Process**:

   The target of the Evaluation Process is to collect and aggregate intelligently the gained operative data from the audit trails coming from the Workflow Process. The results form input again for further decision making, yielding into a new strategy, course engineering or Learning-Objects, depending on the results´ gravity and impact.

The ADVISOR methodology may start with the "Strategic Decision Process" in a top-down manner, but is also open for a bottom-up approach, i.e. Learning-Objects exist in the first place to be accumulated to courses that have impact on strategic issues.

Courseware Engineering[41]: Klein and Stucky compare the development of E-Learning content with Software Engineering and therefore use the term Courseware En-

---

[40]See Chapter 2.5.4
[41]for this Chapter see [163]

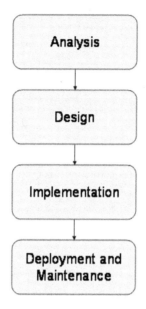

Figure 2.7: Courseware Engineering

gineering. The related methodology is similar to Software Engineering practices and has got four sub-categories shown in Figure 2.7.

The sub-categories in detail:

- **Analysis**:
  Analysis concentrates on requirements definition and tries to answer questions concerning target definition, content and target groups.

- **Design**:
  Design takes the achieved goals from Analysis and targets in a Courseware model (i.e. with the Unified Modeling Language (UML), Hypertext Design Model (HDM), Relationship Management Methodology (RMM) or Object-oriented Hypertext Design Model (OHDM)) with special focus on modular components and component interdependencies for future connections.

- **Implementation**:
  Implementation converts the models from Design into the desired software solution. Courseware Engineering describes a bottom-up approach, beginning with authoring in-the-small, where modular objects are defined and ending in authoring in-the-large

	Sequence	Method	Extent	Hybrid	Tool-support
Plato-Cookbook	feedback	top-down	holistic	+	-
Rosenberg	no feed-back	top-down	-	+	-
Six Steps	no feed-back	top-down	-	+	-
ADVISOR	feedback	top-down and bottom-up	holistic	+	+
Courseware Engineering	no feed-back	bottom-up	holistic	+	-

Table 2.2: Classification of Methodologies

connecting these objects to courses. This authoring has a special focus on meta-data and standardization issues, so that the modular objects can easily be re-used and transparent to third party clients.

- **Deployment and Maintenance**:
Realize the implementation and improvement of errors together with evaluation.

2.3.3.2 Classification of Methodologies

Table 2.2 shows an aggregated view on methodologies presented adding the information, whether it is supported by tools or not. Research concentrated on methodologies in the E-Learning sector only. Methodologies for CBTs or WBTs were considered not important for this survey. Still, also non-holistic methodologies were scrutinized. But as these concentrate on strategic levels for an E-Learning scenario, they were considered important and thus are mentioned.

2.4 General Standardization issues

"The phrase 'learning standard' is one of the most powerful and most mis-understood aspects of the E-Learning revolution. As organizations make signif-icant investments in digital learning content, there is a strong desire to have greater assurances, portability, and re-usability. As organizations focus on providing learners with the 'just right' content and activities, there is a strong

desire to have the ability to more easily store, search, index, deploy, assemble, and revise content. All of these hopes are part of the story of 'learning standards'[42].

The introductory quote already states the common problems when talking about standards. This issue is not only evident in E-Learning, but everywhere else, where global commerce represented by multi-national big players meets the needs for general descriptions. There will always be a trade-off between personal company interests and the need to openness in order to exchange content with other participants. Both extremities exist in the ICT-world and there is no global rule or decision model to predict the outcome in a "standardization war"[43].

Before describing the situation in E-Learning, certain definitions and demarcations have to be made.

2.4.1 Definitions: de-facto/de-iure-Standards, Standards, Specifications

The International Organization for Standardization (ISO) states the following on the topic standardization:

> *"When the large majority of products or services in a particular business or industry sector conform to International Standards, a state of industry-wide standardization can be said to exist. This is achieved through consensus agreements between national delegations representing all the economic stakeholders concerned - suppliers, users and, often, governments. They agree on specifications and criteria to be applied consistently in the classification of materials, the manufacture of products and the provision of services. In this way, International Standards provide a reference framework, or a common technological language, between suppliers and their customers - which facilitates trade and the transfer of technology"*[44].

According to Duval[45], the following requirements need to be fulfilled by standards:

---

[42][57], p. 2

[43]one example each should be sufficient at this point to undermine this statement: the company Microsoft with its operating system Windows (see http://www.microsoft.com/windows) as a "company winner", and the W3C with HTML (see http://www.w3c.org/MarkUp) as a "winner in openness".

[44][143]

[45][79], p. 2

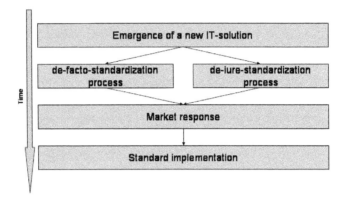

Figure 2.8: Standardization lifecycle

- **Semantic interoperability**:
  A general object should have the same semantic meaning, without respect to the person or entity using it. Duval´s example states, that - wherever a normal shoe is made - size, material and all other properties are exactly the same because of used standards.

- **Openness**:
  With the use of standardized objects, anyone or any entity may use these objects in a correct and reasonable way, as they are intended.

These requirements do not mean to inhibit but tend to increase freedom by giving the user the chance to combine all kinds of elements that bear the selected standard as well. Nevertheless, there are two possible paths in standardization. These two also build the starting point for a standardization lifecycle as shown in Figure 2.8.

If corporate solutions are accepted due to widely disseminated products, a de-facto-standardization[46] process starts. The de-iure-standardization[47] process is open, where stakeholders come together to jointly discuss requirements that yield in a consensual solution. The draft thesis resulting in a de-iure-standard after approval by a standard organization or committee is called Specification. In either case, depending on market response, some "Standard" will be chosen for use.

Again, there is a trade-off between de-facto-standards and de-iure-standards, depending on time, involved power, money on the one hand and level of agreement and will for joint

---

[46]de facto, latin for existing, even without lawful regulations
[47]de iure, latin for existing by law

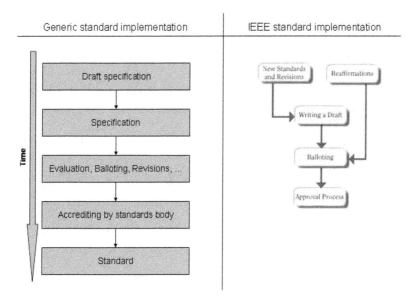

Figure 2.9: Standardization process

contribution on the other hand.

The Figure 2.9 shows a generic and the IEEE[48] way of how to achieve a standard:

Figure 2.9 also shows, besides describing the process, the difference between two key terms, namely "Specification" and "Standard". Specifications and standards are both encouraging a common view on a certain topic. The real difference lies in the formal accreditation by a standardization body, which makes a standard a specification that is confirmed by an independent group concerning quality issues and content. Because of this formal act, standards may be adopted by partners in order to assure data exchange in a syntactically and semantically correct way. ISO´s definition of standards:

> "Standards are documented agreements containing technical specifications
> or other precise criteria to be used consistently as rules, guidelines, or def-
> initions of characteristics, to ensure that materials, products, processes and
> services are fit for their purpose. For example, the format of the credit cards,
> phone cards, and 'smart' cards that have become commonplace is derived from
> an ISO International Standard. Adhering to the standard, which defines such
> features as an optimal thickness (0,76 mm), means that the cards can be used

---

[48]See [130]

worldwide. International Standards thus contribute to making life simpler, and to increasing the reliability and effectiveness of the goods and services we use"[49].

2.4.2 Organizations, Committees, Specifications and Standards involved in E-Learning

As to all standardization issues, the situation is very complex and getting a draft thesis as far as becoming a standard is a rocky road. The Figure 2.10 shows three layers (excerpt), the standardization bodies, the organizations generating specifications in order to get standardized by these bodies according to the process shown in Figure 2.9 and the specifications issued by these organizations:

Detailed information about organizations and specifications can be found in Chapter 2.4.5.

2.4.2.1 Standardization bodies

The following section will give further information about the bodies ISO, IEEE and CEN.

ISO/IEC JTC1/SC36[50]: *"The International Organization for Standardization (ISO) is a worldwide federation of national standards bodies from some 140 countries, one from each country.*

ISO is a non-governmental organization established in 1947. The mission of ISO is to promote the development of standardization and related activities in the world with a view to facilitating the international exchange of goods and services, and to developing cooperation in the spheres of intellectual, scientific, technological and economic activity. ISO's work results in international agreements which are published as International Standards"[51].

ISO is the top organization, representing a large number of local bodies (i.e. DIN in Germany, ANSI in the USA, etc.). Within the ISO, committees and subcommittees work on certain topics. The JTC 1 committee (Information Technology) with its subcommittee SC36 (Learning Technology) are responsible for E-Learning issues.

As ISO is the global standardization body, IEEE is US-centric and CEN is European-centric.

IEEE/LTSC: *"The IEEE (Eye-triple-E) is a non-profit, technical professional association of more than 377,000 individual members in 150 countries. The full name is the*

---

[49][144]
[50][143]
[51][142]

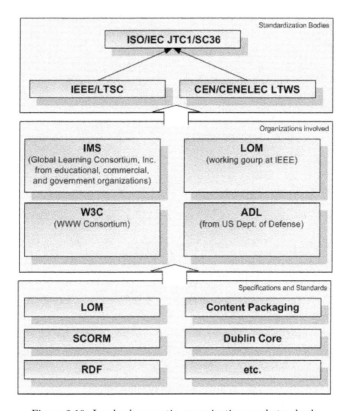

Figure 2.10: Involved consortia, organizations and standards

Institute of Electrical and Electronics Engineers, Inc., although the organization is most popularly known and referred to by the letters I-E-E-E.

Through its members, the IEEE is a leading authority in technical areas ranging from computer engineering, biomedical technology and telecommunications, to electric power, aerospace and consumer electronics, among others"[52].

The IEEE is also organized by structured committees depending on the topic. For E-Learning, the IEEE Learning Technologies Standard Committee (LTSC)[53] is responsible. Within these committees, working groups are arranged to do research in different topics. The IEEE/LTSC working groups are:

- Architecture and Reference Model WG

---

[52][122]
[53][126]

- Glossary WG

- Computer Managed Instruction WG

- Learning Objects Meta-data WG

- Semantics and Exchange Bindings WG

- Data Interchange Protocols WG

- Platform and Media Profiles WG

- Competency Definitions WG

- Digital Rights Expression Language Study Group

After having passed the IEEE standardization process many of the standards will be advanced as international standards by ISO/IEC JTC1/SC36.

CEN/ISSS CENELEC LTWS: *"CEN's mission is to promote voluntary technical harmonization in Europe in conjunction with worldwide bodies and its partners in Europe. Harmonization diminishes trade barriers, promotes safety, allows interoperability of products, systems and services, and promotes common technical understanding.*
In Europe, the Comité Européen de Normalisation (CEN) works in partnership with CEN-ELEC - the European Committee for Electrotechnical Standardization (www.cenelec.org) and ETSI - the European Telecommunications Standards Institute (www.etsi.org) ... Wherever possible CEN works with other European bodies (aerospace, iron and steel, open systems and electronic data interchange) and the International Organization for Standardization (ISO)"[54]. CEN/ISSS, a sub-section in the CEN, was created in 1997 as the focus for its ICT activities[55].

Similar to the IEEE/LTSC, CEN/ISSS Learning Technologies Workshop (LTWS)[56] is the committee dealing with E-Learning. CEN/ISSS LTWS are working very closely with IEEE/LTSC, trying to leverage the results concerning LOM, for example.

2.4.2.2 Organizations involved

The organizations involved take the standards issued by the standardization bodies and go a step further towards implementation in a specific domain. The three organizations mentioned here are thought to be the most important ones and hence are the only ones

---

[54][45]
[55]See [46]
[56][44]

to be described.

ARIADNE: *"The Alliance of Remote Instructional Authoring and Distribution Networks for Europe (ARIADNE) Foundation was created to exploit and further develop the results of the ARIADNE and ARIADNE II European Projects, which created tools and methodologies for producing, managing and reusing computer-based pedagogical elements and telematics supported training curricula"*[57].

ARIADNE´s concept[58] is based on many dislocated knowledge pools that are interconnected via prototypes and methodologies.

One important research issue, the ARIADNE Educational Meta-data specification (the 'pedagogical header'), contributed very much to the IEEE/LTSC LOM specification.

AICC: *"The Aviation Industry CBT Committee (AICC), founded in 1988, is an international association of technology-based training professionals. The AICC develops guidelines for aviation industry in the development, delivery, and evaluation of CBT and related training technologies. The objectives of the AICC include assisting airplane operators in development of guidelines which promote the economic and effective implementation of CBT, developing guidelines to enable interoperability and providing an open forum for the discussion of CBT (and other) training technologies"*[59].

The "AICC Guidelines and Recommendations (AGR)"[60] are the specifications issued by the AICC, including Computer Managed Instruction (CMI), Courseware Interchange, Web-based computer-managed instruction, etc. Especially CMI gives input to other standards and specifications, i.e. IEEE/LTSC CMI WG or ADL's Sharable Content Object Reference Model (SCORM)[61].

IMS: *"IMS Global Learning Consortium, Inc. is developing and promoting open specifications for facilitating online distributed learning activities such as locating and using educational content, tracking learner progress, reporting learner performance, and exchanging student records between administrative systems ... IMS is a global consortium with members from educational, commercial, and government organizations."*[62].

IMS´s aim is not only to provide technical specifications, but also to support their incorporation in products. The core IMS specifications for E-Learning concern[63]

- Meta-data

---

[57][14]
[58][15]
[59][9]
[60]See [11]
[61]See [10]
[62][136]
[63]See [138]

- Enterprise

- Content Packaging

- Question and Test

- Learner Information

- Competency Definition

- Accessibility

ADL: *"The Advanced Distributed Learning (ADL) initiative is a collaborative effort between government, industry and academia to establish a new distributed learning environment that permits the interoperability of learning tools and course content on a global scale"*[64].

The ADL initiative was established by the US Department of Defense in 1997 to modernize learning with the help of ICT and promote training and education between government, industry and academic institutions by means of standardization.

High-level requirements for this effort include[65]

- Content reusability

- Accessibility

- Durability

- Interoperability to leverage existing practices

ADL also is responsible for the SCORM, consisting of two parts

- The Content Aggregation Model (CAM)

- and the Run-Time-Environment[66].

Several specifications for LOs exist within CAM, describing different E-Learning domains. They are[67]:

- Meta-data dictionary (from IEEE/LTSC LOM)

- Content Packaging (from IMS)

---

[64][4]
[65][4]
[66]the Run-Time-Environment provides a means for interoperability between LOs and LMS, [6], p. 1-33
[67]See [6], p. 1-5

- Content Structure (derived from AICC)

- Meta-data XML-Binding and Best-Practice (from IMS)

2.4.3 Standards and their impact on E-Learning standardization issues

The current situation in E-Learning, where software producers and E-Learning content providers want to reach goals and profits quickly, without dealing with standardization issues and the potential for re-use, can be compared to the early days of classic software engineering: products were built on the fly without thinking about deployment or functionalities for end-users. Methodologies and dealing with standardization issues have not been considered. E-Learning should learn from history and should not repeat the mistakes made in these early phases of software engineering.

The need for dealing with standardization issues therefore is evident. It seems that commercial software producers have realized this, because almost every product puts on ads including the integration-possibilities concerning standards. Here only a few:

- **DigitalThink E-Learning Platform:**
  "The E-Learning Platform is the highly available, scalable, accountable, and open technology ..."[68]. *"Standards-compliant content can be integrated and managed through the E-Learning Platform. Learning Management supports the AICC and SCORM specifications, the most widely supported standards in the e-learning industry"*[69].

- **WebCT:**
  "WebCT Vista, Built on Extensible, Standards-Based Enterprise Platform Architecture"[70].

- **Blackboard:**
  "We are working with leaders in the accessibility field to bring our software into compliance with industry standards and federal guidelines for accessibility"[71].

- **Sun Enterprise Learning Platform:**
  "Complies with SCORM 1.1/AICC standards for launching and tracking learning

---

[68]See [163], p. 1
[69][74]
[70][317]
[71][32]

content and includes special utilities for interoperating with content which is not standards-compliant ..."[72].

- **Saba Learning - Enterprise Edition**:
  "Robust, Scalable Learning Management ... supports learning technology standards including AICC, ADL SCORM and IMS to improve interoperability with other learning components ..."[73].

Pawlowski and Adelsberger[74] also identify an obligatory need for implementing E-Learning standards, because of the must for up-to-date content due to the augmented use of ICT and the corresponding timely and spatial flexibility. Standards therefore are the only way to sensibly interconnect the participating entities

- Technologies

- Actors

- Methods and

- Content

Pawlowski and Adelsberger define base requirements that E-Learning standards in terms of the participating entities mentioned must fulfill:

- Possibility for recombination

- Possibility to use entities in another context

- Portability and Interoperability

- Adaptability

- Flexibility

- Simplicity

- Profitability

---

[72][267]
[73][233]
[74]See [213], pp. 2

2.4.4 Implications for end-users: Which standard or specification should you choose?

Taking the information and quotations from the latter Chapter, the following question has to be answered: how is it possible for the end-user - either the company, that wants to invest in an E-Learning product or the learner or administrator, who formulate requirements - to settle on a certain standard or specification? The trend shows a very strong connection with XML in general, but which XML-application will succeed in the end is still a big question-mark. But the vicious circle only begins with the standards or specifications problem, because E-Learning products implement only one of them at the moment. Cohen´s article[75] describes this dilemma and poses questions like *"Will SCORM lead the way?"* but still seeing, that *"... inevitably, the market pressure for interoperability will prevail"*.

Summing it up, at this point no standard or specification, de-facto as well as de-iure, has reached wide-spread acceptance.

Therefore, Chapter 2.4.5 gives a general overview on the most common E-Learning standards and specifications.

2.4.5 The E-Learning "situation"

Figure 2.11 describes the E-Learning "situation"[76]. On top, consortia give the input as an organization coping with E-Learning standards, and coming from the bottom, the corresponding drafts, specifications and standards are shown. The figure is not complete, but the relevant institutions on top were already mentioned in Chapter 2.4.2. This Chapter is concerned with the elements at the bottom. It also reflects the structure of its sub-chapters.

We can distinguish between general document description and E-Learning description on the top level, when talking about specifications and standards. "Resource Description Framework (RDF)" and "Dublin Core" are two standardization efforts concerning general document description and will make up the first part of this Chapter followed by E-Learning description possibilities with its sub-elements "General Standards", "Metadata", "Skills and Profiles" and "Management". The classification of this level of Figure 2.11 is an aggregation of the structure of the IEEE working groups and the specifications

---

[75]See [55]

[76]E-Learning standards will be revisited several times in this thesis (e.g. see Chapter 4.3.1), because they build the foundation for all further ideas.

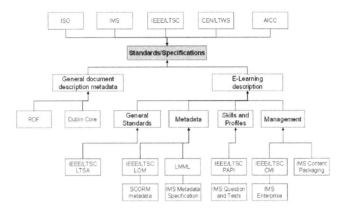

Figure 2.11: Meta-data classification

of IMS[77].

Details on these standards are to be discussed in the following Chapters that reflect the structure of Figure 2.11.

The focus of this Chapter lies on the section "Meta-data". All other categories are going to be described in brief only.

The method chosen[78] to evaluate all standards and specifications is a standardized schema, enabling a final evaluation.

- General information on the initiative or body concerned with the standard or specification

- Current and future status

- Overview on the meta-standard core and elements

- Advantages, difficulties and conclusions

2.4.6 General document description

General document description defines meta-data for categorizing documents like word-processor-documents or html-files. Core purpose is to transform the current WWW into a Semantic Web. Besides this core purpose, general document description is input to

---

[77]See Chapter 2.4.2.1
[78]only for general document description and meta-data

E-Learning meta-data. In the following, the two most important meta-data-descriptions are discussed, RDF and Dublin Core[79].

2.4.6.1 Dublin Core

Dublin Core is a short form of the meta-data standards issued by the "Dublin Core Metadata Initiative".

General information: DCMI originated in 1995, in Dublin, Ohio[80]. DCMI´s mission is to promote and publish meta-data standards[81] and specializes in describing meta-data-vocabularies. The DCMI consists of[82]

- a Board of Trustees, that oversees general activities

- a Directorate, concerned with management and coordination

- an Advisory Board, that gives advice and technical support to the Directorate

- several Working Groups, that are concerned with special topics and defining specifications due to special guidelines.

As already mentioned, DCMI strongly interrelates with other meta-data initiatives in order to leverage positive effects. Related organizations include CEN, IEEE/LTSC LOM, ISO/IEC JTC1/SC36 and the World-wide Web Consortium (W3C).

Current and future status[83]: The Dublin Core defines a meta-data schema for linking networked resources with the consensus of international, cross-disciplinary groups of professionals from librarianship, computer sciences, text encoding, the museum community, and other related fields of scholarship. 15 elements were found that make up the Dublin Core standard. Dublin Core sets its focus on document-like objects, but it can also be applied into other kinds of resources. This can be achieved by its openness towards adding new elements or skipping (all) optional elements. Dublin Core has the following goals:

- Simplicity of creation and maintenance

- Commonly understood semantics

- International scope

---

[79]See Chapters 2.4.6.1 and 2.4.6.2 for the use of RDF and Dublin Core in E-Learning.
[80]See [62]
[81]See Chapter 2.4.7.2 for details on the term meta-data
[82]See [63]
[83]See [112]

Content	Intellectual Property	Instantiation
Coverage	Contributor	Date
Description	Creator	Format
Type	Publisher	Identifier
Relation	Rights	Language
Source		
Subject		
Title		

Table 2.3: The Dublin Core elements

- Extensibility

Overview on the meta-standard core and elements[84]: Table 2.3 shows the 15 Dublin Core elements sorted by three criteria.

The criteria more detailed:

- "Content" describes the resource itself, using title, subject and other mentioned attributes

- "Intellectual Property" defines details about the owner of the content

- "Instantiation" defines the resource-instance concerning format, language, etc. (i.e. the same resource could exist in English and in German)

Advantages, difficulties and conclusions: Dublin Core defines an extremely open standard concerning resource-meta-data. Difficulties between more than one meta-data-namespace are sure to arise. DCMI encounters this with the "Qualifier"-concept. With the help of Qualifiers, some elements´ meaning can be refined[85]. Within "Summaries for Qualifiers", more concrete attributes are qualified with the Dublin Core elements (i.e. "Created" is qualified with the Dublin Core element "Date")[86]. The relevance of Dublin Core in terms of E-Learning is also quite evident and can bring important input to E-Learning meta-data initiatives.

In the future, the RDF-binding of Dublin Core will play an important role in the Semantic Web.

---

[84]See [112]
[85]See [67]
[86]See [66]

2.4.6.2 RDF

RDF is a meta-data specification issued by the W3C. In contrast to the Dublin Core, RDF concentrates on automated processing of the tagged resources together with connection to rights management and digital signatures[87].

General information: The W3C[88] was founded in 1994 at the Massachusetts Institute of Technology, Laboratory for Computer Science (MICT/LCS), in collaboration with CERN, with support from DARPA and the European Commission. The W3C´s mission is to promote and encourage interoperability on the WWW by supplying an open forum and technical specifications and standards. The W3C team mostly is spread on the facilities of its hosts, the MICT/LCS in the United States, l'Institut National de Recherche en Informatique et en Automatique (INRIA) in France, and Keio University in Japan. It is lead by

- a Chief Operating Officer and the Director and founder, Tim Berners-Lee

- the "Technical Architecture Group"

- the "Advisory Board"

One of the numerous standards and specifications is RDF.

Current and future status:

RDF shall maximize the interoperability between web-servers and clients through defining a mechanism for describing resources that makes *"no assumptions about a particular application domain, nor defines (a priori) the semantics of any application domain. The definition of the mechanism should be domain neutral, yet the mechanism should be suitable for describing information about any domain"*[89].

RDF has the following goals:

- possibility to specify semantics for data based on XML in a standardized, interoperable manner

- resources are tagged to be processed in an automated, machine-readable way

Overview on the meta-standard core and elements[90]: *"The foundation of RDF is a model for representing named properties and property values"*[91]. The RDF-model

---

[87]See [296]
[88]See [294]
[89][296]
[90][296]
[91][296]

```
[1] RDF           ::= ['<rdf:RDF>'] description* ['</rdf:RDF>']
[2] description   ::= '<rdf:Description' idAboutAttr '>' propertyElt*
                      '</rdf:Description>'
[3] idAboutAttr   ::= idAttr | aboutAttr
[4] aboutAttr     ::= 'about="' URI-reference '"'
[5] idAttr        ::= 'ID="' IDsymbol '"'
[6] propertyElt   ::= '<' propName '>' value '</' propName '>'
                    | '<' propName resourceAttr '/>'
[7] propName      ::= Qname
[8] value         ::= description | string
[9] resourceAttr  ::= 'resource="' URI-reference '"'
[10] Qname        ::= [ NSprefix ':' ] name
[11] URI-reference ::= string, interpreted per [URI]
[12] IDsymbol     ::= (any legal XML name symbol)
[13] name         ::= (any legal XML name symbol)
[14] NSprefix     ::= (any legal XML namespace prefix)
[15] string       ::= (any XML text, with "<", ">", and "&" escaped)
```

Figure 2.12: RDF-syntax

can be compared to models in other ICT-disciplines like the ER-model. An example of this relation could be "the property DOCUMENT has the value RESOURCE_ID". This is a RDF property-value relation that can also be seen as two entities having a relationship in respect to the Entity-Relationship method. The basic RDF-model consists of three object types:

- **Resources**:
  Any object described by RDF is called a resource. A resource is unambiguously defined by a Unified Resource Identifier (URI).

- **Properties**:
  A Property is a specific attribute or aspect of a resource.

- **Statements**:
  A resource together with a property and a property-value is called statement. A statement can of course have a link to another resource.

Figure 2.12[92] shows the basic RDF-syntax.

See Figure 2.13 for a basic example. A resource is described by a URI coming from the RDF-namespace referenced with the RDF-tag "Description" and the attribute "about".

Advantages, difficulties and conclusions: RDF is often used in combination with the Dublin Core or other proprietary vocabularies. RDF describes the resource in a very abstract way, only showing the connection via a URI to make it machine-readable, whereas Dublin Core put more detail in the resource's meta-data information, concerning an author or title. Hillman notes, the *"decentralized approach recognizes that no one scheme is appropriate for all situations, and further that schemes need a linking mechanism independent of a central authority to aid description, identification, understanding, usability,*

---

[92]taken from [296]

```
<rdf:RDF xmlns:rdf="http://www.w3.org/1999/02/22-rdf-syntax-ns#"
         xmlns:dc="http://purl.org/dc/elements/1.1/">

  <rdf:Description rdf:about="http://media.example.com/audio/guide.ra">
     <dc:creator>Rose Bush</dc:creator>
     <dc:title>A Guide to Growing Roses</dc:title>
     <dc:description>Describes process for planting and nurturing different kinds of rose bushes.</dc:description>
     <dc:date>2001-01-20</dc:date>
  </rdf:Description>
</rdf:RDF>
```

Figure 2.13: Combined use of RDF and Dublin Core

and/or exchange"[93]. This independent mechanism is provided by RDF.
With the help of RDF, multiple applications coming from different domains may be linked
- like the referenced audio recording of Figure 2.13[94] - to any resource - like a curriculum
vitae of the author.

2.4.7 E-Learning

This Chapter deals with standards and specifications concerning E-Learning. Whereas
Chapter 2.4.6 does not have a special domain, we will now discuss, the specifics in E-
Learning.

2.4.7.1 General Standards

General standards in E-Learning describe high-level system design when facing ICT-
supported learning.
From the IEEE/LTSC, a specification is issued in this category called Learning Technology Systems Architecture (LTSA)[95]. LTSA helps to understand a system architecture
from a top level, describing systems, sub-systems and their interrelations. Aim of this
specification is to provide high-level re-usability, cost-effectiveness and adaptability. *"The
architectural framework developed in this standard should not address the specific details
of implementation technologies ... . The standard shall identify the objectives of human
activities and computer processes"*[96].

2.4.7.2 Meta-data

> *"Imagine that you are wired into all the digital learning content on the
> planet. With the magical click of a mouse you can retrieve anything from
> anywhere. Also imagine that you are putting together a course on gardening
> and what you need is a three-minute video clip on hydroponics that takes a*

---

[93][112]
[94]See figure [112]
[95]See [129], p. 7
[96][129], p. 7

discovery learning approach.

*You have to be able to legally reproduce it, it needs to be in a format that works
with other content in your course, and it must run on the computers in your
learning lab. How are you going to find a clip that meets all these criteria?
You could try a Web search, but Web search engines are primarily based on
key words extracted from the content itself. That method won't work for video
clips since they don't contain words, and it won't tell you anything about the
educational approach or most of your other selection criteria. To effectively
find and use e-learning content, you need information about content that is
not necessarily in the content. This is called meta-data*[97].

Meta-data is *"information about information"*[98] or *"structured data about data"*[99] and
therefore gives meaning or semantics to the described information-object, making it accessible for third-party users. If you want to sell an LO, you have to provide certain
details about it, describing the author, the format, creation date, etc. This is information
about your LO and therefore meta-data. Other examples[100] include library management,
where meta-data are assigned to books, i.e. the title, author ISBN, etc.

The use of meta-data also implies another technical requirement, namely the use of modular built LOs. There are at least three reasons to be mentioned here, to produce these
LOs:

1. The creation of small, modular units makes it easier to re-use them, especially in
   terms of learning-on-demand.

2. Modular LOs, in terms of skill-management, are much easier to assign to a person.
   A personalized curriculum showing the current skills may be the result and could
   show the learning gap, the person has to overcome in order to achieve a certain
   knowledge standard.

3. E-Learning is often mixed up with teleconferencing and delivering the content with
   large video-streams. Students get bored with long, non-interactive sequences. Small
   LOs are easy to grasp and improve interactivity, because they have to be clicked on
   at the time the student wants to watch them. And there is no reason to implement
   a sophisticated meta-data concept for a single video file.

---

[97][228]
[98][295]
[99][64]
[100]See [192]

LOs can be defined in the following way: *"An LO can be any entity, digital or non-digital that can be used or referenced in technology-supported learning. An LO can be physical, such as text, a workbook, or a CD-ROM, or online, such as electronic text, a .GIF graphic image, a QuickTime movie, or a Java applet"*[101].
The aims of meta-data are the following[102]:

- enabling field-based (e.g., author, title) searches

- permitting indexing of non-textual objects

- allowing access to the surrogate content that is distinct from access to the content of the resource itself

Learning Object Meta-data (LOM): The IEEE P1484.12 Learning Object Meta-data Working Group[103] dedicates its work to the LOM standard that specifies syntax and semantics to fully describe an LO in terms of meta-data[104].
General information: Information about IEEE/LTSC, the working group dealing with LOM, was already given in Chapter 2.4.2.1.
Current and future status: LOM has become an IEEE standard in November 2002 under the name of IEEE/LTSC 1484.12.1-2002. LOM is specified in a very general way, using Dublin Core for sub-definitions of attributes and may be extended and will probably be basis for other domain-specific efforts to describe E-Learning meta-data[105].
Purpose of Proposed Project[106]:

- To enable learners or instructors to search, evaluate, acquire, and utilize Learning Objects.

- To enable the sharing and exchange of Learning Objects across any technology supported learning systems.

- To enable the development of LOs in units that can be combined and decomposed in meaningful ways.

- To enable computer agents to automatically and dynamically compose personalized lessons for an individual learner.

---

[101][192]
[102]See [112], Hillman references Weibel and Lagoze, 1997, at the end of section 1.1
[103]See [127]
[104][128]
[105]IMS meta-data and SCORM meta-data both instantiate LOM.
[106][128]

- To compliment the direct work on standards that are focused on enabling multiple Learning Objects to work together within a open distributed learning environment.

- To enable, where desired, the documentation and recognition of the completion of existing or new learning and performance objectives associated with Learning Objects.

- To enable a strong and growing economy for Learning Objects that supports and sustains all forms of distribution; non-profit, not-for-profit and for profit.

- To enable education, training and learning organizations, both governments, public and private, to express educational content and performance standards in a standardized format that is independent of the content itself.

- To provide researchers with standards that support the collection and sharing of comparable data concerning the applicability and effectiveness of Learning Objects.

- To define a standard that is simple and yet extensible to multiple domains and jurisdictions so as to be most easily and broadly adopted and applied.

- To support necessary security and authentication for the distribution and use of Learning Objects.

Overview on the meta-standard core and elements: The LOMv1.0 Base Schema consists of the following main categories[107]:

- General category

- Lifecycle category

- Meta-Meta-data category

- Technical category

- Educational category

- Rights category

- Relation category

- Annotation category

---

[107]See [123]

- Classification category

These categories group data elements and therefore LOM data model *"is a hierarchy of data elements, including aggregate data, elements and simple data elements (leaf nodes of the hierarchy)"*[108], where only leaf nodes have values according to their value space and data type. Aggregates and elements do not have individual values. For each data element, LOM defines[109]

- a name

- an explanation

- a size

- an order

- an example

Advantages, difficulties and conclusions: To put it in a nut-shell, LOM will be the basis for all further efforts in E-Learning meta-data, as it has already become an IEEE standard and will probably move forward towards an ISO standard as well. Criticism about meaning and interpretation of LOM elements (i.e. element "semantic density") will surely heat up the discussions, but nevertheless LOM will be used in practice.

SCORM meta-data and IMS meta-data Many of the organizations and standardization bodies work closely together, trying to get the best out of individual research in common specifications. AICC, ADL, IMS, IEEE/LTSC, CEN/LTWS, ARIADNE, DCMI and ISO are the important key players in this context.

Concerning E-Learning meta-data, as mentioned in the Chapter before, LOM, as a standard, will lead the way. This Chapter, describing SCORM meta-data and IMS meta-data, therefore will be very short, as they both leverage LOM with some own specific additions. The following citations clearly point out this development:

- **IMS meta-data**:

    "The following table is based on the IEEE LTSC LOM Working Draft 6.1: Base Scheme (2001-02-13). Names have been changed to be all lower case ... IMS additions and modifications are noted ..."[110]

---

[108][123]

[109]For the full list of aggregates and elements of LOMv1.0 Base Schema see Table 1 in [123], pp. 10.

[110][137]

- **SCORM meta-data**:

  "It is built upon the work of the AICC, IMS, IEEE, ARIADNE and others to create one unified "reference model" of interrelated technical specifications and guidelines designed to meet Department of Defense's high-level requirements for Web-based learning content. ... The SCORM references IMS Meta-data Information Model ... based on IEEE/LTSC LOM Specification ..."[111]

Learning Material Markup Language (LMML) 1.1 LMML is an academic effort towards an E-Learning meta-data specification of the University of Passau, Germany.

General information: *"The Learning Material Markup Language is an XML-based markup language designed for educational contents. It provides sub-languages for various educational fields and yet remains further extensible"*[112].

Current and future status: LMML originated in version 1.0 and is currently in the stage 1.1[113].

Overview on the meta-standard core and elements: LMML groups elements in the following way[114]:

- ContentModules

- MediaObjects

- StructureObjects

- StructureModules

Advantages, difficulties and conclusions: LMML will not be discussed further as it seems that development has ended.

2.4.7.3 Services, Skills and Profiles

Service, Skills and Profiles describe specifications and standards for the actors surrounding the LOs. They include administrators, students, teachers, tutors, etc. But not only description about the actors themselves have to be included, but also rights management regarding authoring, publishing and grading and skill management.

IEEE/LTSC´s Public and Private Information (PAPI) for example *"specifies the syntax and semantics of a 'Learner Model', which characterizes a learner (student or knowledge worker) and his or her knowledge/abilities. This Standard includes elements for*

---

[111][5], p. 2-12
[112][264]
[113]Further development cannot be found in the source [264].
[114][265]

recording knowledge acquisition, skills, abilities, learning styles, records, and personal information "[115].

2.4.7.4 Management

Management specifications and standards enable combination and administration of LOs into courses, being able to exchange content between one or more LMS and thus providing interoperability.

IEEE/LTSC CMI[116] is a representative for this category.

2.4.8 Further institutions concerned with standardization topics

This Chapter concludes with an enumeration of further institutions involved in E-Learning concludes this Chapter:

- K12-Learning Consortium
  http://canvas.ltc.vanderbilt.edu/lc/

- American Society for Training and Development, E-Learning Courseware Certification
  http://www.astd.org/

- European Commission
  http://europa.eu.int/comm/education/elearning/index.html

- Universal Learning Format (ULF)
  http://www.saba.com/standards/ulf/Overview/Frames/overview.htm

- Microsoft: Learning Resource Interchange (LRN)
  http://www.microsoft.com/elearn/

2.5 Dimensions for E-Learning Applications

The following Chapters describe several requirements that can be seen as dimensions that have to be considered when implementing an E-Learning Application.

---

[115][124], p. 8
[116]See [125]

2.5.1 LMS and LCMS

This part addresses implementation of the ideas from Chapter 2.4. Definitions in this area and current systems and platforms are looked at.

LMS or LCMS build the basis for implementing an E-Learning solution. Functionality should include

- Administration/Assessment

- Communication

- Providing learning specific tools

- Presenting content

- Skills management/Tracking

· Besides these functionalities, the following requirements should be considered[117]:

- Accessibility

- Flexibility

- Extensibility

- Reusability

- Interoperability

- Scalability

- Security

- Standards compliance

- Leveraging of existing corporate infrastructure.

There are a lot of synonyms for LMS and LCMS, some are E-Learning system, E-Learning Portal, etc. also depending on some countries specifics. In this thesis, a system environment for E-Learning is called LMS.

Literature provides the following definitions:

- *"LMS ... is a suite of functionalities to deliver, track, report and manage learning content, student progress and student interaction"*[118].

---

[117]See [16]
[118][6]

- LMS include *"administrative functionalities supporting registration, application, pro-filing, personalization and recording of data"*[119].

- *"Software that automates the administration of training events. The LMS registers users, tracks courses in a catalog, and records data from learners; it also provides reports to management. An LMS is typically designed to handle courses by multiple publishers and providers. It usually doesn't include its own authoring capabilities; instead, it focuses on managing courses created by a variety of other sources ... A software application that allows trainers and training directors to manage both the administrative and content-related functions of training. An LCMS combines the course management capabilities of an LMS (learning management system) with the content creation and storage capabilities of a CMS (content management system)"*[120].

- *"We're in the midst of an e-learning revolution, which brings with it rapid change ... Stage 1: Generic content libraries ..., Stage 2: Learning management systems ..., Stage 3: Outsourced e-learning platforms ..., Stage 4: Learning content management systems ..."*[121].

In the following Chapter, a generic LMS architecture is introduced. Chapters 2.5.3 and 2.5.4 discuss two dimensions concerning LMS that extend the existing approaches. They are process-orientation and the need for a methodology.

2.5.2   E-Learning architecture

A generic E-Learning LMS-architecture, comprising all necessary features, is sketched in Figure 2.14.

The LMS itself has got only a Personalized Web Portal giving access to users, other LMS or proprietary Authoring and Admin Tools, communicating with E-Learning standards vocabularies. One layer below the Portal, a Application Server manages business logic by combining other applications, that interact with each other. The architecture should be open towards inclusion of other Application Programming Interfaces (APIs). Java 2 Enterprise Edition (J2EE) compliant Application Servers or other middleware products are a possibility for this task.

---

[119][20], p. 296, translation
[120][18]
[121][227]

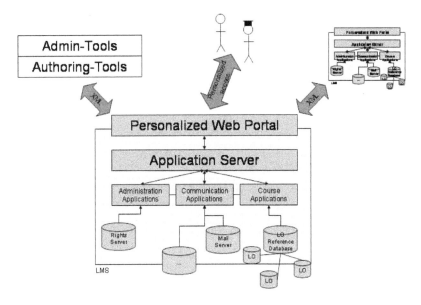

Figure 2.14: LMS architecture

2.5.3 Process oriented E-Learning

Process-orientation had great impact on BPM bringing lots of advantages to educational institutions. Advantages include:

- Structured methodology

- Dynamic view of learning scenarios over time

- Integration of learning services along a value-chain

- BPM-models are knowledge objects themselves serving as input for corporate learning

- Possibility to evaluate learning scenarios

- Documentation for dissemination via intranet

- Decision-tool through simulation possibilities

- etc.

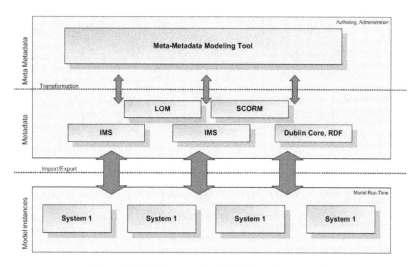

Figure 2.15: Process-oriented E-Learning scenario

With adapting the process-idea for E-Learning these advantages plus gaining totally new perspectives can be instantly inherited.

The modeling methods are nothing but defining meta-data semantics, and instantiating these meta-models may give E-Learning standard-compliant XML code that can be used universally.

Impact for process-oriented E-Learning is displayed in Figure 2.15:

2.5.4 Methodologies: Coherence of BPMS, PROMOTE and AD-VISOR

Figure 2.3 already showed the interdependencies between current technologies. They have to be kept in mind in order to maximize system integration.

Factors are:

- General factors

    - Integration of interdependencies to other ICT-disciplines

    - Integration of methodologies

    - Identification of added-values

- E-Learning factors

- Hybrid methodology

- Openness und scalability towards change management

- E-Learning strategy's influence on general strategy

For this matter, existing methodologies BPMS[122], PROMOTE[123] and ADVISOR[124] are
to be further scrutinized.

Especially the relationship PROMOTE-ADVISOR has added-value potential according
to the concepts of Chapters 2.2.4.1 and 2.3.3.

2.6 Future development of current E-Learning with respect to the standards development

Tim Berners-Lee and the W3C are trying to take the WWW into a new level called
Semantic Web. The Semantic Web shall bring order into the unstructured WWW as it
exists now. Anything will be a meta-data-tagged resource, and finally the user will be
able to retrieve the content he is looking for and information suppliers can publish their
information as knowledge in a very proper way.

ICT-disciplines will follow, and E-Learning may be a pioneer in this matter. Semantically
tagged E-Learning resources will be included in the new WWW to make personalized
Learning-on-demand a matter of seconds.

I believe that the meta-data and standards discussion will succeed in a positive way soon,
meaning, that not only a new trusted and authentic Semantic Web will be born, but also
that a new "information-society" will lead the way. This development is reflected by the
Roadmap to Semantic E-Learing.

2.6.1 Meta-data issues

It is quite clear that the meta-data issue in E-Learning will play a key role in future
development. It is quite interesting to see the top-down development in the E-Learning
area. Standards like IEEE/LTSC LOM emerge quite early at a mature status, forcing
companies to adopt the standard-topic, like clearly pointed out in Chapter 2.4.3.

It could be, that de-iure-standards will be able to force ICT under their yoke. This could

---

[122]See [156]
[123]See [157]
[124]See [34]

be a benefit for both end-users[125] and companies[126] giving the greatest degree of freedom for both parties. Unlike in other ICT-disciplines where the rapid corporate developments overtook research (i.e. Workflow Management, Office Products, etc.), E-Learning could lead the way to a sensible outcome[127].

Future developments include[128]:

- Use of standard meta-data tags only in accordance to individual needs

- Standards will be included into E-Learning products

- Powerful searching will become a standard feature within LMS

- Repositories will emerge to store and manage learning content and meta-data tags for personalized learning, a.k.a. learning-on-demand

- Standards-based meta-data tagging will leverage interoperability between E-Learning and KM products

2.6.2 Learning-on-demand

Taking the future meta-data developments into account, the individual user will be able to personalize his learning matters in real-time in large E-Learning repositories, based on standard descriptions.

Besides the access to large repositories, standard skill-ontologies[129] have to be defined, so that personalized learning called learning-on-demand can grow to its full potential by providing only the content needed. Having reached this state of maturity and rapid development in wireless communication technologies, E-Learning can take off to new dimensions without borders.

---

[125] *"Metadata tagging also benefits individual learners. As E-Learning grows in popularity users will soon be able to purchase a wide array of off-the-shelf content. And meta-data tagging will provide a consistent way to locate the information they want."*, see [17]

[126] *"Metadata tagging enables organizations to describe, index, and search their learning resources-and that's essential for reusing them."*, see [17]

[127] *"Buyers are demanding standards, and vendors are stuck in a tough spot when buyers put 'standards compliance' on their requests for proposal,' says Wayne Hodgins, chief learning officer for software developer AutoDesk and chair of the IEEE standards task force."*, see [19]

[128] according to [17]

[129] Skill ontologies have to be viewed from two different sides. Firstly, a skill ontology describes required skills for an LO. Secondly, skill ontologies describe the skill level for a person in a Learner Profile. This deviation is often called skill-gap.

2.7 New architectural approach in E-Learning: Web-Services

The E-Learning community has realized the need and impact of new technologies like the Semantic Web and Web-Services. This creates the necessity for a re-orientation in terms of architectures and applications with the benefits of openness and interoperability to better serve customers' needs. The developments in E-Learning are quite promising when looking at XML standards like LOM but still lack RDF-bindings to be applicable to a Semantic Web of service-oriented architecture concepts. Nevertheless, big summits[130] about E-Learning have two main topics at the moment:

- Standards

- Web-Services

Standards have already been discussed and so the following part will be dedicated to the second topic: Web-Services.

It has always been the dream of Software Engineers to reuse existing code in a way, that required program logic should only be added to already programmed templates or basic code. This development is reflected in the evolution of Software Engineering over the years by introducing object-orientation, establishing the software development process as engineering discipline through the use of UML and standard methodologies like the "Rational Unified Process" or the introduction of reusable repositories like the "Standard Template Library". All these efforts did not seem to work out as suggested or are still in evolution. To embrace today's importance of internet technologies, a new scientific discipline in this context emerged, called Web-Services. Web-Services are the next step in software development evolution, taking the one-to-many to a many-to-many approach, providing many distributed repositories to choose chunks of services via Extensible Markup Language (XML) interfaces over the internet. This finally shall make non-computer-experts' dreams come true: they will be able to produce personalized applications without having to code one single line, "some mouse-clicks will be sufficient".

This stands for a jump from thin-clients and fat-servers to distributed service integration via standard-internet protocols[131]. This development also has general ideas of the Semantic Web community in common. It determines business automation as a top requirement of the future internet, so that XML annotated and therefore machine-readable data can

---

[130]See http://www.elearningresults.com as an example.
[131]See [261], p. 435

	Distributed Computing	Web-Services
Paradigm	Client-Server	Peer-to-Peer
Consumption	Human-to-Human	Computer-to-Computer
Level of sophistication	Content information	Personalized information
Coupling	Tight coupling	Loose coupling
Size	Monolithic	Service components

Table 2.4: Comparison of Distributed Computing approaches vs. Web-Services

be transformed into information and knowledge to serve a greater purpose.
Obvious advantages of Web-Services include[132]:

- Error avoidance through machine-processing

- Process acceleration

- Simplification of interfaces to the actual know-how

- Cost reduction, if transformed correctly

- Perfect adaptation and customization of users' needs through the use of reusable, decomposed and distributed services at run-time

- Software as a Service

- Dynamic Business Interoperability

- Accessibility

- Efficiencies

- Universally Agreed Specifications

- Legacy integration

- New Market Opportunities

Table 2.4 is a subsumption and comparison of classic Distributed Computing approaches (i.e. CORBA, (D)COM, RMI, etc.) vs. Web-Services.

Chapter 2.7 and Appendix A introduce and motivate efforts for research in the integration of Web-Services and E-Learning.

---

[132]See [261], p. 436, and [317]

Appendix A features information and definitions on the term "Web-Service" in general. The aim is to create a taxonomy of terms and technologies associated with Web-Services to be able to categorize and explore different architectures proposed by standards bodies, such as Universal Description, Discovery and Integration of Web-Services (UDDI), Simple Object Access Protocol (SOAP), and Web-Services Description Language (WSDL), and global players, such as IBM, Microsoft or Sun.

After having dealt with Web-Services in general, Chapter 2.7.1 concentrates on requirements for E-Learning, in case of using Web-Services. The basic idea is to create a top-down approach where each step is clearly defined by a methodology. Therefore, resources and relations between them have to be annotated semantically, bringing a link to the Semantic Web as a foundation for Web-Services. KM serves as means to reach this foundation.

Chapter 2.7.2 delivers a proposed working scenario with the service-oriented framework PROMOTE and gives a future outlook, including a semi-automatic scenario mapping a KM Process to a SOAP protocol file.

Chapter 2.7.3 concludes with next steps that have to be taken.

2.7.1   Web-Services in E-Learning

The title of this thesis already implies a certain research area, namely E-Learning[133]. But it is also important to point out the relationship to another area, namely KM. The conclusion to be drawn is the following: when faced with implementations of KM or E-Learning, it is of primary interest to include the business strategy by taking a top-down approach. This includes the Business Process landscape of the targeted implementation first and the linking to ICT resources only as a consequence of this landscape. Moreover KM includes a methodology taking care of the top-down approach.

The benefit of the symbiosis of E-Learning and KM is a semantically rich description of the business, its resources and their interdependence. And this again builds a perfect foundation for a linking to the Semantic Web that also takes KM matters into internet technologies.

2.7.1.1   The relationship between Knowledge Management and E-Learning

Since the uprising of strategic decision support through ICT, information systems have taken the task of supplying decision makers with the relevant information at the right time and the right place. In recent years, a new scientific approach was created to fulfill these needs: KM became the new sanctuary and software vendors promised to solve every

---

[133]For this Chapter see [181]

problem by managing the resource knowledge. Often functionality has been traded in for strategic issues and the "circle of KM" was replaced by a "vicious circle of KM".

As a part of KM, the term organizational learning was coined to point out, that knowledge has to be managed on the one hand but also has to be distributed as part of employee-training, without giving further details. Later on, E-Learning emerged as a self-standing discipline.

Although both KM and E-Learning are obviously quite similar, integration-efforts of both scientific communities are quite rare. Both technologies are about the management of resources, called knowledge object or LO, and have to present them to the end-user in a typical kind of way: either by providing knowledge portals to retrieve "the right information at the right time and place" or by setting up an online course. It probably is a rather philosophical issue, whether KM and E-Learning are to be treated separately, either arguing, that KM were a part of E-Learning or vice versa. This thesis tries to look ahead of all of these discussions for the integration momentum. This momentum may take KM and E-Learning from being quite static to dynamic content repositories giving users on-demand, context-aware "just-for-me" knowledge or learning content.

Most importantly, let us mention methodologies. Integrating strategic issues is probably the most important factor, as all of the mentioned technologies are interdisciplinary, combining management of human and financial resources only enabled by ICT. To keep track of all these input factors, standard documentation, evaluation and management and tool integration as well are a "must" for success.

In the following, some citations about combining methodologies, strategies and efforts to integrate KM and E-Learning are listed:

- Fraunhofer IESE calls *"technology enabled learning and Knowledge Management a very promising strategy"*. Therefore, IntView-KM methodology was introduced to *"set-up a combined learning and Knowledge Management environment ... in packaging small chunks of knowledge into courseware modules"*[134].

- Lytras et. al. introduce the *"Multidimensional dynamic Learning Model"*, describing a cube with KM, E-Learning and Integration as dimensions. The KM and E-Learning dimension contribute to an integrative model by managing objects and Knowledge Management processes on the KM-axis, by *"incorporating learning styles, learning needs and templates"* on the E-Learning-axis and by providing collaboration tools and knowledge generation through linking to real business operations on the Integration-axis. *"The combination of the two life cycles, the Knowledge Manage-*

---

[134][105]

ment framework and the e-learning life cycle, the knowledge objects are transformed dynamically to learning products through specific consideration. ... This approach has to be based in integrated approaches, which include ontologies Knowledge Management, semantics and annotations"[135].

- Lytras emphasizes the importance of meta-data annotation to make LOs knowledge assets for reuse by introducing a meta-data schema[136].

- Maurer et. al.[137] argue, that E-Learning has to be a part of KM, to be able to face future information overflow, presented by an "Omnipresent Computer" that brings together individuals to share their knowledge in a collaborative way to gain value.

- *"There is a great correlation between learning and knowledge"*. Knowledge resources are vital assets for a company and have to be indexed for providing the correct information through search capabilities. This means, that these knowledge resources, according to access-policies, support business processes. These features form the basic functionalities of KM. Learning has to teach users, that the knowledge is understood in the correct way, and that competencies and skills can be built up according to the company's wishes. So the linking part of KM and E-Learning is knowledge. Therefore, Back et. al. mention E-Learning contributions to KM (acquisition, sharing and creation of knowledge) and KM contributions to E-Learning (human resources management, E-Trainings, E-Collaboration, JICT E-Learning)[138].

- Rosenberg[139] refers to KM as a pyramid with three layers: document management, information creation/sharing/management and enterprise intelligence and calls implications for E-Learning "huge". Advantages are the use of structured information with "productivity enhancing tools". The main advantages of an integration are that *"knowledge databases are accurate and available"* and users are able to *"self-select what they want or need"*.

- Kearsley[140] sees organizational learning as central factor between KM and E-Learning, the *"capability of an organization to improve its effectiveness based upon its experience"*. There lies great importance in "accumulated knowledge and skills" in

---

[135][186]
[136]See [185]
[137]See [189]
[138]See [20]
[139]See [229]
[140]See [160]

contrast to learning on an individual level. This is where technology comes in. It can enhance communication and is able to disseminate information via a KM-tool.

- *"KM is about delivering the right knowledge to the right people at the right time"*. Rossett et. al. see KM as catalyst *"to shift the wealth of individual knowledge into organizational resources"*. KM takes responsibility of managing these resources, whereas learning fore mostly is developing "brainpower". So, *"where training builds capacity to help people respond IF a need emerges, KM creates resources that are there WHEN they are needed"*[141].

As these quotations clearly show, literature on the topic "integration of KM and E-Learning" can be found, but the quality of assumptions or tool-support are still very theoretical.

The following enumeration collects important issues and adds additional requirements to an integrated KM and E-Learning system:

- Issue one: Need for a methodology to merge strategy with human resource management and ICT

- Issue two: Large amounts of information need to be described by standard meta-data descriptions to extract the highest value. This also reflects the general direction of the Semantic Web community to make information machine-readable

- Issue three: The semantic structure of information is the heart of a KM-E-Learning system. It must contain standard annotations for the objects themselves and must also include meta-data information about their relationships. This raises questions, which form of representation should be used: XML, RDF, ontologies, taxonomies, topic-maps, mind-maps

- Issue four: Integration of tools and repositories has to be done in a service-based and process-oriented way, in contrast to the use of one big application to ensure flexibility, extensibility and adaptability of the target framework.

- Issue five: a tendency from individual to collaborative knowledge with the need for sophisticated collaboration-tools to build a conjoint organizational memory (OM) exists. This OM shall be presented in a personalized way (Just-for-me), so that the user is only confronted with relevant information (personalized portals).

---

[141][230]

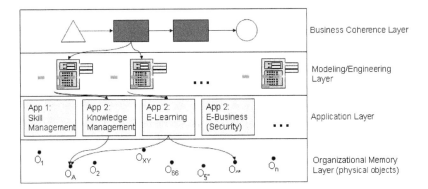

Figure 2.16: Knowledge Management and E-Learning

When these issues or requirements are satisfied, they are greatly relevant for being input for the Semantic Web. The integration of these two technologies also sets the foundation for another emerging branch of today's hot disciplines, namely the Semantic Web. The Semantic Web is dependent on many input factors, like business processes, working environment, skills and service-oriented interaction between these entities Implementing KM and E-Learning are the right means to reach these goals.

The Semantic Web's approach introduces a bottom-up methodology to annotate resources, create ontologies and implement services on top. This thesis takes a top-down approach from an economical point of view, to start with a business plan, describe business processes and ontologies and conclude with description of resources, built on BPM and KM.

Figure 2.16 shows the economically-driven top-down scenario, beginning with business-processes describing the domain expert-knowledge, which is further scrutinized through engineered domain-specific models, which together form the desired framework (in this case KM and E-Learning). The OM layer serves as object repository for whatever framework is modeled.

2.7.1.2 Web-Services and the Semantic Web

Before deploying Web-Services, the structure and resources of the application field have to be described semantically. Resources and interdependences have to be shown in a standard way with meta-data. Only when resources are annotated in such a way, they can be (re-)used and connected in an execution workflow. Web-Services therefore rely on another concept called Semantic Web. This Chapter is an excursion to this topic rounding up the presented ideas and relationships between E-Learning, KM and Web-Services.

machine-processable, semantically rich resources: the Semantic Web					
Web-Services			Linking and execution	SOAP, UDDI, WSDL	PROMOTE Portal
BPM and KM			Creating ontologies	RDF, OWL, DAML+OIL	PROMOTE models
E-Commerce	E-Something	E-Learning	Creating metadata	XML, LOM, IMS	XML, ADL
Scientific disciplines			**Description of resources**	**Technologies**	**PROMOTE**

Figure 2.17: The Semantic Web

The Semantic Web vision was initiated by the "father" of today's WWW Tim Berners-Lee. The Semantic Web is the better version of it, containing semantic information, that makes machine-processing possible. The W3C defines it as *"the abstract representation of data on the World Wide Web, based on the RDF standards and other standards to be defined. It is being developed by the W3C, in collaboration with a large number of researchers and industrial partners"*[142].

One of the first articles was published in Scientific American in May 2001, beginning with a scenario using a "Semantic Web". The following citations are taken from this article[143] and express the main ideas:

- *"The Semantic Web is not a separate Web but an extension of the current one, in which information is given well-defined meaning, better enabling computers and people to work in cooperation".*

- *"these developments will usher in significant new functionality as machines become much better able to process and 'understand' the data that they merely display at present".*

- *"Like the Internet, the Semantic Web will be as decentralized as possible".*

- *"The real power of the Semantic Web will be realized when people create many programs that collect Web content from diverse sources, process the information and exchange the results with other programs. The effectiveness of such software agents will increase exponentially ... The Semantic Web promotes this synergy".*

The Figure 2.17 takes some technologies related to the Semantic Web and puts them into a structured taxonomy that will be the foundation for the ideas of this thesis.

Bringing Figure 2.16 and Figure 2.17 together, the Semantic Web is a collection and interdependence of underlying technologies. The approach in this thesis[144] is top-down,

---

[142]See [296]
[143]See [29]
[144]See Chapter 4.

defining a strategy first that engineers Business Processes and KM interdependences in order to depict and organize the organizational landscape. This creates a set of semantically modeled information, defining the application scenario; in this case, it is an E-Learning scenario. Taking these models into account, XML or RDF representations set the basis for transformation into standard compliant models that can be used as input for Web-Services. This makes the relationship of the Semantic Web and Web-Services complete[145]. Most of the information presented here can only be summarized as vision. Whether the Semantic Web or Web-Services will become reality in the near future depends on several variables, like the ongoing standards-development process and the implementation in real scenarios.

However, there is strong evidence, that the vision will become real:

- One positive hint is the global acceptance of XML as means for information exchange and the use of the internet as physical medium for transporting the data.

- This tendency is underlined by the fact, that only very few standards consortia really are involved (W3C, OASIS).

- All existing and coming standards have XML bindings (RDF, UDDI, WSDL, SOAP, LOM, etc.)

- and strongly recommend to use the HTTP protocol to communicate[146]

- Other Software Engineering approaches failed in supplying this kind of open distributed internet-based architecture[147]: *"Unix RPC requires binary-compatible Unix implementations at each endpoint, CORBA requires compatible Object Request Brokers (ORB), RMI requires Java at each endpoint and DCOM requires Windows at each endpoint"*, whereas SOAP *"is a an XML wire format, that places no restrictions on the endpoint implementation technology choices"*.

2.7.1.3 Requirements using Web-Services in E-Learning

The next topic to be discussed in the context of this Chapter is the role of E-Learning and its relation to Web-Services. There are certain requirements an E-Learning application has to fulfill to be Web-Service compliant. Table 2.5 shows the evolution of E-Learning applications.

---

[145]Column "PROMOTE" anticipates the connection of the Semantic Web and the scenario to be discussed later.
[146]See [47], p. 60, and [224], p. 301
[147]See [121], p. 12

Applications	Needed standards
CBT, WBT	Plain courses: no standards description
LMS	Resource description, Content Packaging: LOM, IMS, SCORM, etc.
Enhanced LMS	Object-oriented services: J2EE (or similar) compliant n-tier architecture, extensible
Distributed E-Learning	E-Learning with Web-Services: SOA, UDDI, WSDL, SOAP, etc.

Table 2.5: Historical development in E-Learning applications

The historical development ranges from CBT and WBT application in the past to distributed E-Learning applications with Web-Services. Apart from the historical connection, also the "needed standards" correlate with each other. The aim is to deploy Web-Services, for this the following requirements have to be considered:

- **Resource description via standard meta-data (LOM, IMS, SCORM, etc.)**: E-Learning objects have to be assigned categories: i.e. course, lecture, module, graphic, audio, etc. The use of the objects depends on the type of category[148].

- **Object-oriented services reference resources**: Services can be categorized as well, depending on the type of employment: administration, management, learning, sequencing, etc.

- **Web-Services use these services**: Resource description alone is not sufficient. Relations between resources, ontologies, process description and human resources are a vital input as well[149]. The process-oriented view of information and data flow also reflects a service-oriented view for execution of a Web-Service workflow. This again sets the connection to KM, because these applications reflect a bottom-up approach. The proposed connection to KM using a methodology[150] fixes this problem and applies strategy-issues.

---

[148]For more information on Learning objects and taxonomies, see [324]
[149]See [328]
[150]See Chapter 2.7.2.1

Stack Layer	Technology	PROMOTE
Discovery	UDDI	Knowledge Resource and Services Model
Description	WSDL	KMP (Knowledge work-flows)
Messaging	XML-RPC, SOAP	SOAP information out of KMP
Transport	HTTP, SMTP, FTP	HTTP

Table 2.6: The PROMOTE Web-Services stack mapping

2.7.2 PROMOTE - A service-oriented Framework for delivering E-Learning and the connection to Web-Services

Chapter 2.7.2 takes the theories discussed in Chapter 2.7.1 and tries to set the link to a practical scenario with the KM-platform PROMOTE. This scenario was chosen due to several reasons (see also Figure 2.17):

- PROMOTE is a process-oriented tool for delivering KM

- E-Learning scenarios can be modeled in the PROMOTE context showing a first effort towards engineering knowledge in E-Learning

- A top-down methodology sets the strategic outline[151]

- Via Business processes, the operative structure and procedures are modeled and documented

- Services, resources and KM-Processes are explicitly modeled; a mapping to the basic Web-Services stack is possible

- The models are represented in XML and can be transformed into standard compliant XML-code

- The PROMOTE-engine enables execution of the KM models

The PROMOTE working scenario will serve as "light" role model for the two instances of E-Learning Engineering eduWeaver and DKElearn in Chapters 5 and 6[152].

Table 2.6 maps the PROMOTE modeling methods with the basic Web-Services stack

---

[151][167] addresses the top-down-agenda as well and states that Web-Services at the moment lack the strategic influence.

[152]In fact some Modeling Methods of PROMOTE are used in DKElearn.

conceptually. In the following, PROMOTE is introduced showing current status and future potential for use in the E-Learning Engineering framework.

2.7.2.1 Introduction to PROMOTE

PROMOTE[153] is an EU project dealing with KM and running in the IST program, nr. IST-1999-11658[154]. The overall goal of the project is to develop an integrated framework for process-oriented Knowledge Management, to validate it by developing a product named PROMOTE and to test it with end-user companies from the financial and insurance sector.

PROMOTE[155] is based on business processes, as the objective of any KM strategy has to support the business goals which will be achieved by business processes. Generally spoken, KM activities are successful if they improve process performance, e.g. by more efficiently producing a product or by increasing the number of products sold. PROMOTE is process-oriented, breaking KM down into modeling constructs covering structured, semi-structured and unstructured knowledge. A KM-Process (KMP) is defined as the set of activities that implement knowledge flow between individuals in a company.

Modeling and implementing the knowledge flow between people using ICT ends up in an OM[156] with defined interfaces, access rights and knowledge evolution. PROMOTE concentrates on the implicit knowledge, since people are the knowledge owners. Consequently, when building an OM the basic design question is how to support the exchange and generation of people's implicit knowledge. The PROMOTE methodology combines both Business BPM and KM.

As a process-oriented approach for KM is followed in PROMOTE (regarding the respective business processes as well as shifting from business process- to knowledge process modeling), it is obvious to derive the PROMOTE-methodology from the existing BPMS-methodology. This methodology consists of five basic steps (see Figure 2.18).

Apart from these basic five steps, the PROMOTE platform is based on a three layer architecture: the Knowledge Layer, the OM Layer and the ICT Layer. The Knowledge Layer is seen as the application layer, where special knowledge is needed to execute the Business Processes. The required knowledge is mainly stored at the ICT Layer by using different tools. The approach of PROMOTE is to introduce a third- the OM Layer that lies between the Knowledge Layer and the ICT Layer. This approach ensures high flexi-

---

[153]See [35]

[154]See [148]

[155]See [223]

[156]Do not confuse the abbreviation of Organizational Memory OM with the abbreviation for Object Model OM.

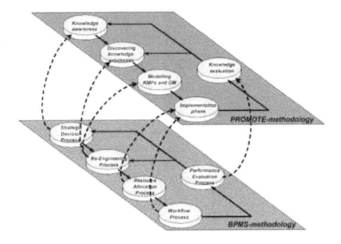

Figure 2.18: PROMOTE methodology

bility, tool independency and openness.

In order to build a PROMOTE-KM System, several steps according to the methodology have to be taken (in sub-processes "Discovering Knowledge Processes" and "Modeling KMP-s and OM")[157]: Business Processes with knowledge-intensive tasks have to be designated. These knowledge-intensive tasks are further analyzed and described using various model types to define an OM. For each knowledge-intensive task, a Knowledge Structure (Topic Map) is created to describe the taxonomy of the resources. In the next step, Skill Profiles are assigned to the Knowledge Structure with the possibility to determine "Should"- and "Is"-Skills. To build the OM, information exchange is described by so-called KMPs, that define the building-, identification-, access-, storage-, distribution-, and evaluation-process of an OM. Each activity of a KMP again refers to an object of the Knowledge Structure and can be seen as a service-based process. The modeled environment is executed by the PROMOTE-engine and visually represented to the user at run-time via a web-interface.

Model types to describe the OM include:

- Static Models

    - Working Environment

    - Skill Documentation

---

[157]See [154]

- – Knowledge Structure

- – Community Model

- Dynamic Models

- Business Process

- Knowledge Management Process

- Knowledge Process

- Hybrid Models

    - – Knowledge Landscape

    - – Knowledge Resource Model

Possible working scenarios of PROMOTE include:

- Support of E-Business processes

- Configuration of KM-tools

- Enhancing business process optimization

- Personalized knowledge portals

- Supporting Content Management

- Evaluation through Balanced Scorecards

- PROMOTE as basis for service-based KM through Web-Services

2.7.2.2 E-Learning Scenarios with PROMOTE

Several conceptual ideas exist to use the KM-platform PROMOTE in an E-Learning and Web-Services context. The following application areas would be possible:

- Automatically created on-demand courses out of certain knowledge structures

- Creation of personalized courses through Web-Services workflows

- Adaptation of PROMOTE models for inclusion of security and intellectual property rights issues

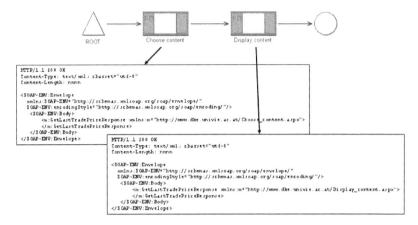

Figure 2.19: KM processes mapped to SOAP messages

- Extension of PROMOTE for the possibility of evaluation with Balanced Scorecard method

- KMP-s with export transformation to SOAP messages (see next Chapter)

2.7.2.3 Future potential of PROMOTE: KMP and Web-Services

In the following, one of the above mentioned scenarios is scrutinized further conceptually. This KMP-to-Web-Services scenario could include the following steps:

- Modeling of a simple KMP

- Creation of sample Web-Services (or search in UDDI directories for reasonable services instead)

- Use WSDL interfaces from service description models to create a SOAP message call for a knowledge intensive task, see Figure 2.19[158]

- The PROMOTE platform processes the messages

The scenarios do not include publication of Web-Services in a UDDI directory or describing the interface with WSDL, they focus purely on the SOAP transformation[159]. The Web-Services lifecycle introduced in Appendix A looks like the following:

---

[158]The code shown in this figure is arbitrary and does not correlate with choosing or displaying content.
[159][121], p. 43, calls this a point-to-point implementation

- Client

    - UDDI is not part of the scenario, the user knows where to find and how to deploy a Web-Service

    - KMP has to be modeled

    - SOAP specific information has to be added (URI, types, etc.) from service description models

    - KMP invokes SOAP message

- Provider

    - Implement PROMOTE methodology

    - Service development

    - Provide services on Web-Service platforms

2.7.3 Potential for Web-Services

Finally, two facts have to be pointed out: first, as already mentioned, UDDI, WSDL and SOAP will be the basic XML standards for Web-Services; other specification concerning security, intellectual property rights or better semantic description of relations will start on top of this basic Web-Services stack. Second, so far, Web-Services use a bottom-up and technology-driven approach; consortia like ebXML try to address this problem, but it is not clear at this point, whether it will be considered for standards development. The PROMOTE scenario is just one example, of how a top-down approach, modeling Business Processes and KMP-s, may be realized[160].

2.8 Summary

Chapters 1 and 2 have dealt with theoretical matters and literature surveys in order to present the scientific methods and the application scenario E-Learning in a very detailed way. Tight connections and future prospects for E-Learning to other disciplines like KM, the Semantic Web and Web-Services were pointed out.

Chapters 3, 4 and 6 take all these discrete parts of information to form an E-Learning Framework and furthermore an E-Learning Engineering approach and a partial proof of

---

[160]This approach is independent from the DKElearn library presented in Chapter 6

feasibility concerning the description of learning resources that can be deployed by Web-Services.

The puzzle to be assembled consists of the following ideas that will be resolved by the E-Learning Engineering Framework:

- Methodology integration for consistent implementation of strategies and mapping of organizational requirements onto technical solutions

- B2B interdependencies for being able to provide Peer-to-Peer collaborations

- Document exchange via XML-based standards and specifications

- Presentation of E-Learning specific modeling methods for description of learning resources

- Representation of modeled learning resources as Semantic Web compliant resources

- Incorporation of the E-Learning Engineering framework into a service-oriented architecture using Web-Services

- Prototypical test-beds will show that RDF learning resources can be processed by any client that is able to "speak" SOAP

Chapter 3

The E-Learning Framework

3.1 Prologue: Structuring Content from the Instructor's point of view

Before stepping into defining an actual framework for E-Learning scenarios, some preliminary thoughts on the conceptual ideas of this thesis shall be introduced.

Among the many roles of users that participate in an E-Learning environment, the role "instructor" is of major importance and has to be supported and involved properly.

In Chapters 5 and 6 - based on the general findings of Chapters 3 and 4 - two solutions are sketched that define two different models of how the instructor can construct a course. Both show possible interrelations between instructors and learning resources (content). Figure 3.1 depicts this scenario.

It is important to say, that instructors should not be aware of the technologies and underlying technical dependencies. Therefore, E-Learning is a blackbox and enables teaching supported by Educational Technologies with usable and easy interfaces. By pressing only few buttons or by deploying predefined wizards, instructors should be able to leverage the full potential of E-Learning solutions.

In order to reach this goal, a complex and generic framework has to support the scenario along several dimensions (see the rest of this Chapter 3) and has to provide easy management on the basis of visual engineering methods; depending on the use case, these visual engineering methods may differ (see Chapters 5 and 6) either in the classes that are used for visualizing a scenario or in the technical surroundings (i.e. they use XML or RDF).

This thesis takes two instances of visual engineering methods into account:

1. The instructor is aware of the structure and the contents of his courses. The degree of

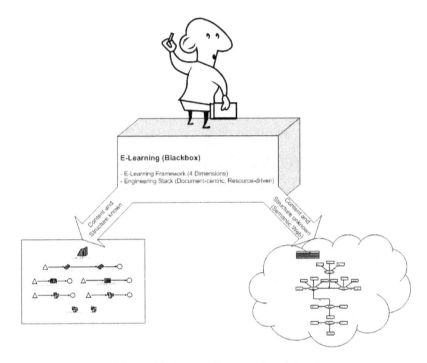

Figure 3.1: Relationship between instructor's and learning resources

awareness is high, so the instructor knows details about the actual learning resources, details about the schedule, organizational details, etc. The resources that make up the courses were authored by the instructor with the help of authoring tools (e.g. Microsoft Powerpoint).

2. The instructor is not (fully) aware of the structure and the contents and even may not have an actual course in mind. The degree of awareness is low or medium, so the instructor knows general requirements surrounding a course, the domain of research or teaching and experts in the field to contact. In a sense, the role of the instructor in this case can be compared to a semi-informed learner. The resources reside somewhere in the Semantic Web and may be retrieved on the basis of their ontological description.

Both methods describe visual engineering methods and refer to the ability to model the learning scenario according to (manually) researched learning resources.

Possibility one reflects a Document-centric approach, implying that the knowledge

	Document-centric Learning	Resource-driven Learning
Content Creator	instructor	instructor or anyone or anything that is able to parse and interpret learning ontologies
Content	personalized content, structure and sequencing according to the needs of the instructor	remote content, structure accoring to an external ontology
Type of Graph	learning process graphs	resource graphs
Course Granularity	predefined in the instructor's institution (e.g. Course/Module/Lecture)	unknown or according to an external ontology
Target Group	instructors from all domains	experts
Interoperability	low level	fully interoperable
Openness	content may be restricted for accessing	open content
Effectiveness	this setting (probably) uses a centralized data storage for learning resources; the effectiveness of learning therefore is restricted to the power and expressiveness of the combination of these learning resources	this setting has the Semantic Web as a decentralized pool for learning resources; the effectiveness in terms of combining an infinite number of learning resources therefore is higher but depends on the power of searching and retrieving for relevant learning resources

Table 3.1: Comparison of two content-scenarios from the instructor's point of view

about the course content and structure is already known to the instructor; this can be said to be the "typical" scenario for an instructor planning a course at an educational institution including retrieval capabilities for existing learning resources (for information about the Backloading concept see Appendix C).

Possibility two reflects a Resource-driven approach, implying that the knowledge about the learning scenario resides in the internet; this possibility is considered to be suitable for a learning scenario where instructors and learners share a common goal of interest and are able to learn in a community (the prototype only includes descriptive means).

The differences between these two scenarios are listed in Table 3.1.

3.2 Chapter Outline

Every problem has a solution methodology and an accompanying solution technique. This statement is true for all kinds of problem areas, like traveling, building houses, measuring growth and turnovers, programming an application and of course learning. Today, many of these problems are resolved using concrete solution techniques without thinking of the problem itself and its solution methodology. IT, internet programming languages and technical systems are seen as the only keys to unlock a concrete problem neglecting vital dimensions rendering the solution to a different kind of problem again. Taking the situation of financial institutes into account, judicial guidelines (e.g. BASEL II) to a great extent define the requirements of the IT solution[1]. Exactly these "situations" are relevant in an E-Learning context as well looking at guidelines produced by the European Union[2]. Nevertheless, supporting problems with IT solutions is a must-criterion in our global market economies, because the complexity and the number of potential users of an application scenario is enormously high. One can say, that in the context of management paradigms like strategic measurement, business processes or learning have to be transformed into IT-supported management scenarios. Each management paradigm therefore has its own technological solution. In case of learning, Educational Technologies will be the key. Depending on the application, actual instantiations of learning with the help of Educational Technologies can be derived, like fully virtual learning (E-Learning) or Blended Learning, combining on-campus (classroom) education with virtual learning.

In order to reach an IT solution for a learning scenario as mentioned in the latter paragraphs, a structured methodology and a common "picture" or framework is inevitable. Figure 3.2 outlines the interrelations to reach an agreement in this context.

Sophisticated and complex scenarios like learning scenarios have to be abstracted from the real world. For this matter, the concept of a "Framework" is introduced. With the help of four dimensions that are specific to learning any given scenario can be aligned to this framework; and hence a methodology and a solution technology can be assigned.

The proposed E-Learning Framework helps to sketch a roadmap - a historical evolution - from traditional teacher-centered classroom learning without technological support to student-centric technology-supported scenarios, until eventually a Knowledge Society based on life-long learning is reached.

---

[1]See [178]
[2]See Chapter 3.4

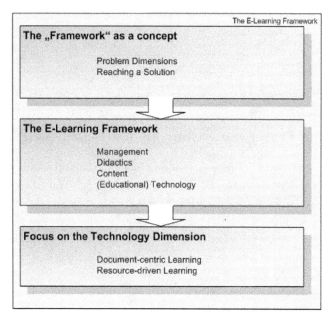

Figure 3.2: Overview

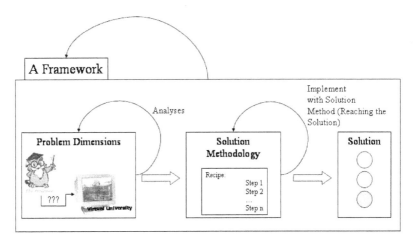

Figure 3.3: Interdependence between problem and solution incorporated into "A Framework"

3.3 The Framework Concept for E-Learning

But before being able to IT-support a problem solution, a framework - an abstract model of the real world with variables for every necessary dimension also taking care of the underlying methodology and the solution technique - has to be introduced in order to define roles and interfaces to satisfy all requirements.

In case of IT-supported Learning only few holistic frameworks exist. Normally, the problem is tackled from the basis implementing a solution with certain solution methods - generally specifying these methods as Educational Technologies.

Compared to frameworks from other disciplines like Business Engineering (Zachmann Framework[3], ARIS Framework[4] and House of Business Engineering[5], E-BPMS[6], GERAM[7], CIMOSA[8], etc.), an E-Learning Framework has to satisfy the same requirements. Most of these frameworks are stacks, assigning different functions and roles to each layer.

Looking at E-Learning in particular, various stack Frameworks exist as well. Especially efforts and approaches from accredited standards consortia and similar global institutions

---

[3]See [332]
[4]See [235]
[5]See [234]
[6]See [171]
[7]See [30]
[8]See [52]

like the ISO-IEC JTC 1[9], the IEEE Learning Technology Standards Committee (LTSC)[10], Advanced Distributed Learning (ADL)[11] and the IMS Global Consortium[12] shall be mentioned at this point.

The tasks, namely creating a framework and considering all aspects of a problem is the job of the discipline Business Informatics - that is adding a sense of engineering and methodology to IT-supported management scenarios. The main tasks according to Figure 3.3 are

- Defining the Problem Dimensions (domain specific requirements)

- Introducing a Solution Methodology

- Reaching the Solution (execution of the domain specific requirements with the help of IT)

In the following, these three tasks are discussed in detail.

3.3.1 Defining the Problem Dimensions

Many technology-centered approaches exist to categorize learning. Traditional on-campus (classroom) learning offers several possibilities for teachers to pass knowledge to students. Basically speaking this has to be done in a teacher-centric way with frontal-lectures.

Except from the teachers' knowledge itself and the information coming from study books, all other dimensions are implicit: the didactical schema, management of students, management of grades, creation and evaluation of tests or exams, etc.

The emergence of IT-supported learning - often described as E-Learning or Blended Learning - offers a whole new paradigm to conciliate this knowledge. This also implies the explication of the implicit dimensions mentioned in the latter paragraph, because learning supported with Educational Technologies can only process machine readable content that has to be described formally with the help of models. Currently, forms of electronically supported learning adhere very much to document or course centric structures, where XML is the means of switching drill-and-practice learning objects (LOs) from one Learning Management System (LMS) to another. But the power of IT-supported learning probably has to be leveraged differently, because traditional didactical approaches do not apply to online scenarios.

Therefore, the first task is to define the Problem Dimensions:

---

[9]See [146] and Chapter 2.4.2.1
[10]See [134] and 2.4.2.1
[11]See [7]
[12]See [141]

- Management

- Content

- Didactics

- Technology

The proposed E-Learning Framework is not a stack but consists of these four dimensions. Any concrete learning scenario - like on-campus learning, distance learning or any other possible combination of dimensions - instantiates this framework. Detailed information will be given in Chapter 3.4.

3.3.2 Introducing a Solution Methodology

Today, IT-supported learning is set on a stage, where LOs can be interchanged between LMS with the help of XML E-Learning applications meaning that one LO or document can be passed onto another system, where it has to be customized to fit the needs of the proprietary system to finally being used. This is a great step forward, as interchangeability and reuse of content is a main goal of IT-supported learning. But the vision of future learning has to be sketched differently: a user - being any person involved in a learning process like a student, tutor or teacher - logs on to some system and automatically is plugged into his personal life-long learning "matrix":

- Didactical patterns are automatically chosen because of the user's personal learning history - didactic dimension.

- The user can browse something like a global learning grid for topics from arbitrary colleges or universities that interest him and dependent sources are automatically added - content dimension.

- Evaluation and promotions are added to the personal profile - management dimension.

A Solution Methodology that is able to fulfill all the posed tasks has to be generic in character, so that addenda and extensions can be made. The methodology can be seen as a recipe or an instruction sheet consisting of several steps. Accompanying the methodology, a Solution Method defines the language of the constructed models that is responsible to map domain requirements automatically to IT requirements. Depending on the participating roles within the execution of a methodology (e.g. manager, instructor, student,

administrator, etc.) the type of the methodology may change from a top-down approach
to a bottom-up approach.

3.3.3 Reaching the Solution: Roadmap to Semantic E-Learning

We are only on the way to reach this vision. Starting with an actual scenario and concrete domain requirements, each dimension is instantiated and filled up to a certain level
(level of management effect, level of technology use, etc.) in a way already pre-defining
the Solution Method. Therefore, every scenario has its own specific mixture of learning
flavors forming an unambiguous scenario. Depending on the level of Technology that
shall support the scenario, standardization and machine readable content - the abstract
models of the scenario - have to be quite sophisticated to bridge the gap between domain
requirements and technical implementations.

Starting from the situation today, one possible roadmap towards Reaching the Solution
could be (see Figure 3.5):

- Step 1: Traditional Learning

- Step 2: Drawbacks of today's approach - called Document-centric Learning in this
  Chapter - result from the exact adaptation of on-campus learning supplying students
  with existing slideshow-documents.

- Step 3: The Internet technology on the other hand is decentralized and puts the
  student in the driver's seat: students should be able to book and collect relevant
  LOs by themselves presenting a problem- and student-centered approach - called
  Resource-driven Learning in this Chapter. Technologically Resource-driven learning
  embraces Semantic Web technologies and addresses resources as central concept
  references by Uniform Resource Identifiers (URIs)[13].

- Step 4: The future of (life-long) learning ...

With the help of the E-Learning Framework, each step of this path can be visualized and
categorized up to the final achievement of the future vision.

3.4 Introducing the E-Learning Framework

This Chapter is fully dedicated to defining an E-Learning Framework based on the ideas
of the generic framework introduced in Figure 3.3.

---

[13]See [183]

Looking at other publications with the topic "E-Learning Framework" it can be stated that non IT-driven approaches are rare:

1. Khan's E-Learning Framework[14] concentrates on eight dimensions to define an E-Learning application.

2. Tuohy[15] addresses education system building blocks (teachers, infrastructure, curriculum and content, teaching and learning tools, administration).

3. IBM[16] published an E-Learning portfolio with two dimensions: process, content and technology on the one axis and access and design, implement/integrate and run on the other axis.

4. Shen et al.[17] address mostly technical issues to enable students to process automated questions and teachers to analyze the learning progress.

5. Siqueira et al.[18] have developed a "semi-complete" framework based on configurable components.

6. Phelps et al.[19] present several steps for different approaches to the use of IT in teaching and learning.

7. Sun Microsystems[20] presents a layered approach differentiating between a Presentation, a Common Service, an E-Learning Service and a Resource Tier for creating E-Learning applications.

8. New Zealand's Ministry of Education[21] introduced a high-level direction for E-Learning capabilities consisting of visions, principles and action areas.

9. Baumgartner[22] defines a framework based on the dimensions social organization, learning/teaching and activity.

10. Seufert and Euler[23] define a framework of sustainability for E-Learning with the dimensions didactics, technology, organization, culture and economical efficiency embedded into defining a strategy.

---

[14]See [161]
[15]See [283]
[16]See [118]
[17]See [251]
[18]See [254]
[19]See [215]
[20]See [273]
[21]See [204]
[22]See [24]
[23]See [247]

11. The E-Learning specific technology stacks issued by consortia mentioned in the Introduction.

In the context of the proposed E-Learning Framework, items 1 and 10 from the latter enumeration mostly apply to the required scope. Therefore the four mentioned dimensions Management, Didactics, Content and Technology are a reasonable approach.

Figure 3.4 depicts the E-Learning Framework and determines four dimensions and its embedment into a strategic dimension that implicitly shows two other important aspects of the use of an E-Learning Framework:

- The ability for quality assurance and traceability[24].

- Hence the use of the transparent E-Learning Framework for planning and strategy.

The E-Learning Framework itself with the four dimensions Management, Content, Didactics and Technology has to be applied to different strategic layers: in case of the strategic educational and E-Learning activities set by the European Commission[25], national States/Governments have to implement these guidelines according to national law; the Educational Institution as executing entity has to actually execute these guidelines operationally.

The arrangement of the dimensions does not imply any specific coherence amongst them. As already mentioned in Chapter 3.3.1 a concrete learning scenario instantiates the E-Learning Framework: e.g. on-campus (classroom) learning would focus on the dimensions Didactics and Content; the dimensions Management and in particular Technology are neglected to a certain degree. Figure 3.5 sketches three different learning scenarios according to the E-Learning Framework. Chapter 3.5 will address two intermediate scenarios according to the Roadmap to future E-Learning, where the Knowledge Society and life-long learning are reality.

Each dimension is supported by a methodology itself - embedded into a Methodology of the Educational Institution - and some way of describing the scenario formally, namely by providing a visual modeling method, the common platform that achieves understanding among domain experts and technical solution providers. The whole E-Learning Framework is embedded into several layers that are enforced by certain Guidelines. Taking the situation of European Union (EU) into account, the EU executive instruments produce general guidelines that have to be implemented in the national states. The following enumeration demonstrates these interdependencies:

---

[24]See [107]
[25]See [89]

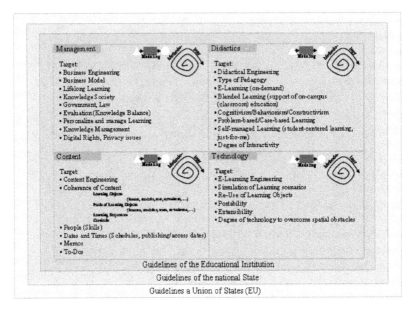

Figure 3.4: The E-Learning Framework

- Guidelines of a Union of States (EU): Bologna process[26], Erasmus program, European Credit Transfer System (ECTS)[27]

- Guidelines of a national State: national laws for implementing curricula, EU Guidelines

- Guidelines of an Educational Institution: implement own Guidelines and Guidelines of the national state and EU Guidelines

Figure 3.5 shows the roadmap to life-long learning starting with traditional learning without IT support (top tight, Step 1), stepping over Distance Learning (top right, "(Step 1)"), IT centered Document-centric learning (Step 2) and Resource-driven learning (Step 3) as intermediary steps (bottom right) and eventually ending with all dimensions of the E-Learning Framework filled and fully considered (bottom left, Step 4).

In the following, the four dimensions are discussed in detail.

---

[26]See [91]
[27]See [90]

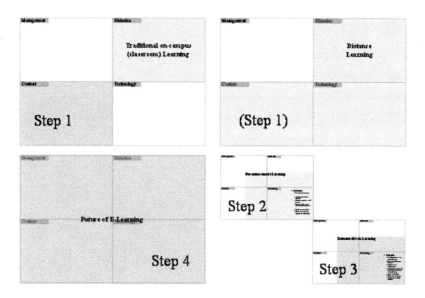

Figure 3.5: Learning scenarios according to the E-Learning Framework with respect to the developments of the Roadmap to Semantic E-Learning

3.4.1 Management

Today, E-Learning is still an isolated discipline creating an own ICT domain. On a technical level, mature E-Learning standards like the IEEE Learning Objects Metadata (LOM) standard[28] seem to overcome the hurdles of integrating other Learning Objects (LO) into proprietary LMS, but on an organizational level, integration into e.g. Enterprise Resource Planning (ERP) systems is still rather a dream than reality[29].

The Management Dimension intends to position an E-Learning scenario into an organizational context. Today, E-Learning solutions lack the connection to a business strategy and the ability for evaluation in terms of measures. Furthermore, A planning dimension for E-Learning projects is missing, because the lack of a structured methodology to create courses and how to treat them in terms of technological implementation forces people to create their own and proprietary E-Learning island[30].

As Figure 3.4 already suggests, the Management Dimension and the layered requirements in terms of Guidelines urge to produce a common understanding among Educational In-

---

[28]See [127]
[29]See [22]
[30]See [190]

stitutions, national States and greater unions like the European Union. The goal - e.g. promoted by the European Union - is to reach life-long learning within a Knowledge Society and therefore standardized access and resource pools of LOs, Learner Profiles and general Guidelines have to be provided.

Possible application scenarios within the Management Dimension are summarized by the following enumeration.

- Curricula Management

  - Is a course combination syntactically or semantically possible?

- HR Management and Simulation

  - Which number of staff members do I need for a course?

  - Can I do the course with department A and/or B?

  - Simulation of the flow of a learning process

  - Student support

  - How long a student should be supported?

  - How many average mails are necessary to answer requests?

  - Is a 24/7 response likely?

- Calculation of Costs

  - How much does a course with two teachers cost?

  - What are the costs of a student?

In order to achieve the exploitation of this dimension, the following targets have to be considered:

- Business Engineering

- Business Methodology

- Business Model: Part of Business Engineering showing trading partners and the flows that are generated among them.

- Life-long Learning: New paradigm in learning defining learning as a process that lasts from birth to death of a human learner. In contrast to the paradigm that is used up to now, where learners only share punctual learning experiences that are not connected (e.g. school, university, etc.)[31].

- Knowledge Society: *"to become the most competitive and dynamic knowledge-based economy in the world, capable of sustainable economic growth with more and better jobs and greater social cohesion"*[32].

- Government, Law: Guidelines of governmental institutions and other participating stakeholders often pose restrictions on a scenario. They have to be included into the Business Model.

- Evaluation: Speaking especially of the Austrian national Guidelines and Laws within Higher Education institutions, evaluation (with the help of Knowledge Balances) and contracts concerning fulfillment (from German "Leistungsvereinbarung"[33]) are a vital issue between the Rectorate[34] and the Government and have to be considered within the overall Methodology.

- Personalize and manage Learning: Each participating role has to be able to personalize and manage its own Learner Profile and experiences and skills within the process of life-long learning.

- Knowledge Management: In order to achieve life-long learning within a Knowledge Society, data and information have to be semantically annotated to become knowledge.

- Digital Rights, Privacy issues: Educational Technologies enable the automatic processing of machine-readable content. It is of vital importance in this context that digital rights and privacy issues are not violated. E.g. the process of publication of information has to be retraceable for the owner, etc.

3.4.2 Content

Traditionally and obviously, content exists in a learning context. All the data and information passed between instructors and students can be defined as content. Evolutionary speaking, content and the presentation of content have changed: scripture and printing

---

[31]See [88]
[32]See [87]
[33]See [33]
[34]See [205]

were two major inventions concerning publication of content to a mass audience. Computers and Educational Technologies mark another milestone that reflects the paradigm shift to life-long learning and the shift from Documents-centric to Resource-driven learning. Therefore, the participating roles in a new learning scenario have to think about the adequate publication of content today: written content has to be transformed to online LOs from one context to another[35] (the new technology paradigm - from sequential style like written books to networked resources like the (Semantic) Web - has to be considered). In order to achieve the exploitation of this dimension, the following targets have to be considered:

- Content Engineering

- (Content Methodology)

- Coherence of Content: The context in which an LO is to be embedded has to be considered.

- Learning Objects: LOs have to be defined on different levels of abstraction (lesson, module, test, news item, etc.) so that they become generic modular units.

    - Pools of Learning Objects
    - Learning Sequences

- Curricula: Are a set of LOs and sequences of LOs together with semantic information about skills, schedule information, etc. that may define one critical interface to the Management Dimension.

- People (Skills): Learner Profiles are a vital input to life-long learning, because prerequisites may be considered on the individual learning path.

- Dates and Times: Schedules, publishing/access dates are vital for the context of a LO.

- Memos and To-Dos: Information about LOs themselves has to include semantically enriched notifications, memos or To-Dos.

3.4.3 Didactics

Several termini technici can be used within this dimension. They are often treated as homonyms, namely pedagogy (education), didactics[36] and methods to implement peda-

---

[35]See [276]
[36]See [78]

gogy and didactics. The Didactics Dimension in the E-Learning Framework covers all of these aspects: it is concerned with teaching and learning and the incorporation of teaching and learning into an educational context.

In order to achieve the exploitation of this dimension, the following targets have to be considered:

- Didactical Engineering

- Didactical Methodology

- Type of Pedagogy

- E-Learning (on-demand)

- Blended Learning (support of on-campus (classroom) education)

- Cognitivism/Behaviorism/Constructivism

- Problem-based/Case-based/Contextual Learning

- Self-managed Learning (student-centered learning, just-for-me)

- Degree of Interactivity

3.4.4 Technology

As already mentioned, the Technology Dimension in E-Learning is quite mature having produced explicit standards like LOM and having issued de-facto standards or specifications like the ones of the IMS Global Consortium or the SCORM Profile by the ADL.

Current efforts and courses in E-Learning can be categorized as document-centric. This implies that they are reduced to using proprietary Learning Management Systems (LMS). Fortunately, most of the leading LMS already implement standard interfaces for importing courses (IMS Content Package, etc.). Unfortunately, these standard interfaces are only able to transfer data or documents and still lack information about meaning (e.g. is there more on a certain topic, who wrote the article and how can I contact and maybe meet this person, etc).

The latter scenario as another instance of the E-Learning Framework (resource-driven) reflects the vision of the Semantic Web but can also be applied to E-Learning: current didactical approaches restrict E-Learning to hierarchical and document-centric scenarios reflecting the XML paradigm but Semantic Web technologies could leverage the networked structure of technologies like RDF that could make personalized and resource-based scenarios possible.

Trying to show the feasibility of resource-driven E-Learning, a roadmap towards a resource-driven focus within the Technology Dimension is a next step towards reaching the vision of life-long learning[37].

In order to achieve the exploitation of this dimension, the following targets have to be considered:

- E-Learning Engineering

- E-Learning Methodology

- Simulation of Learning scenarios: The modeled environment may be one interface to the Management Dimension. It can provide substantial input for better management decisions.

- Re-Use of Learning Objects: Depending on the technology, LOs may be reused in another context. The way of finding LOs in proprietary LMS or Semantic Web like learning pools is defined by the technology.

- Portability: The learning content should not be restricted by the end-user's device. Depending on the didactical scenario, reasonable learning paths may be done with a mobile device, other learning paths can only be achieved within a physical classroom.

- Extensibility: Especially in the context of Semantic Web resources, the amount of LOs can be indefinite. Therefore extensibility and scalability in terms of space and computing time is a major issue.

- Degree of technology to overcome spatial obstacles

3.5 Roadmap to Learning with Educational Technologies

As already mentioned, Document-centric Learning and Resource-driven Learning are intermediate steps on the way to the Knowledge Society (see Figure 3.5). Document-centric Learning marks a stage in Learning supported by Educational Technologies where syntactically annotated LOs can be transferred between two different systems. Resource-driven

---

[37]See [182]

Learning adds semantic information to Document-centric Learning scenarios by assigning skills, responsible roles, schedules and other information to reach a Semantic Learning comparable to the concepts the Semantic Web adds to the current World-wide Web. Table 3.2 summarizes the differences between these two types of learning according to the dimensions of the E-Learning Framework.

Criterion	Document-centric Learning	Resource-driven Learning
Management		
Methodology	Top-Down methodology	Hybrid methodology
Planning	Planning and execution with the help of modeling.	Planning and enactment control with the help of modeling.
Learning Management	An institution manages learning.	The individual manages learning.
Content		
Knowledge	Knowledge/Content is pre-determined.	Knowledge resides in the individuals' minds and in the networked Semantic Web.
Didactics		
Didactics	Didactics depend on type of Content (Cognitivism, Behaviorism).	Didactics can be applied/chosen (Problem-oriented self-managed learning; Constructivism).
Interactivity, Collaboration, Personalization and type of media publishing[38]	Low degree and asynchronous and synchronous publishing for mass audiences.	High degree and Content-Personalization.
Central concept	Institution, Teacher; Curriculum-based	Student; Life-long Learning
Succession of LOs	Mostly sequential or hierarchical.	No successions but complex interdependencies between LOs networks.
Technology		

---

[38]See [43]

Standards	Tagging of Resources within a self-contained application. Portability and Extensibility depend on application.	Tagging of Resources with globally accessible URIs. Portability and Extensibility are dependent on the power of the defined ontology.

Table 3.2: Comparing Document-centric Learning to Resource-driven Learning

Historically speaking it is vital to point out the developments in learning in the publishing sector in a more general way. Long before out contemporary calculation of times scripture became the first "modeling" method to express ideas and thoughts. Later, printing revolutionized the mass production and dissemination of scripture.

Each of these new technologies was hardly accepted in the beginning but changed the way of communicating an learning immensely. It took some time to really being able to exploit the whole power of the new medium. This also holds true as well for computer technology and Learning supported by Educational Technology.

Three scenarios for learning express this path of evolution in terms of the right use for Educational Technologies:

1. Traditional on-campus (classroom) learning.

2. Blended Learning (Document-centric Learning).

3. E-Learning in a Semantic Web (Resource-driven-Learning).

4. The Future: Life-long learning.

What steps do exist today to realize Resource-driven Learning:

- IMS Global Consortium RDF Specifications[39] in collaboration with KMR in Stockholm[40].

- Peer-to-Peer projects like Edutella[41] or EducaNext[42] that introduce learning resources market places.

---

[39]See [140]
[40]See [166]
[41]See [197]
[42]See [83]

- Learning Design and Web-Didactics as didactic-focused approaches without in-depth technical implementation scenarios as a basis for an ontology for Semantic Learning. Within the E-Learning Framework, these two approaches would fill out the Didactic dimension with low emphasize on Content and Technology.

3.5.1 Traditional Forms of Learning

Learning and related scientific disciplines pedagogy and didactics pose very complex problems on teachers and learners, because logic reasoning and analytical methods do not always apply to scenarios with human-related interaction: these scenarios are mostly unpredictable.

As already pointed out in Table 3.2 the newly introduced medium "computer" with contemporary Educational Technologies note a paradigm shift from traditional on-campus (classroom) learning with teacher-centric scenarios to virtual learning where students are the center of consideration.

Coming from Behaviorism and Cognitivism the didactic challenge today is making Constructivism possible, where students have the ability to manage complex and maybe problem-based learning scenarios.

The following two Chapters describe Document-centric and Resource-driven Learning as intermediary steps to reaching life-long learning.

3.5.2 Document-centric Learning

Document-centric Learning reflects the contemporary State-of-the-Art situation in Educational Technology supported Learning and can be compared to what is called Blended Learning. The focus lies on the interchangeability of contents or documents from one LMS to another one. Current E-Learning standards and specifications and related XML-bindings reflect this type of learning exchange by introducing typical stack structures: LOs of lower granularity consist of LOs of higher granularity; e.g. the IMS Content Package Specification, that is currently available for most LMS, aggregates a number of files or documents (LOs) into a hierarchic structure similar to a course.

Chapter 5 describes Document-centric Learning together with a test-bed.

3.5.3 Resource-driven Learning

The drawbacks of Document-centric learning are caused by the technology focus on XML: documents that are described by XML can easily be exchanged between LMS. The prob-

lem is that both the LMS and the XML application are proprietary solutions and have
to be reprogrammed in case of changes. Furthermore, XML does not have a concept for
identifying and locating LOs: LOs that are described by XML applications are defined by
the XML-file itself. And finally, the semantic information and concatenation and linking
to other vocabularies is not possible.

Therefore, the next step in learning should overcome these drawbacks. A possible solution
can be compared to approaches currently proposed by the Semantic Web community. Taking the E-Learning Framework into account, the exploitation of all dimensions in terms
of modeling and annotation and the linking of information between the dimensions lift
E-Learning scenarios to a knowledge based and enabled application.

Talking of technological solutions, such a Resource-driven scenario has to be founded on
a comprehensive ontologies and not on light weight XML vocabularies - meaning flat
XML-like structures with the URI concept like RDF Site Summary (RSS)[43], Dublin Core
Metadata (DCMI)[44] or even existing LOM. The inter-references and networked information has to be extended on the large scale. Speaking of Educational Technologies in this
context, the next generation of ontology languages, namely the Web Ontology Language
(OWL), will be able to contribute to these problems positively.

Chapter 6 describes Resource-driven Learning together with a test-bed.

3.6 Summary

This Chapter presented an E-Learning Framework that helps to categorize E-Learning
scenarios. Several scenarios were introduced showing a roadmap to future life-long learning. The focus was placed on the Technology Dimension. The historical development in
this dimension states a stage with focus on XML document sharing (Document-centric
learning), to a stage with focus on RDF (Resource-driven), to a stage where intelligent
OWL ontologies may finally reach a world, where applications are able to parse and induce new knowledge from ontology-based descriptions of the real world.

Based on the findings of the E-Learning Framework, Chapter 4 instantiates the Framework conceptually and shows that - supported by an E-Learning Engineering Framework
- complex learning scenarios can be modeled. Eventually, Chapters 5 and 6 again instantiate the E-Learning Engineering Framework and show exemplary test-beds.

---

[43]See [275] and [220]
[44]See [26] and [69]

Chapter 4

E-Learning Engineering

As mentioned, Chapter 4 together with 5 and 6 make up the scientific antagonists theory (E-Learning Engineering Framework) and practical proof. Two different test-beds with eduWeaver and DKElearn are based on the E-Learning Engineering Framework showing feasibility of Document-centric and Resource-driven Learning respectively.

4.1 Chapter Outline

The theory - as a first step in this Chapter - has to evaluate several technological aspects concerning Knowledge Representation Formalisms so that visual modeling methods (meta-models) can be derived. This topic is discussed in Appendix B showing historical developments and focuses on technologies related to the Semantic Web. Besides the static knowledge representation discussion, dynamic enactment is topic of Appendix A. Both - Knowledge Representation Formalisms and the dynamic enactment with the help of Web-Services - are input to the concepts of the E-Learning Engineering Framework.

On top of that, a generic approach is presented theoretically; main topics will be the presentation of an E-Learning framework together with a methodology that places the approach into a B2B context. The outline of this Chapter is depicted in Figure 4.1.

The generic approach addresses top-down business needs with the help of Business Engineering. More technically speaking, this is done with the help of KM[1]: starting from Business Process Engineering and optimization, technical processes, learner and learning processes and the connection to ontologies. Figure 4.2 shows a typical scenario that links business requirements with technical implementation with the help of E-Learning:

- Learner Profiles and skills for resources have to be levied

---

[1]See Chapter 2.3.3

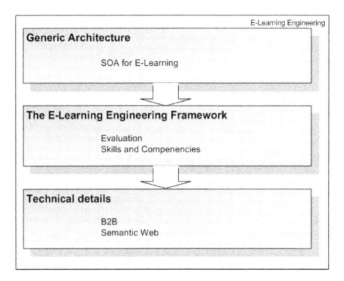

Figure 4.1: Overview

- Skill gaps have to be evaluated

- Learning processes have to be formulated

- Mapping of the skill gap evaluation and learner processes

- Embedding of the E-Learning scenario into a B2B context

Appendix B tries to find the optimal way to represent all the KM related resources (skills, LOs, etc.) beforehand. Chapters 4.3 and its sub-chapters explore all other requirements (process-orientation, methodology incorporation, etc.) in order to be able to fit the represented knowledge into a dynamic framework for E-Learning where a person gets the right LO at a designated time. This is only possible by abstracting relevant parts of the real world by modeling the entire E-Learning context.

Chapter 1.2 mentioned two stages of E-Learning Engineering: stage one delivers a methodology and the engineering methods and stage two embeds the engineered E-Learning scenario into a run-time environment. Moreover, the generic E-Learning Engineering framework has to address the mentioned deficiencies of State-of-the-Art E-Learning and has to remap it as described in Chapter 2 to a generic framework as sketched

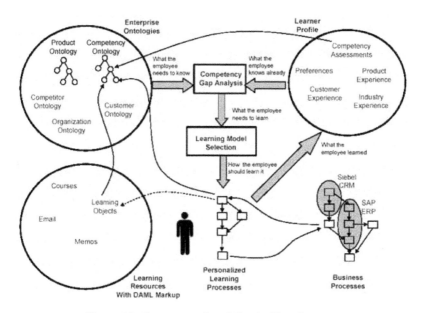

Figure 4.2: Competency based Just-in-Time learning

in Figure 4.2[2].

The generic E-Learning Engineering approach in this thesis therefore has to conceptually link several domains:

- Organizational structures and business processes coming from BPM

- Knowledge structures (including LOs) and flows and the associated skills coming from KM

- Learning specific information like learning processes coming from E-Learning

The linking on the conceptual level is depicted in Figure 4.3.

Bringing this conceptual level into the engineering context into the domain of E-Learning, this thesis extends the E-BPMS[3] framework approach.

Figure 4.4[4] shows the different levels of Business Engineering schematically. The red dots show the interface between the Course Modeling Process and the Target System Level

---

[2][328], p. 1
[3]See [171]
[4]See [179]

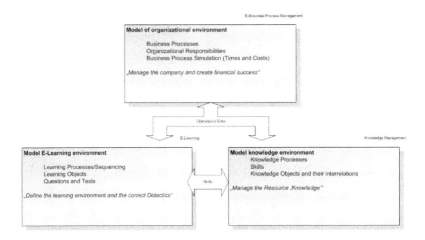

Figure 4.3: Generic E-Learning Engineering Framework - Conceptual Level

marking the focal interest of this thesis[5]. All other topics and themes are mentioned in short in the following two paragraphs.

First and simplified[6], one can say that after having clarified strategic issues, the organizational structures are modeled in the Business Modeling Layer. More precisely, the Course Modeling Layer adds the E-Learning information to the organizational structures and flows; e.g. the Business Process "Reach a higher Level of Skills for an Employee" is supported by a learning process in one activity. The Target System Level has to cope with modeled information in form of XML/RDF including the information into its environment. The generic approach in this thesis opens all possibilities for target systems; in E-Learning, they are e.g. LMS or WBT. However the implementation with Web-Services is favored, especially when thinking about a B2B scenario into which E-Learning needs to be integrated. The lowest level, the Learning Process, depicts all workflow instances from the Target System Level.

Second, accompanying methodologies bring life into a Business Engineering cycle. Chapters 2.3.3.1 and 2.3.2 already showed the proposals of this thesis: coming from the generic BPMS methodology, PROMOTE introduced tight relationships between the BPMS and the PROMOTE KM methodology in Figure 2.18. These holistic recipes for Business Engineering on a global business scale embrace the different levels. But several other circles

---

[5]The red dots also clearly mark the focus on the Technology Dimension of the E-Learning Framework either in a Document-centric or in a Resource-driven way.

[6]The word "simplified" only implies a very basic and non-complex example, without regard to skills or organizational responsibilities etc.

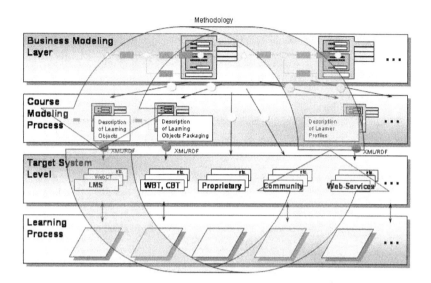

Figure 4.4: Business Engineering in E-Learning

of procedures are embedded into them: above all Chapter 2.3.3.1 mentions a course engineering methodology that gives instructions about how to build an E-Learning course; another sub-methodology is ontology engineering[7] that leads the way through the difficult process of creating a domain vocabulary. In this matter, this thesis takes existing ontologies as input[8]. Rounding up the use of methodologies in Business Engineering, they enable to evaluate the strategic goals with the help of audit trails that were generated by the execution of each Learning Process. There the methodology cycle starts again, because the audit trails enable the optimization of the organizational business processes.

4.2 The E-Learning Engineering Framework - additional semantics on the Management Dimension

This Chapter introduces two additional scenarios for an E-Learning approach in the context of the Management Dimension of the E-Learning Framework briefly.

In a sense of a semantically enriched learning environment these scenarios give information and may also obtain information from an E-Learning Engineering based scenario.

---

[7]See [274], pp. 34-46
[8]See footnote 245

First, an evaluation approach with the help of a Balanced Scorecard is presented, second, KM the need for managing Skills and Competencies is introduced.

4.2.1 Evaluation approach in a B2B scenario

There are multiple methods to evaluate a BPM scenario. All these methods originate from Strategic Management and include mechanisms like Return-on-Investment, Business Process Evaluation or the Balanced Scorecard (BSC)[9] method.

This Chapter introduces ongoing research efforts at the DKE to introduce a BSC for E-Learning. The intention is to use the collected information that is produced from the execution of the models of the generic approach for measures in a BSC. For this matter, the classic perspectives "Financial Perspective", "Customer Perspective", "Learning and Growth Perspective" and "Internal Process Perspective" were changed to

- Student Perspective

- Image Perspective

- Process Perspective

- Potential Perspective

The BSC approach (cause and effect diagram) is depicted in Figure 4.5 for the strategic vision "Reach a Top-Ten position among the best universities globally". The main goal and addressee is the student. All other measures cause effects for the top-level measures associated with the student.

The heart of the BSC for E-Learning - as for every BSC - lies in the formulation of measures for the strategic goals sketched by the pyramids in Figure 4.5. Potentially interesting measures are:

- General measures

  - Cycle times for Web-Services workflows

  - Number of workflows per student

- E-Learning measures

  - Cycle time of learning processes

  - Overall success on the basis of grading

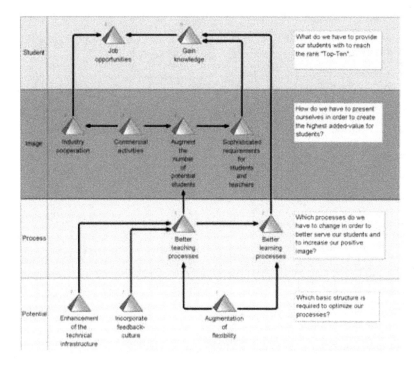

Figure 4.5: BSC for E-Learning

Future research to continue this work in progress will include enhancements in the cause and effect diagram and the definition of measures for E-Learning applications like the eduWeaver and the DKElearn Modeling Method for automatic creation of Knowledge Balances.

4.2.2 Skills and Competencies

Figure 4.3 already pointed out a vital interface between KM and E-Learning besides structuring knowledge resources, namely skills. Skills have to be provided, evaluated and linked to knowledge flows in the course of KM. Especially in combination with Human Resource Management, skills are also a key ingredient for life-long learning, because they provide the main input for the E-Learning strategy and education of knowledge workers. The following scenario introduces a possibility to match existing skill profiles in a company with the skill profile of a knowledge worker, so that a learning gap can be computed

---
[9]See [152] and [153]

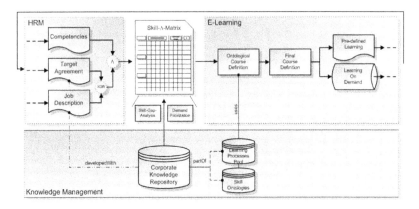

Figure 4.6: The Skill Delta Matrix

and consequentially the correct E-Learning activities can be launched. The knowledge worker can be both, an internal employee or an external applicant for a job vacancy. The scenario can be read in detail by reviewing the thesis of Praml[10] and fits perfectly into the E-Business Engineering framework as it uses already introduced tools PROMOTE and ADVISOR.

Figure 4.6 introduces the conceptual model for this purpose. Three different concatenated entities are depicted: the Human Resources Management, KM and E-Learning. The Human Resources Management provides general management of employees, storing competency profiles, target agreements about these profiles and job application profiles. All of the information comes and is stored in a corporate knowledge repository that is provided by the second player in this model: KM. Besides the information about competencies coming from skill ontologies, the knowledge repository also provides the information for learning processes. The link between KM and the Human Resources Management is the proposed Skill Delta Matrix that computes the skill gap between existing and actual knowledge of the knowledge worker. The skill gap and the learning demand priorization set grounds for the selection of LOs in the following providing either pre defined learning or Learning on Demand.

All the required activities within the Skill Delta Matrix themselves are defined by a KM Process. Many other KM Processes for managing the knowledge resources in this context are neglected. Future scenarios may include the management of all courses resulting from skill gaps or creating standard courses out of the most used Learning on Demand courses.

---

[10]See [217]

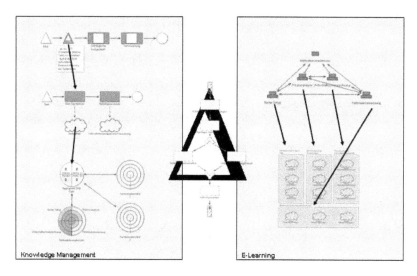

Figure 4.7: Modeling the Skill Delta Matrix

On the other hand, Learner Information Ontologies[11] provide standard modeling methods for describing E-Learning courses. Figure 4.7 depicts the scenario for the Skill Delta Matrix with PROMOTE and ADVISOR modeling methods clearly showing the integration momentum for E-Learning and KM. A resulting E-Learning course structure symbolized upon the Delta shows the created learning process that results from the calculation of the skill gap and the Ontological Course Definition.

4.3 The E-Learning Engineering Framework - additional semantics on the Technology Dimension

This Chapter gives two additional scenarios for the Technology Dimension of the E-Learning Framework that are vital for the DKElearn Modeling Method.

First, the connection to B2B applications and Workflow Management Systems is drawn, second, the relationship between E-Learning and the Semantic Web is given.

Plainly spoken, E-Learning has got perfect characteristics for serving as application scenario regarding the Semantic Web and Web-Services. On the one hand, potentially everyone - in the process of life-long learning - should have the possibility to get access to E-Learning resources, and on the other hand, the resources themselves are heterogeneous

---

[11]See Chapter 6.2.3.3

and may come from any location or provider. The obvious conclusion lies in the concatenation of "everyone" and the resources that "everyone" needs. This scenario needs many different ingredients; nearly all of them have already been at least mentioned in this thesis:

- E-Learning is embedded in a B2B scenario and therefore needs to be integrated into business strategies and methodologies based on interoperable XML-based standards

- E-Learning is distributed over the internet

- E-Learning uses ontologies to represent inter-relations and resources

- Users and systems are heterogeneous and locally independent

In order to produce a generic approach towards a Service-oriented Architecture (SOA) in E-Learning within a B2B scenario, some prerequisites have to be discussed first. Appendix B about Knowledge Representation Formalisms will help to understand and determine how to represent E-Learning resources and interdependencies. But still, other theoretical issues have not been discussed up to this point:

- B2B, process-orientation and Workflow Management Systems (WfMS)

- E-Learning in the Semantic Web

- A methodology and an E-Learning framework as already mentioned in Chapter 2.3.3.1

- Querying over more than one ontology resulting in a "target vector" ontology representing the ideal LOs for a given person

4.3.1 B2B, process-orientation and Workflow Management Systems

This Chapter[12] discusses the relevance of embedding E-Learning into a process-oriented B2B[13] scenario and the impact of WfMS towards Web-Services. Compared to BPM this discipline could be called E-Learning Management as a sub-class of Business Engineering. Business Engineering currently is mature to provide a modeled environment of the business

---

[12]The parts B2B and process-orientation in this Chapter are discussed very generally only. But the topics are needed in order to fully explain technical embedment of the topic WfMS.

[13]Often, B2B application scenarios are also related to other technical terms like Enterprise Application Integration (EAI) or grid-computing referring to enterprise-wide and integrated scenarios. In this thesis, such scenarios are only mentioned in the combination with the term B2B.

process landscape; like an architect who can provide plans for building and constructing a house. What is still missing is the ICT support for executing the models at run-time. Historically speaking, Business Engineering's ICT supported Management has its roots in data-driven scenarios (information management, Decision Support Systems, Data Warehouses, etc.). Currently, process-orientation and holistic Business Engineering enable knowledge-driven scenarios, especially with additional dimensions apart from financial view (Balanced Scorecard, Knowledge Management, etc.). The process-orientation enables the mapping of activities into a given process-context; it is possible, to tell who is responsible for a given activity and vice versa. The modeled processes landscape is the basis for transformation to technical ICT supported technical workflows[14]. This knowledge-driven approach can still be augmented by any other context, e.g. Semantic Web compliant ontologies or relations to B2B partners.

Taking into account the advantages of Business Engineering from Chapter 1.1.1.3, it can be stated, that process-orientation is an abstraction layer inserted between the organizational layer and the technical layer[15]. The need for this abstraction layer with processes is raised by many arguments:

- The knowledge-driven approach - as mentioned - enables B2B collaborations with the help of public interfaces[16]

- Globalization and efficiency of procurement processes for product production are driving factors to succeed in highly competitive markets

- The "customer is king"-paradigm (private and corporate) demands flexibility and immediate reaction. The workload may be transferred to the customer, who can order personalized products over internet portals

- Need for optimal costs based on efficient business processes

- The process landscape documents the Know-How and the mapping between organization and ICT

- Business Processes provide an *"process abstraction layer"* to serve as an interface between technical applications and organizational requirements, making it possible to manage enterprise wide scenarios[17]

---

[14]Even process-oriented Software Engineering is possible; this means that the organizational structures as a whole yield into technical requirements.
[15]Compare to the ideas of PROMOTE, Chapter 2.7.2
[16]E.g. see Chapter 2.2
[17]See [221], p. 177

- Activities within Business Processes are small chunks that also need little pieces of executable code, called services. Activities have to be able to decide at run-time which service they will bind. These coupled services need to be integrated along the Business Process[18]

- The fact, that small services are atomic parts of a Business Process, also enables creation of different process versions depending on the end-user's hardware (PC, PDA, cellular phone, etc.)

- Possibility for execution of context-specific ad-hoc processes for any user (internal or external, mobile or local, etc.)

Having created a so-called Business Model with the help of Business Engineering, all relevant information is described statically with the help of the meta-data provided by the models. This is the exact point, where ICT supported Management jumps in providing the ICT-connection. Traditionally, Business Models can be executed with the help of

- WfMS[19]

  - Autonomous WfMS

  - Embedded WfMS

  - Integrated WfMS

- Standard Software[20]

  - Enterprise Resource Planning Software

  - Groupware Systems

  - Document Management Systems

  - etc.

- Individually created software

---

[18]See [174], p. 55

[19]See [150], p. 117; WfMS traditionally need the following Business Models: (1) a business process, (2) an organizational context and (3) the technical infrastructure. The WfMS controls the flows among these models. Extending the Workflow paradigm with Semantic Web ideas, other domain ontologies may provide richer semantics. The execution of Business Models shows the tight connection between the disciplines WfMS and Business Process Engineering, see [218], p. 17. Unfortunately, this coupling is not yet supported by a standard interface; for some approaches, see [321], p. 221. Inter-dependencies and constraints between the business model and the workflow model are also question to research; related approaches to integrate them into both directions can be seen in [97], pp. 61-76, and [150], Chapter 7.

[20]See [150], Chapter 5

The listed execution environments however use the client-server paradigm. It seems reasonable to transform it into a Peer-to-Peer SOA using Web-Services. But there are some drawbacks of using SOA Web-Services over client-server based internet[21]:

- HTTP is a request-response protocol and therefore is synchronous

- HTTP is stateless

- SOAP over HTTP is bound to these drawbacks

Web-Services - especially in a B2B context where reliability, scalability, asynchronous messaging, etc. are needed[22] - therefore require a middleware capable of SOA-requests by using a message driven paradigm that manages both synchronous and asynchronous services[23]. These facts and the definition by Karagiannis "Web-Services are workflows over the internet" immediately relate WfMS to Web-Services. The question remains: do Web-Services Workflow engines exist? Before answering this question some information about WfMS.

- WfMS and Business Engineering are tightly coupled disciplines, where WfMS covers the technical infrastructure for modeling and executing technical models of business processes. It is vital to add that Business Engineering - in contrast to classic Taylorism that is concerned with how to optimize a single activity - uses process-orientation for combining and integrating activities from different entities into a value chain[24]. Before thinking about technical processes executed by WfMS, the organizational processes have to be re-engineered for optimal efficiency concerning times and costs. A transformation has to take place that converts the organizational business process to a technical E-Business process[25]

- A holistic methodology has to combine process engineering and execution of business models as workflows and the corresponding evaluation

- Standard descriptions of workflows do not exist as such; each vendor proposed his own meta-model for describing workflows[26]. De-facto standards could have emerged from IBM's MQSeries Workflow Definition Language (FDL)[27] that merged into

---

[21]See [191]
[22]Especially ebXML (see Chapter 2.2) is addressing these problems; see [187]
[23]See [191]
[24]See [25], p. 17
[25]See [150], p. 261
[26]See [150], p. 129
[27]See [176]

the Web-Services Flow Language (WSFL)[28] adopting FDL for Web-Services within the Web-Services Conceptual Architecture (WSCA). The WSCA and Microsoft's XLANG merged to BPEL4WS[29] that was submitted to OASIS and is continued by the Web Services Business Process Execution Language (WSBPEL) Technical Committee[30].

Returning to the Workflow and Web-Services, the answer to the above posed question concerning Web-Services Workflow engines is "Yes", for at least IBM's BPWS4J (`http://www.alphaworks.ibm.com/tech/bpws4j`), Microsoft's BizTalk Server (`http://www.microsoft.com/biztalk/beta/`) and Collaxa's BPEL Orchestration Server (`http://www.collaxa.com/developer.download.html`, recently acquired by Oracle) already exist. The next question is though: Are there existing approaches for combining Business Engineering, the workflow paradigm and Web-Services? This question has to be answered positively as well, although there are only a few solutions[31].

To put it in a nutshell: Business Engineering combined with a methodology - in this case embedded in an E-Learning scenario - serves for strategy formulation and evaluation and for modeling of the descriptive state of resources and their inter-relation. Concerning the execution of the Business Model several options exist; two of the most reasonable ones are coupling Business Engineering with WfMS and the coupling with SOA scenarios and Web-Services. Contemporary literature invented a new term for such an application: E-Services. E-Services can be seen as E-Business related, "small" online-applications fulfilling a certain use-case with the help of a SOA approach[32].

4.3.2 E-Learning in the Semantic Web

E-Learning was chosen as application scenario, where Knowledge Representation technologies set the foundation for applications and agents to query existing structures. Whereas Chapter 2 discussed the topic E-Learning generally, this Chapter takes E-Learning further into the direction of the Semantic Web and Web-Services providing the foundation for

---

[28]See [175]

[29]See Chapter 2.3

[30]See `http://www.oasis-open.org/committees/tc_home.php?wg_abbrev=wsbpel`

[31]See [177]

[32]Like all other definitions in computer sciences, the term E-Services can not be defined properly in one sentence. E-Services are a *"natural outgrowth of E-Commerce ... technologists view E-Services as Web-delivered software functionality, often characterized under the rubric of Web-Services"* (see [260], p. 28) and *"An e-service is any asset that is made available via the Internet to drive new revenue streams or create new efficiencies"* (see [216], p.)- E-Services seem to replace the E-Business E-Terms, especially E-Commerce and stress customer-satisfaction as core goal (see [232], p. 37).

the E-Learning Engineering framework.

The State-of-the-Art situation in E-Learning is a bit behind compared to the developments in the Semantic Web. Although XML-based standards exist, RDF-based technologies are still in their beginnings[33]. Also applications are still monolithic and do not conform to emerging Peer-to-Peer technologies based on SOA ideas coming from Web-Services. Methodologically speaking, E-Learning - like many other ICT disciplines including the Semantic Web - is technology-centered (see Figure B.3). This is where KM comes in to cover strategic issues and business processes together with description of human and ICT resources and their interconnection.

The vision of this thesis is to use KM as strategic management discipline instantiating Business Engineering for E-Learning set in a B2B scenario: breaking down business tasks to learning activities so that they reference LOs annotated in a Semantic Web-like style. Workflow-like middleware is then able to control and manage Semantic Web-Services for E-Learning to create on demand personalized courses depending on a user profile. The breaking down of the different tasks and all other associated ontological information will be modeled with a modeling method that takes input from the Knowledge Representation Formalisms discussed in order to create a sound and complete knowledge base for E-Learning.

Chapter 4.3.2.1 therefore discusses the State-of-the-Art situation in E-Learning and starts the discussion on the E-Learning modeling method that is able to produce dynamic courses over the Internet.

4.3.2.1 Representation Frameworks and approaches in E-Learning

Many different views and figures exist when talking about key players in E-Learning. They were already discussed in Chapter 2.4. This Chapter revisits the main ideas and focuses on efforts towards the Semantic Web and E-Learning. Figure 4.8 depicts these key players according to the evolution of a standard. A standard is developed because of academic and scientific interest in a first stage; the documents that are produced are called specifications. Consortia with academic and industry involvement then take up these specifications to produce best-practices and APIs and so-called profiles[34]. A profile is a distinctive set of specifications bundled to serve a certain E-Learning scenario[35]. The Shareable Content Object Reference Model SCORM (http://www.adlnet.org/) and the

---

[33]See [200]

[34]Note: do not confuse the use of the word "Profile". Until now, three different types of "profiles" have bee defined: (1) the Web-Services Profiles, e.g. the WS-I Basic Profile (see footnote 302), (2) Profiles of certain users, e.g. Skill-Profiles and (3) Profiles in E-Learning, e.g. SCORM.

[35]E.g. Academic versus industry profiles and applications.

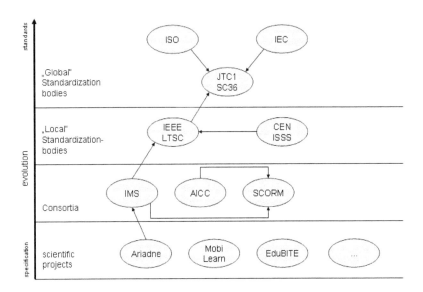

Figure 4.8: Evolution of E-Learning standards

specifications provided by the IMS Global Consortium (http://www.imsglobal.org/)
are the two examples in E-Learning. After passing the specification stage, local standardization bodies pass them through lengthy evaluation processes to produce standards.
Finally, global standardization bodies elevate these standards to global ones. The Learning Objects Meta-data (LOM) specification has been the first to reach the level of an
IEEE 1484.12.1 - 2002 standard (http://ltsc.ieee.org/wg12/index.html).
Unfortunately, the E-Learning specifications and standards still exist only as XML-bindings,
which do not make them that interesting in terms of the Semantic Web[36].

Fortunately, efforts exist to tackle these issues:

- The RSS LOM provides a translation from IEEE LOM to RSS (http://www.downes.
  ca/xml/rss_lom.htm) to allow learning repositories to work together.

- The KM Research (KMR) Group at the Centre for user oriented ICT design of
  the Numerical analysis and computer science (NADA) at the Royal Institute of
  Technology in Stockholm, Sweden, is creating an RDF binding of the IEEE LOM
  standard (http://kmr.nada.kth.se/el/ims/meta-data.html).

- The Open Knowledge Initiative of the MIT, the Educational Activities and Learn-

---

[36]See also Chapter 2.4.7

ing Practices (EALP) (http://demo-emcc.mit.edu/oki/project.html), is dealing with research of pedagogy, learning styles, and the implications of computer
aided education.

- The project Edutella (http://edutella.jxta.org/) is developing dynamic learning repositories on the basis of Peer-to-Peer technologies and embracing Semantic
Web representation technologies.

The first step shown in Figure 4.9[37] is to map the E-Learning information models to Semantic Web technologies[38]. The main arguments why to use RDF(S) can be summarized
in the following enumeration[39]:

- RDF provides interoperability because different types of data use a single storage
model

- Reuse of existing meta-data standards is enforced (e.g. vCard[40] RDF binding, etc.)

- Relationships among vocabularies can easily be formalized and are therefore machine-
readable

- Ontology engineering and vocabulary formulation is a fundamental part of RDFS
and extensions (DAML+OIL, OWL, etc.) and vocabularies can be modeled in a
standard way

- Extension of RDF does not cause interoperability problems. Only a new RDFS has
to be introduced

- Means for describing meta-meta-data (i.e. reification) is already included

- Graph-representation is a reasonable and understandable way to document ontologies

Further steps - after having produced knowledge bases in that way - E-Business models
have to make use of this semantic resource base. Approaches like

- ebXML (http://www.ebxml.org/)

- Business Process Execution Language for Web-Services (BPEL4WS) (http://www.
oasis-open.org/news/oasis_news_04_29_03.php)

---

[37]A generic ontological visualization is used.
[38]XML structures have to be resolved with RDF structures simply because the Semantic Web depends
on RDF (see [200]).
[39]See [200]
[40]See footnote 441

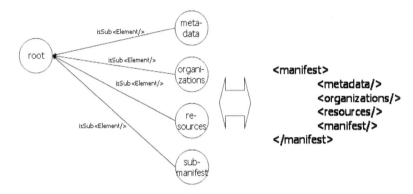

Figure 4.9: Mapping of a (networked) ontology to a (hierarchic) XML structure

- DAML-S (http://www.daml.org/services/)

- Elasticknowledge proposes a system for competency-based just-in-time learning that uses competency ontologies and semantic Web-Services to deliver LOs to learners in a corporate environment (http://www.elasticknowledge.com/pub_elearning.html)

are concerned with business models and the execution of business workflows by Web-Services. Finally, the whole knowledge processes together with the organizational environment have to be executed in some way, either by individually created software, by WfMS, by Web-Services or a combination of them.

These enumerations definitely show that the topics B2B, RDF-bindings, ontologies and Web-Services will be the key issues in E-Learning in the coming years, changing the "E-Learning Island" into an easy to integrate technology and E-Learning services into a Business scenario (see Figure 4.10).

4.3.2.2 Existing E-Learning ontologies

Taking Chapter 4.3.2.1 into account, this Chapter discusses and presents current Semantic Web approaches in E-Learning[41]. The standards or specifications that already point into

---

[41]This Chapter and the generic approach will not discuss or argue about the quality of the information model of the existing E-Learning specifications. This is done at least because of two reasons: (1) the evolution of a standard takes time, involves a lot of discussion and urgently needs to consolidate many different views, e.g. the discussion about LOM elements like Educational.SemanticDensity are neglected, and (2) the concept of this thesis per se is generic and new specifications can easily be fitted in. The fact, that E-Learning already has an existing standard (LOM) and some other mature specifications (Content Packaging), was seen as sufficient to use them as a basis for a proof of concept.

direction into the Semantic Web world are:

- **LOM[42] for LOs**:

  The IMS Global Consortium is currently working on an RDF-binding for LOM[43] in cooperation with the KMR Group at the "Centre for user oriented ICT design" at the NADA[44]. The LOM RDF binding is (almost) compatible to Dublin Core RDF binding; it shall be noted that the RDF binding is an interpretation of the LOM information model and also incorporates additional semantics; therefore full compatibility between the XML-binding and the RDF binding is lost: transformation from XML to RDF is only possible providing additional contextual information[45].

- **Content Packaging[46] for aggregated LOs**:

  The IMS Global Consortium is also working on an RDF-binding for the Content Packaging specification[47] also in cooperation with the KMR Group at the NADA[48]. However, the status of the Content Packaging RDF binding is not as mature as the LOM RDF binding.

The LOM and Content Package RDF bindings can be seen as ongoing efforts to include, reuse and map existing[49] Dublin Core vocabularies[50] like the vCard RDF binding[51] and the Dublin Core RDF binding[52].

These two approaches[53] are at this point of time the only two concerning RDF-bindings of E-Learning standards or specifications.

For a holistic KM-driven scenario with service-oriented E-Learning the existing ontologies have to be embedded into a greater picture; the modeling environment of DKElearn tries to provide a conceptual solution (see Chapter 6). Especially the document-driven style of LOM XML-bindings has to be transformed into RDF-driven networks of state-

---

[42]See [131]

[43]See [140]

[44]See [103]

[45]See [201] and [198]: e.g. XML models are interpreted in automatic ordering; The corresponding RDF model needs to encode ordering information additionally.

[46]See [132]

[47]See [139]

[48]See [102]

[49]See [198] for semantic design issues for the LOM mapping.

[50]See [201]; note the liaison between Dublin Core and LOM ([71])

[51]See [306]

[52]See [70]

[53]The KMR Group (http://kmr.nada.kth.se/tools.html) is participating in the project Edutella and also produced a Conceptual Browser Conzilla (http://www.conzilla.org/), the learning component archive Standardized Content Archive Management (SCAM). (http://sourceforge.net/projects/scam/) and the E-Learning meta-data editor ImseVimse (http://kmr.nada.kth.se/imsevimse/index.html).

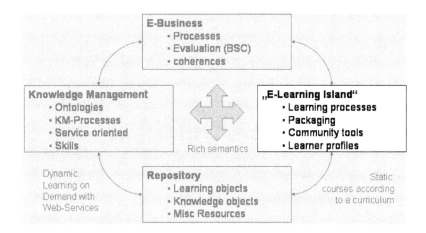

Figure 4.10: State-of-the-Art E-Learning situation

ments in order to be able to query over more than one LO[54].

The Austrian meta-data specification: To show that the meta-data community is active and working, a use-case of the Austrian government is presented.

In this context, the ongoing efforts on the political scene in Europe coming from the European Commission known as the E-Learning Action Plan[55] and the local implementations by the Austrian Federal Ministry for Education, Science and Culture (BM:BWK)[56] have to be mentioned. The E-Learning Action Plan focuses on Europe to become a knowledge-based society.

Every member state of the EU has to contribute to this Action Plan by implementing certain guidelines. This Chapter shortly discusses the developments of the Austrian BM:BWK.

According to the Dublin Core and LOM, a meta-data specification[57] for the Austrian E-Learning portal http://www.bildung.at was created. This portal intends to integrate all Austrian E-Learning content resources by urging all content providers in the public sector to annotate their LOs and publishing them into a content pool.

Similar projects can be found within the whole European Union to fulfill the E-Learning Action Plan.

---

[54]See [198]

[55]See http://europa.eu.int/comm/education/programmes/elearning/index_de.html for details.

[56]See http://www.bmbwk.gv.at/start.asp for details.

[57]See [169]

4.3.2.3 Non-existing E-Learning ontologies

For matters of completeness, this Chapter mentions further E-Learning specifications that will be needed[58] for creating a complete E-Learning framework. They are[59]:

- **General Standards**:
  LTSA or other specifications describing E-Learning architecture do not exist as RDF-bindings and are currently not in progress. The question remains, whether stand-alone XML-bindings will have any prospect, because SOA and Web-Services are currently State-of-the-Art in this sector.

- **Meta-data**:
  LOM and Content Packaging specifications concerning RDF-bindings exist or are work in progress.

- **Services, Skills and Profiles**:
  Services and especially skills and profiles of learners are a very important issue, because dynamic allocation of learner specific LOs depend on learner information concerning interest, learning history, passed exams, etc. The development in this section is by far not as mature as in the meta-data section. This also implies that no efforts concerning RDF-bindings exist.

- **Management**:
  The issues in this section are similar to the ones from the General Standards section.

The lack of important ontologies with RDF-bindings - mostly information about learners -has to be treated by KM related developments. Chapters 4.2 and 6 will provide more information.

4.3.3 Querying several ontologies with an RDF-binding

Several statements about querying ontologies have to be made in advance:

- It has already been stated in Chapter 1.3 that the development concerning ontology representation is in its beginnings. RDF(S) still is State-of-the-Art and is not considered to be a full-scale ontology language but is said to have sufficient power to serve for test-beds of the introduced generic model. DAML+OIL or OWL therefore are not taken into account from this point on.

---

[58]See end of Chapter 4.3.2.2

[59]See Chapter 2.4.7 and [266] for general information about E-Learning standards and http://ltsc.ieee.org for ongoing standardization developments

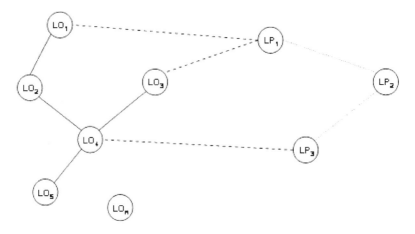

Figure 4.11: Relations between LOs and Learner Profiles

- The existing RDF-bindings for LOM and Content Packaging are still work in progress. Projects like Edutella and partners are one of the very few consortia to deal with RDF-bindings in E-Learning. State-of-the-Art situation still are XML-bindings.

- Interfaces or APIs are not mature or do not fully support semantic querying of RDF models. Depending on the power, complex semantic interrelations are hard to process. Due to deficiencies, the full impact of RDF(S) may be reduced to hierarchically structured schemata[60].

With these statements in mind, this Chapter conceptually deals with the question of how to combine resources defined in different ontologies. The following two key questions[61] have to be answered by the generic model are the following:

- Which is the best LO for a set of arbitrary restrictions?[62]

- Which LOs fit a Learner's Profile?[63]

Schematically speaking, Figure 4.11 depicts the second question in a very simplified way neglecting any quality of the relations (e.g. grading, level of granularity of LOs or sequencing of LOs):

---

[60]Compare to the development of RDF-bindings for simple [69] and qualified [68] Dublin Core Metadata Element Set.

[61]These two questions purely focus on learning scenarios. Of course other questions like "What does an LO for specific skills cost?" or "How many LOs does an instructor need to create or manage to fulfill his contract?" have to be considered as well.

[62]See [199], p. 2

[63]The question is only reasonable without predefined learning processes (Learning on Demand).

- LOs have relations among themselves defining something like a curriculum (solid arcs).

- Learner Profiles (LPs) exist and also may have some relations (small dotted arcs).

- Relations between LOs and LPs are the key to answering the question (dashed arcs) indicating that LPs have already accessed certain LOs.

Compared to relational paradigm this information would be stored in m:n relations between LOs and LPs. In RDF(S), RDFS sets the semantic restrictions (i.e. LOM RDF-binding) and RDF defines the resources according to the RDFS schema. Unlike the records stored in databases, a storing mechanism for RDF resources is not predefined per se. Resources may reside in separate RDF-files (either holding one or n resources), in databases or any other resource pool with a RDF interface[64]. This is where existing APIs set restrictions: of course a pool of resources has to be the basis for querying; ideally the pool of resources is composed out of LOs originating from an arbitrary location[65] meaning that LOs described in distributed RDF resources have to be combined. The issues concerning RDF APIs will be again addressed in Chapter 6.3.

Underlying theory for querying RDF graphs themselves is a matter of graph theory. Unlike standard querying in databases, scientific research concerning RDF tries to find modeled queries resulting again in RDF graphs[66]. An own vocabulary for these result graphs has to be defined[67]. Concerning the power and ability to dynamically and semantically query resources with different vocabularies, the implementation of RDF graph theory in connection with RDFS or higher level ontology languages such as OWL[68] remains one of the biggest challenges in the Semantic Web.

4.4 Summary

This Chapter discussed the E-Learning Engineering Framework on a conceptual level as one instantiation of the E-Learning Framework presented in Chapter 3. With the help of Appendices A and B, the concept is based on a static (Knowledge Representation) and a

---

[64]See [198]; a coupling between static description of LOs via RDF and dynamic processing of LOs by Web-Services is one reasonable scenario (see Chapter 6.3).

[65]Brokerage of LOs and electronic markets is a vital issue in today's E-Learning. For further reading consider Bernd Simon's publications at http://wwwi.wu-wien.ac.at/people/Simon.html, especially [253]

[66]See [301] and [298]

[67][301] references a vocabulary defined by the Jena Semantic Web toolkit (http://jena.hpl.hp.com/2003/03/result-set)

[68]For RDFS vs. OWL see related discussion such as [297]

dynamic (Web-Services).

Furthermore, interdependencies to a greater business scope (B2B, ERP, BSC and competencies) were shown. Finally - already with respect to a concrete technical solution - the current situation of E-Learning specifications in the context of the Semantic Web was presented, showing a rather mediocre state of maturity at the moment. The following Chapters 5 and 6 actually make use of the E-Learning Engineering Framework.

Chapter 5

E-Learning Engineering and Enactment with eduWeaver

This Chapter sketches one instance of an E-Learning Engineering Framework as outlined in Chapter 4 with a Document-centric character called eduWeaver.

5.1 Chapter Outline

eduWeaver Modeling Method was developed within the EDUBITE project[1]. History and detailed description are not part of this thesis. eduWeaver - as one instance of Document-centric Learning - shall only constitute as an existing method to show a concrete test-bed within this learning paradigm.

Figure 5.1 shows the structure of this Chapter. First, the eduWeaver meta-modeling methods are defined and described. Along with the description comes a concrete modeled scenario to illustrate the modeling methods that can also be simulated by stepping through a learning process. Second, two transformation scenarios are shown.

5.2 eduWeaver Modeling Methods

The eduWeaver Modeling Methods were developed as generic technique to describe (sequences of) LOs with an interface to the IMS Content Package. Therefore, arbitrary courses from different domains can be modeled as pointed out in Chapter 5.2.2.

Figure 5.2 shows the current situation represented by a stack of Educational Technologies ordered by the responsible consortium that reflects the conceptual architecture of the

---

[1]See http://www.edubite.ac.at/

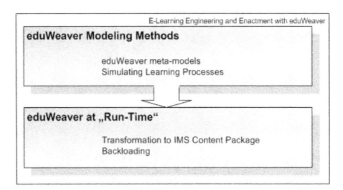

Figure 5.1: Overview

meta-models within eduWeaver.

eduWeaver was developed to bring different domain experts in the context of ERP together so that they are able to describe their courses generically. EduWeaver normally suggests a top-down methodology beginning with planning a learning scenario, creating LOs and connecting the learning scenario with the LOs. These generic models are provided with a standard interface to IMS Content Package so that the planning steps are rounded up by the learning activities at Run-Time.

Many other scenarios except from the interface to IMS Content Package can be thought of in this context, which is exactly the motivation to introduce the intermediary modeling step; otherwise - e.g. if domain knowledge represented via LOs would be transformed directly into a technical environment like an LMS - these transformation scenarios would not be possible. The de-contextualization and re-contextualization as described in Chapter 5.3.2 are simply not possible. These transformations are the added-value of such a modeled environment and can be entitled as "spin-off product"[2].

The strengths of eduWeaver therefore are:

- **Planning and management platform for instructors**:
  The main challenge in learning with Educational Technologies is the usability of the technology: users as well as instructors should be able to use these technologies even if they are non-ICT experts. In this context visual modeling methods serve as translation between domain and technical requirements. Therefore the first advantage of eduWeaver is the provision of an easy to understand visual modeling method with a structured methodology that eases the planning process of a learning

---

[2]See Chapter 4.2 as an example.

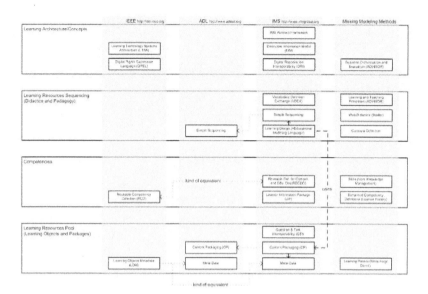

Figure 5.2: Blended Learning stack - State-of-the-Art situation in E-Learning

scenario. Based on the structured learning scenario different transformations into other contexts are possible.

- **Technical transformations**:
  Transformations into a technical context are concerned mostly with standardized document and LO exchange. Typically, XML applications as described in Chapter 2.4.7.1 are potential output. Chapter 5.3.1 and 5.3.2 show one concrete example.

- **Non-technical transformations**:
  Depending whether didactical issues are already included in technical standards, transformations into a non-technical context include skill-dependent scenarios (novice or expert courses), didactical scenarios (problem-based or drill and practice) and many other scenarios (e.g. gender-specific transformations).

5.2.1 The ADONIS meta-modeling platform and the instance eduWeaver

The following Chapter is concerned with the actual eduWeaver Modeling Method and the realized meta-models based on the ADONIS meta-modeling platform[3] instantiating the E-Learning Engineering Framework according to Figure 4.4 within the Document-centric paradigm.

5.2.2 The eduWeaver meta-models

The eduWeaver meta-models at this stage include the following visual modeling methods[4]:

- Course

- Module

- Lesson

- LO Usage

- LO Pool

In the future, eduWeaver may be extended e.g. to also serve managers and curriculum designers by adding respective modeling methods, so that courses can be arranged into a greater scope like a curriculum. A structured methodology and visual modeling methods are especially interesting in the context of *e*Europe[5].

Schematically focusing on actual courses, learning sequences and LOs, the top-part of Figure 5.3 depicts a typical structure of a course with the help of eduWeaver modeling method[6] reflecting the E-Learning Modeling Layer from Figure 3.5.

As already mentioned, the eduWeaver Modeling Methods are able to describe any learning scenario in arbitrary domains. They were tested at the University of Vienna in the following Departments:

- **Scope Business Informatics**: Faculty of Informatics, Department of Knowledge Engineering[7].

- **Scope Marketing**: Faculty of Business

- **Scope Theoretical Chemistry**: Faculty of Chemistry

---

[3]See Chapter 6.2.1
[4]See [23]
[5]See Chapter 3.4
[6]See [23]
[7]The example in Figure 5.3 is taken from this scope.

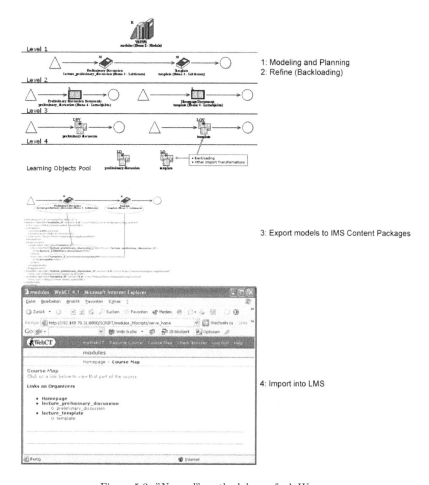

Figure 5.3: "Normal" methodology of eduWeaver

Figure 5.4: Simulation: Preview a learning process

5.2.3 Simulating Learning Processes with eduWeaver

Simulation scenarios as pointed out in Chapter 2.5.3 and 3.4.1 may appear on different levels: on a management level, simulation may help executives to plan learning scenarios budget-wise by helping them to compare different possibilities. This chapter introduces a simulation concept on the level of visualizing a learning process[8].

Particularly in the context of Backloading as described in Chapter 5.3.2 it can be extremely helpful to preview the automatically generated learning processes immediately, even before importing them into an LMS.

The learning processes preview may be used in the LO Usage model and references the corresponding resources in the LO Pool model as shown in Figure 5.4. A learning process - beginning with a **Start Object** - is processed sequentially highlighting each learning activity that it passes. Depending on the existence of a resource in the LO Pool model, the actual resource is invoked with the help of an internet browser. As Backloading is merely producing learning sequences, decisions or parallel process parts may not be simulated with the help of the eduWeaver Process Simulator.

5.3 eduWeaver at "Run-Time"

Based on a modeled eduWeaver environment, two transformations are presented in the next two Chapters.

---

[8]The eduWeaver Learning Process Simulator is based on the ADONIS (see Chapter 6.2.1) Process Stepper.

5.3.1 Transformation to IMS Content Packages

This Chapter describes the "normal" way of using eduWeaver as an instructor:

1. Plan the structure of a course

2. Refine details of the models concerning LOs

3. Export the modeled environment into an IMS Content Package

4. Import the IMS Content Package into an IMS compliant LMS

Figure 5.3 depicts this scenario.

5.3.2 Backloading

At this point an interesting concept shall be discussed in brief, namely the concept of Backloading[9]. Especially in the Document-centric learning paradigm it is naturally to cope with a large amount of existing content files, authored with Microsoft Office products to a great extent. Powerpoint slides are the de-facto standard for presenting content in front of a (large) audience. Backloading intends to support instructors in a Bottom-Up combined with a Top-Down way to incorporate and publish these content files automatically into an LMS. Figure 5.5 shows the steps that have to be taken.

As an intermediary step, the content is transformed into a de-contextualized set of text modules that are automatically transformed into E-Learning models. This enables instructors and managers to re-contextualize the text modules with the help of templates to get actual LOs. At the moment it is reasonable to provide an IMS Content Package template, so that the re-contextualized LOs can be imported into an LMS. Other possible templates may include PDF files or LOs with other didactical settings (beginners courses with all the information, intermediate courses with all the information except text, expert courses with the possibility to browse manually, etc.) as mentioned in the enumeration in Chapter 5.2.

Backloading thus gives added value to nearly all participants of a learning scenario:

- **Instructor**: The instructor can re-use legacy presentation slides in the context of E-Learning.

---

[9]See Appendix C for details.

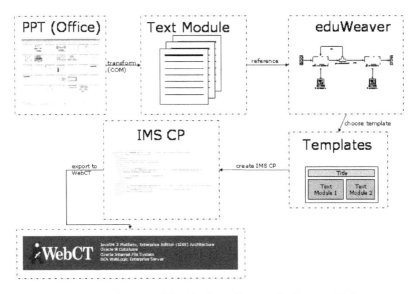

Figure 5.5: Concept of Backloading - Bottom-Up Import of LOs

- **Manager**: Managers like curricula-responsibles or deans can use the modeled information for the decision process.

- **Administrator**: Administrators "source-out" import- and export of arbitrary and unstructured Files.

Technically, several steps have to be followed to reach Backloading (in accordance with Figure 5.5):

1. A client application has to perform the actual transformation

   - Extract actual information of the Powerpoint File into a generic format[10]; see Code-Example 5.1

   - Create an eduWeaver transformation file that saves the structure and sequence of the slides together with the reference to the actual object; see Code-Example 5.2

2. Import the eduWeaver transformation file into eduWeaver creating two models

   - LO Usage

---

[10]This prototype transforms each slide into a GIF-picture with the help of the Universal Document Converter Trial Version to be found at `http://www.print-driver.com/`

```
Sub Print_PowerPoint_File_with_UDC()
        Dim prsPres As PowerPoint.Presentation
        Dim ppApp As PowerPoint.Application
        Dim i As Integer

        On Error Resume Next
        ppApp = New PowerPoint.Application
        prsPres = ppApp.Presentations.Open(globalfilename, 1, 1, 0)
        prsPres.PrintOptions.ActivePrinter = "Universal Document Converter"
        Call prsPres.PrintOut(0, -1, 0, 1, 0)
        Call prsPres.Close()
        Call ppApp.Quit()
        ppApp = Nothing
        For i = 1 To slidecount

            <...>

        Next
    End Sub
```

Code-Example 5.1: Powerpoint Transformation and creating images of slides

- LO Pool

3. Concatenate the LO Usage Pool to the Lesson in the desired way

4. Export to IMS Content Package as described in Chapter 5.3.1

5.4   Summary

This Chapter described one concrete instance of an E-Learning Engineering Framework with a focus on Document-centric Learning mentioning the main advantage of making hierarchical LOs inter-changeable.

As sketched in Chapter 3, Document-centric Learning is the precursor of Resource-driven Learning that is described in Chapter 6.

```
Sub WriteToADL()
    Dim sw As StreamWriter = New StreamWriter(globaldirectory &
        "\TransformPowerpoint.adl")
    Dim i As Integer
    Dim MyGuid As Guid
    Dim i_GUID As String

    MyGuid = Guid.NewGuid()

    <...>

    For i = 1 To slidecount
        i_GUID = i.ToString + "__" + MyGuid.ToString
        sw.WriteLine("INSTANCE <" & i_GUID & "> : <LO (eduWEAVER)>")
        sw.WriteLine("ATTRIBUTE <Einstiegspunkt (CI 1)>")

        <...>

    Next

    <...>

    sw.WriteLine("RELATION <Nachfolger>")
    sw.WriteLine("FROM <" & slidecount & "__" & MyGuid.ToString & "> :
        <LOV (eduWEAVER)>")
    sw.WriteLine("TO <Ende> : <Ende (eduWEAVER)>")
    sw.Close()
    MsgBox("TransformPowerpoint.adl created.")
End Sub
```

Code-Example 5.2: Create eduWeaver transformation file

Chapter 6

E-Learning Engineering and Enactment with DKElearn

This Chapter sketches one instance of an E-Learning Engineering Framework as outlined in Figure 4.4 with a Resource-driven character called DKElearn.

This scenario however creates the need for a totally new architecture leaving the client-server paradigm. Any entity - a human or an intelligent-application agent - now has the possibility to query and process a Semantic Web. These entities are called peers, equally interconnected hosts that are able to perform as a client and as a server as well. Figure B.9 presented the "Web of Trust" and the main problem with Peer-to-Peer architectures: trust. This seems to be ok for Business-to-Consumer (B2C) or Consumer-to-Consumer (C2C) as many applications in the music and film industry demonstrate. In a B2B context[1], where authentication, digital signatures and contracts are the basis for collaboration, Peer-to-Peer architecture has to be lifted onto a higher level of trust than in B2C or C2C scenarios. One way of dealing with this in E-Learning is to introduce a framework of modeled knowledge[2].

The theoretical model is created only on one level: existing E-Learning ontologies serve as input; neither the quality of the information model nor the didactical impact and reasonability is questioned[3]. The main target is to transform the models into Semantic Web compliant structures like RDF(S) documents.

---

[1] See [168], p. 22

[2] See Chapter 4.2

[3] E.g. the element "semantic density" within the LOM information model is widely discussed and interpreted. This thesis will not treat these discussions, because the focus lies on the E-Learning framework and the feasibility of creating an LO out of querying ontologies etc.

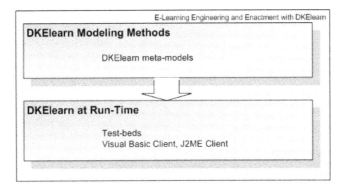

Figure 6.1: Overview

6.1 Chapter Outline

For this approach it has been already stated that several dimensions will be cut back, including the use of a methodology and evaluation restraining it to ICT related issues. A modeled reference environment showing all concepts and dependencies of the E-Learning Engineering framework will be given, above all static knowledge representation with the DKElearn Modeling Method focusing on Semantic Web and ontologies. In order to evaluate the generic approach from Figure 4.4, the feasibility of the Business Engineering approach in E-Learning has partially been realized via some prototypical test-beds.

Figure 6.1 shows the structure of this Chapter. First, the DKElearn meta-modeling methods are defined and described. Along with the description comes a concrete modeled scenario to illustrate the modeling methods. Second, the test-beds that get their static information from the modeled DKElearn environment are discussed.

Some of these static ontologies will be input to test-beds in order to evaluate the quality of the modeled representations. This Chapter is about the description of the DKElearn Modeling Method, the standards transformation and these test-beds.

Figure 6.2 depicts the architecture that is required for the generic approach, where the Business Engineering cycle is the heart of it. It is embedded into a SOA to fit the Web-Services approach. The term "generic" in this context is used, because the meta-models to be used do not come out of a fixed set but can be specialized to whatever requirements.

Note again that this architecture also depicts a paradigm shift from a client-server model to a SOA enabling Peer-to-Peer or B2B messaging model. This also revolutionizes existing E-Learning architectures[4]. At the moment, most LMS and LCMS providers

---

[4]Compare a SOA approach with an LCMS architecture depicted in Figure 2.14.

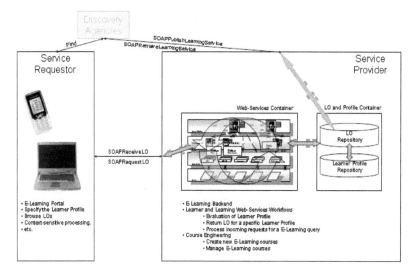

Figure 6.2: E-Learning architecture for the generic approach

build monolithic application with poor standards interfaces. The step towards SOA in E-Learning therefore will have to be huge[5].

The meta-models have to at least serve the following purposes in order to describe the E-Learning ontology and interdependencies:

- Model the B2B context

  - Business Models

  - Business Processes

- Annotate LOs[6]

- Annotate Learner Profiles

- Model Web-Services workflows

Other possible meta-models include:

- Model service quality

- Include mechanisms to model security, privacy and authentication matters

---

[5]The IEEE LTSC published the LTSA (see [129]). It separates an E-Learning application into five layers. This meaning of architecture in this context is not related to client-server architectures or SOA.

[6]LOs will be described by LOM and the Content Packaging specification.

- Include Digital Rights Management

The bold orange arrows imply possible data-flows that are managed within the modeling environment by Web-Services flows indicated by process models. The bold-dotted orange arrow indicates a possible link to Discovery Agents, either for Web-Services of LOs. The Discovery Agents may be UDDI nodes for finding new Web-Services or LO content pools for deploying extra content to engineered courses[7]. Moreover, the orange arrows mark the functionality that will be described in Chapter 6.

The bold orange arrows imply possible data-flows that are managed within the modeling environment by Web-Services flows indicated by process models. The bold-dotted orange arrow indicates a possible link to Discovery Agents, either for Web-Services of LOs. The Discovery Agents may be UDDI nodes for finding new Web-Services or LO content pools for deploying extra content to engineered courses[8]. Moreover, the orange arrows mark the functionality that will be described in Chapter 6.

These process models depict and manage the Web-Services workflows with the help of SOAP messages. The Web-Services Container is responsible for the execution and monitoring of these processes and returns audit-trails according to the evaluation step from underlying methodology. One possible evaluation scenario is described in the following Chapter. The following enumeration summarizes the actions by highlighting the executed items with bold faced font:

- Project management and strategic issues

- Creation and implementation of a methodology

- **Ontology Engineering**[9] **and creation of the meta-models (Chapter 6.2.2)**

- **Modeling the E-Learning environment (Chapter 6.2.3)**

- Execution of the modeled environment **(Chapter 6.3; test-beds)**

- Evaluation of the modeled environment

- Re-Engineering of the modeled environment and the quality of the meta-models on the basis of the evaluation

The items that will be executed comply with the orange arrows in Figure 6.2.

---

[7]See Chapter 4.3.2.2, where the BM:BWK sets up an Austrian wide content pool.

[8]See Chapter 4.3.2.2, where the BM:BWK sets up an Austrian wide content pool.

[9]Ontology Engineering is omitted for the greatest parts. LOM and Content Packaging are taken from the existing standards and specification efforts.

6.2 DKElearn Modeling Methods

The DKElearn modeling environment[10] is the core of the generic approach as depicted in Figure 6.2. It is primarily concerned with providing the Knowledge Representation Formalisms[11] that are required for Business Engineering in E-Learning. As already mentioned, the term "generic" in this context especially refers to the exchangeability of meta-models for describing the E-Learning domain aspects. For this approach, Dublin Core and VCARD RDF-bindings[12] were chosen to represent LOs. Learner Profiles - as no RDF-bindings exist - will be modeled only in a very simple way. The workflow methods are strongly related to the technologies from the basic Web-Services stack (UDDI, WSDL and SOAP).

Furthermore, the integration into a methodology is neglected. It is reduced to basic steps that include tasks:

- Modeling the business context

- Modeling the E-Learning context[13]

- Modeling the Web-Services workflows

Evaluation is not considered. Partly, the modeled environment will serve as input for some test-beds. The DKElearn Modeling is a prototypical implementation and therefore does not claim to be complete.

6.2.1 The ADONIS meta-modeling platform and the instance DKElearn

First, general requirements for a modeling environment are listed (the bold-faced enumerations imply important requirements for DKElearn):

- General requirements[14]

    - Client-Server architecture with database storage

    - Versioning

---

[10]Business Engineering in E-Learning is a not very common approach. For one approach see [170]

[11]See Chapter Appendix B

[12]LOM and the Content Packaging specification were not used because of their current and unfinished status.

[13]See [179]

[14]See [162], p. 63

- User Management

  - Single user management
  - Group management
  - Rights management for model-access

- Ontology modeling[15]

  - Acquiring ontologies
  - **Storing and maintaining ontologies**
  - Querying and browsing ontologies

- **Standards support**[16]

  - Support for modeling existing vocabularies

- Ontology storage system[17]

  - Management
  - Adaptation
  - Standardization
  - Usability (Zooming, etc.)

For the creation and customization the ADONIS meta-modeling platform[18] was chosen. Several reasons can be listed to underline this choice:

- The platform is a mature product

- It supports distributed multi-user access

- Modeled information is stored centrally in a database

- Online customization allows the creation of any meta-model that is based on an object-oriented structure

- The models can easily be transformed to match Semantic Web specifications

---

[15]See [60], p. 5
[16]See [162], p. 63/64
[17]See [162], p. 67/68
[18]See [36] and Chapters 2.3.3.1 and 2.5.4

The requirements for a modeling environment are all fulfilled. Focus and main interest lies in the "Storing and maintaining ontologies" and in "Standards support".

The following Chapter is concerned with the actual DKElearn Modeling Method and the realized meta-models.

6.2.2 The DKElearn meta-models

The DKElearn Modeling Method has to support modeling on different levels. Figure 6.3 sketches the relationships between ontologies and the DKElearn Modeling Method for the domains Semantic Web ("pure") and E-Learning. With the help of the engineered environment, the foundation for "learning-on-demand", "E-Learning Courses" and communication with ERP Systems will be structurally supported. Learning-on-demand hereby means, that - based on a certain Learner Profile and corresponding LOs - a personalized E-Learning course can be realized, i.e. by browsing learning resource pools. The learning-on-demand approach is to be seen in contrast to E-Learning Courses that follow predefined structures like learning processes, i.e. on the basis of a curriculum. A connection to ERP Systems or other EAI scenarios is also possible but are not in the focus of this thesis. Approaches in this B2B context are ebXML or BPEL4WS.

The DKElearn Modeling Method is based on the "E-Business Modeling Framework" based on E-BPMS Framework by Kühn and Bayer[19].

The DKElearn Modeling Methods[20] on the basis of Knowledge Representation Formalisms are:

- Meta Ontology Builder

  - Meta-Ontology Modeler (for vocabulary definitions, e.g. Dublin Core RDF binding)

  - RDFS meta-model

  - RDF meta-model

- Business Information ontologies

  - Working environment for organizational responsibilities concerning Business Processes

---

[19]See [171]

[20]The DKElearn Modeling Method is a subsumption of several modeling methods. They are ADVISOR, PROMOTE and the E-Business Modeling Method, [171].

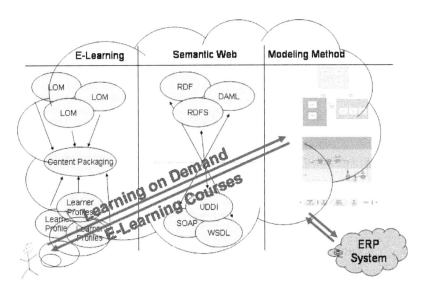

Figure 6.3: Semantic Web-Services in E-Learning

- Business Models[21] for showing the relations among key business partners, products, service and information flows

- Business Processes

- KM ontologies

  - KMPs (see Chapter 2.7.2)

- E-Learning Resource ontologies

  - Learning Objects and Content Packages for describing the infrastructure of LO pools

  - Learning and Teaching Processes (Sequencing)

- Learner Information ontologies

  - Skill profiles

  - Learner information (history)

- Workflow Information ontologies

---

[21]See [282], p. 32

- Description of services infrastructure (e.g. UDDI; see Chapter 2.7.2)
- Web-Services workflows including learning and teaching processes

These modeling methods all represent meta-models instantiated from a meta-meta-model. Benefits of this modeling approach are:

- Top-down approach

- Models are documents (ISO 900x, process-oriented software engineering, etc.)

- Business Engineering

  - Engineering of Business models

  - Engineering of technical resources and workflows

- Modeled environment is input for execution at Run-Time

All modeling methods related to E-Learning LOs and LPs need to support RDF(S) at least on a basic level and should be able to export RDF graphs for further use in applications[22].

6.2.2.1 The meta-models in detail

Taking Figure 4.4 into account, the proposed meta-models can be applied to the four levels of Business Engineering in E-Learning in the following way:

- Business Modeling Layer

  - Business Information ontologies

  - KM ontologies

- Course Modeling Process

  - Meta Ontology Builder

  - E-Learning Resource ontologies

  - Learner Information ontologies

  - Workflow Information ontologies

---

[22]RDF(S) seems to be the most promising technology at the moment. Although, all other efforts, especially coming from standardization bodies (http://www.cenorm.be/isss/workshop/lt/ebrochure/ebrochure-number6.pdf) have to be watched closely.

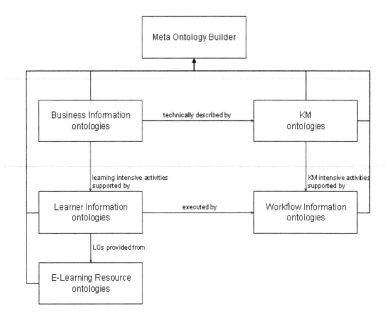

Figure 6.4: Coherence of DKElearn meta-models

The Target System Level and the Learning Process layer are not supported by meta-modeling, because they are responsible for execution. Any E-Learning platform (L(C)MS) with standards support for integration of LOs can be used to support the Learning Process layer.

Figure 6.4 schematically depicts the coherence of the DKElearn meta-models.

Conceptually speaking, the schema of any meta-model can be statically modeled and represented in RDF by the Meta Ontology Builder RDFS meta-model. The RDFS meta-model can be seen as a first step of creating a meta-model for meta-models (meta2 modeling method). The current status however does not support this functionality; at this point of time, the Meta ontology Builder only enables to model RDF(S) graphs. The modeled RDF graphs are used as a basis for deploying LOs and LPs by simple Web-Services as shown in Figure 6.2. Basically speaking, the test-beds to prove the feasibility of the generic approach for E-Learning only support the handling of RDF(S) graphs deployed by prototypical Web-Services.

Therefore it is considered reasonable to show only the relevant excerpt concerning RDF(S) and their relation to Web-Services in action.

6.2.3 DKElearn reference environment

Chapter 6.2.2 lists the meta-models that have been created for the DKElearn library. It has to be noted that the connection of the different models only exists conceptually, as physically three different modeling libraries were concatenated:

- PROMOTE[23]

- ADVISOR[24]

- E-Business Modeling Method (DKElearn plus RDF meta-models as described in Chapter 6.2.3.1)

In order to show a holistic modeling scenario, this Chapter produces a reference environment where the treatment and functionality of LOs, LPs and Web-Services workflows are discussed in detail representing the core result of this thesis. All other ontologies models that are provided for the reference environment have to be considered only on a theoretical level reflecting the experiences made during the Master of Business Informatics (MBI) project at the Virtual Global University (VGU)[25]. The reference environment also merely shows typical models and modeling classes and is not concerned with completeness and integrity and therefore only visualizes the modeling information of DKElearn as a showcase. The scientific impact only can be considered for the E-Learning Resource Ontologies. The methodology has to be aligned according to the E-Learning Engineering approach showed in Figure 4.4. The Business Information Ontologies have to be mapped into the Business Modeling Layer, all other ontologies have to be mapped to the Course Modeling Process.

The conceptual coherence between the meta-models was depicted in Figure 6.4, Figure 6.5 shows the same coherence on the actual instances of the meta-models that DKElearn provides with the LOs and LPs in its center. In the following, each model is described in detail.

6.2.3.1 Business Information Ontology

The Business Information Ontologies have the purpose of describing the organizational structures and process flows within a company. The meta-models are

- Business Process Model

---

[23]See Chapter 2.7.2
[24]See Chapters 2.3.3.1 and 2.5.4
[25]For detailed information about the MBI project and the VGU refer to the web-site http://www.vg-u.de and [179]

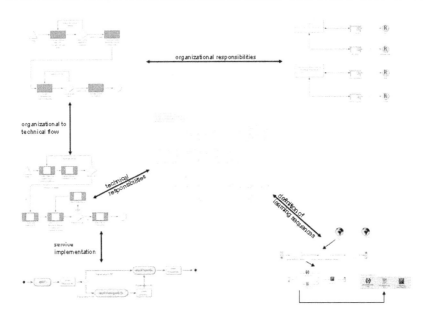

Figure 6.5: Coherence of DKElearn models

- Working Environment Model

Information about responsibility of a user's role concerning a business activity is also included.

Business Processes consist of several modeling classes:

- Process Start represented by a grey triangle

- Activity represented by a blue rectangle

- Decision represented by a grey diamond

- Process End represented by a grey circle

- Succession represented by an arc

Working Environments comprise the following classes

- User represented by a desk

- Roles represented by blue circles

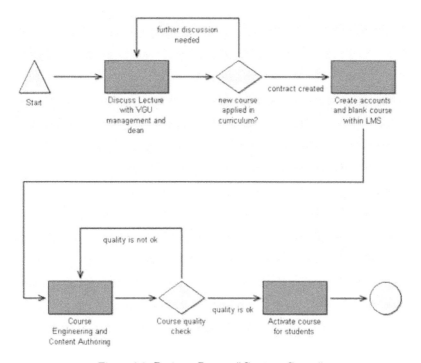

Figure 6.6: Business Process "Create a Course"

- Organizational Unit represented by a rectangle

- Has Role represented by a dotted arc

- User belongs to Organizational Unit represented by a solid arc

The Business Process "Create a Course" depicted in Figure 6.6 was chosen, because all other depending constructs and interdependencies within DKElearn can be shown. Figure 6.7 shows the Working Environment for the reference scenario. Each activity in the Business Process is linked to the Working Environment, e.g. Mr. Miller is responsible for the activity "Activate course for students" and Hannes Lischka is responsible for the activity "Course Engineering and Content Authoring".

6.2.3.2 KM Ontology

The KM Ontology taken from PROMOTE is responsible for modeling all KM flows and structures that manage the OM and therefore is the link between organizational and

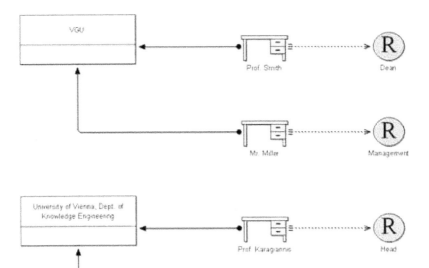

Figure 6.7: Organization chart

technical information. The information is also represented in processes and just like the
Working Environment depicts organizational responsibilities for Business Process, skills
represent technical responsibilities for KM Processes.

The KM Ontology consists of the following meta-models:

- KM Process Model

- Skills Model

- Knowledge Structure Model

- Knowledge Resource Model

For the E-Learning Engineering framework only the KM Process Model was used, be-
cause the Skill Model and especially the Knowledge Structure Model and the Knowledge
Resource Model will be sufficiently represented by the E-Learning Resource Ontologies.
KM Processes consists of several modeling classes (see Figure 6.8):

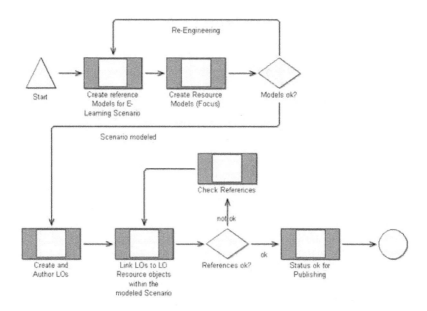

Figure 6.8: KM Process "Course Engineering and Content Authoring"

- KM Process Start represented by a yellow triangle

- KM Process End represented by a yellow circle

- KM Process decision represented by a yellow diamond

- KM Activities represented by blue rectangles with incorporated yellow rectangles

The KM Process "Course Engineering and Content Authoring" defines the knowledge activities for the Business Process activity "Course Engineering and Content Authoring". The technically responsible skill points to the resource http://www.dke.univie.ac.at/~ hlischka from the E-Learning Resource Ontology depicted in Figure 6.11.
Each knowledge activity is supported by a link to an expert or by a Web-Services workflow from the Workflow Information Ontology depending on its execution. In case of the activity "Create reference models for E-Learning Scenario" a modeling expert has to fulfill the task; in case of "Check references" a Web-Services workflow provides the solution (in this case manually).

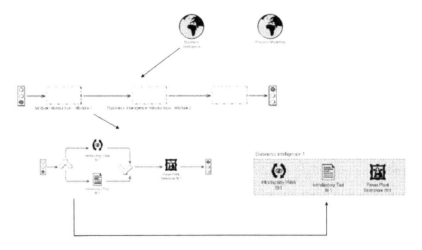

Figure 6.9: Learner Information Ontology

6.2.3.3 Learner Information Ontology

Depending on a top-down (pre-defined learning) or bottom-up (Learning on Demand) learning approach, the Learner Information Ontology defines the sequence of LOs. The meta-models of the Learner Information Ontology originated in the ADVISOR project and Modeling Method.

The Learner Information Ontology[26] consists of the following meta-models (see Figure 6.9):

- Training Map

- Training Sequence Model

- Media Library (Resource Pool)

The examples of the Media Library shown in the following are of three types:

- RDFS graphs for modeling vocabularies

- RDF graphs for modeling instances of LOs and LPs

The E-Learning Resource Ontology consists of the following meta-models:

- RDFS model

---

[26]Detailed description about the meta-models and modeling classes can be obtained from a conference journal, see [21], and are out of the scope of this Chapter.

- RDF model

The two meta-models for RDFS and RDF are integrated into a single modeling method, because it sometimes is reasonable to show schema and instance information in one model. The export functionalities for RDFS and RDF are separate functions.
The modeling classes for RDF(S) are:

- `RDFLiteral`

- `RDFSClass`

- `RDFResource`

- `Namespaces`

- `RDFSProperty`

- `RDFProperty`

Figure 6.10 depicts the LOM RDFS-binding partially. The model shows:

- Namespaces represented by `Namespaces` objects (top rectangles)

- Concepts represented by bold faced ellipses together with the name and RDFS vocabulary (e.g. rdfs:Class)

- Properties as arcs between the concepts with RDFS vocabulary (e.g. rdfs:label)

The corresponding DKElearn RDFS serialization is equivalent to the one proposed by the IMS Global Consortium[27] and is listed in Code-Example 6.1.
Figure 6.11 depicts the learning resources. The model describes a learning scenario with one instructor, two LOs and one student:

- Namespaces represented by `Namespaces` objects (top rectangles)

- Resources (LOs and LPs) represented by ellipses together with the URIs

- Properties represented as arcs between the resources and literals with vocabulary depending on the imported namespaces (e.g. vocabulary from Dublin Core like `dc:title`)

- Literals represented by rectangles defining the property values

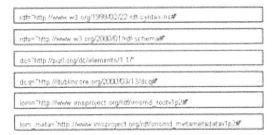

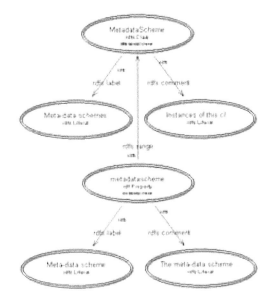

Figure 6.10: Excerpt of an RDFS model

```
<?xml version="1.0"?>

<rdf:RDF
xmlns:rdf="http://www.w3.org/1999/02/22-rdf-syntax-ns#"
xmlns:rdfs="http://www.w3.org/2000/01/rdf-schema#"
xmlns:dc="http://purl.org/dc/elements/1.1/"
xmlns:dcq="http://dublincore.org/2000/03/13/dcq#"
xmlns:lom="http://www.imsproject.org/rdf/imsmd_rootv1p2#"
xmlns:lom_meta="http://www.imsproject.org/rdf/imsmd_metametadatav1p2#">

<rdfs:Class rdf:ID="MetadataScheme">
<rdfs:label>Meta-data schemes</rdfs:label>
<rdfs:comment>Instances of this class represent meta-data schemes.
</rdfs:comment>
</rdfs:Class>

< ... >

<rdf:Property rdf:ID="metadatascheme">
<rdfs:label>Meta-data scheme</rdfs:label>
<rdfs:comment>The meta-data scheme used by the document.</rdfs:comment>
<rdfs:range rdf:resource="#MetadataScheme"></rdfs:range>
</rdf:Property>

</rdf:RDF>
```

Code-Example 6.1: RDFS-binding serialization example

```xml
<?xml version="1.0"?>

<rdf:RDF xmlns:rdf="http://www.w3.org/1999/02/22-rdf-syntax-ns#"
xmlns:rdfs="http://www.w3.org/2000/01/rdf-schema#"
xmlns:VCARD="http://www.w3.org/2001/vcard-rdf/3.0#"
xmlns:DC="http://purl.org/dc/elements/1.1/" >

<rdf:Description rdf:about="http://mail.dke.univie.ac.at/~hlischka">
<VCARD:FN>Hannes Lischka</VCARD:FN>
<VCARD:BDAY>1974-10-17</VCARD:BDAY>
<VCARD:ROLE>instructor</VCARD:ROLE>
<DC:creator rdf:resource="http://131.130.70.72/mbi/bi_kp/bi_kp2/slide1/
index.php"></DC:creator>
<DC:creator rdf:resource="http://131.130.70.72/mbi/bi_kp/bi_kp2/slide2/
index.php"></DC:creator>
<DC:creator rdf:resource="http://131.130.70.72/mbi/bi_kp/bi_kp2/slide2/
index.php"></DC:creator>
</rdf:Description>

<rdf:Description rdf:about="http://unet.univie.ac.at/~a0000000">
<VCARD:FN>Peter Wisdom</VCARD:FN>
<VCARD:BDAY>1980-01-01</VCARD:BDAY>
<VCARD:ROLE>student</VCARD:ROLE>
<DC:relation rdf:resource="http://131.130.70.72/mbi/bi_kp/bi_kp2/slide1/
index.php"></DC:relation>
</rdf:Description>

<rdf:Description rdf:about="http://131.130.70.72/mbi/bi_kp/bi_kp2/slide1/
index.php">
<DC:title>BI 1</DC:title>
<DC:format>www-Site</DC:format>
<DC:type>Course Business Informatics 1</DC:type>
<DC:description>This is a basic course about Business
Informatics; Chapter 1</DC:description>
</rdf:Description>

< ... >

<rdf:Description rdf:about="http://unet.univie.ac.at/~a0000001">
<VCARD:FN>Paul Longtimestudent</VCARD:FN>
<VCARD:BDAY>1970-01-01</VCARD:BDAY>
<VCARD:ROLE>student</VCARD:ROLE>
</rdf:Description>

</rdf:RDF>
```

Code-Example 6.2: RDF-binding serialization example

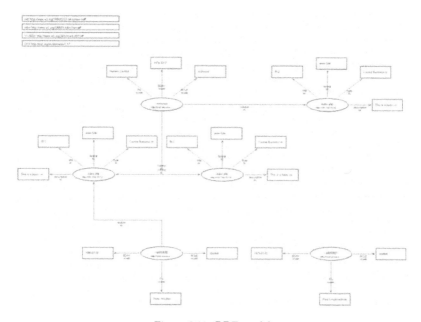

Figure 6.11: RDF model

The corresponding DKElearn RDF serialization is listed in Code-Example 6.2[28].

The RDF-binding serialization is still a work in progress. A support for reification and containers is not yet realized. The example graph from Figure 6.11 will also be input for Chapter 6.3. This simplification of an E-Learning scenario was preferred to use the LOM RDF-binding, because the LOM RDF-binding is still lacking maturity and documentation. Furthermore, the simple model helps to understand the concept of the generic approach in a better way.

The semantics of the used model is as follows:

- The vCard RDF-binding is used for description of LPs

    - VCARD:FN states the full name

    - VCARD:BDAY specifies the birth date (YYYY-MM-DD)

    - VCARD:ROLE distinguishes between students and instructors

---

[27]See [140]. Note that the serialization syntax is based on [307]; the RDF Validator, see [299], is already based on the revised RDF Syntax Specification, see [300].

[28]Validated by W3C's RDF Validator [299]

- The Dublin Core RDF-binding is used for description of LOs and properties between LOs and LPs

  - `DC:creator` references the creator of an LO

  - `DC:title` labels an LO

  - `DC:format` defines a format (in this case only www-Site is used)

  - `DC:type` defines the category of the LO

  - `DC:description` gives a short syllabus of the LO

  - `DC:relation` states that a student has already taken an LO; vice versa, if a `DC:relation` between an LO and an LP is missing the student has not yet applied

The RDF resources listed in this file are:

- Instructor "Hannes Lischka", student "Peter Wisdom" and student "Paul Long-timestudent"

- Two LOs from the type "Course Business Informatics" (Chapter 1 and 2)

- The instructor has created both LOs

- Peter Wisdom has already applied for the course concerning Chapter 1; Paul Long-timestudent has not yet applied for an LO

6.2.3.4 Workflow Information Ontology

Figure 6.12[29] depicts the third meta-model instance type that is presented as an example for input to the Run-Time: the Web-Services workflow model (also called interaction model).

The Workflow Information Ontology consists of the following meta-model:

- Web-Services workflow model

The modeling classes are:

- Start of the workflow (black filled circle)

---

[29]Both transition statements of the decision after the object "show Resources" are labeled "Parameter=URI". The model does not depict the fact that the decision also implies the choice of different buttons in the user interface.

Figure 6.12: Simple Web-Services workflow model

- End of the workflow (black filled circle with extra surrounding circle)

- An action that is to be performed (light grey objects)

- User interface information (white rectangles)

- Transition arcs between actions

The workflow describes the sequence of Web-Services that define the E-Learning application. In this case the workflow is about getting LPs out of a RDF resource file and its associated LOs; the LOs are then rendered by a web browser. Note that at this time the workflow model has only representational function, where an action has a reference to a WSDL interface. A meta-model-model describing services and corresponding WSDL interfaces is not yet implemented.

6.3 DKElearn at Run-Time

This Chapter takes the E-Learning Resource Ontology of the DKElearn Modeling Method into Run-Time conceptually and points out the actual test-beds that were implemented. Figure 6.13 therefore instantiates the generic approach of Figure 6.2[30]. The generic E-Learning Framework instantiates the full idea depicted in Figure 6.2 only on a technical level:

- Providing modeling methods for resources that are manually copied into the Web-Services container

- These resources are deployed by Web-Services

- The Web-Services are invoked by client applications

- The bold orange arrows symbolize modeled messages - SOAP in this case - between the SOA tiers. The message models only exist conceptually

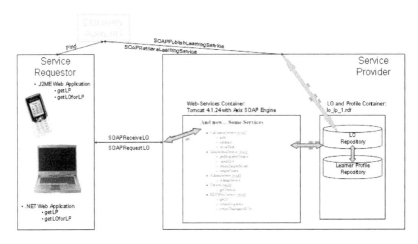

Figure 6.13: Run-Time and Test-beds for E-Learning architecture for the generic approach

Certain issues about the Run-Time that only implement few test-beds have to be mentioned:

- The discussion whether to use a .NET or a Java (J2EE) environment is satisfied solely by showing the feasibility of interoperability between .NET Web Applications and Java Web-Services[31]

- Real enactment in DKElearn is only grazed with the representation of Web-Services workflows. Web-Services workflows generally and in E-Learning will mark the next interesting step in the evolution of ICT[32]

- No real pool for LOs and LPs exists. There is a single resource file in the Axis web folder With the help of the engineered models - as already suggested in Figure 6.3 - two different types of E-Learning can be executed as shown again in Figure 6.14.

- Learning on Demand

- Pre-defined E-Learning Courses

The test-bed-workflow from Figure 6.12 supports a simple Learning on Demand where instructors and students can view their profiles and assigned resources.

---

[30]See [180]
[31]See [325] for further discussion
[32]See Chapter 4.3.1 and the discussion of [3] concerning workflows in E-Learning.

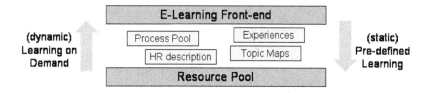

Figure 6.14: Dynamic and static learning

6.3.1 DKElearn test-beds

In order to deploy Web-Services RDF resources dynamically, an RDF API has to be added to the Run-Time for the generic approach. Basically speaking, supporting RDF with APIs is an academic/scientific research area. This implies that the solutions may be immature, not well documented and available in non-commercial products like Java, PHP or Python. The following resources list APIs, tools, parsers or other related RDF products:

- http://139.91.183.30:9090/RDF/references.html#RDF_Parsers

- http://www.ilrt.bris.ac.uk/discovery/rdf/resources/#sec-apps

- http://www.wiwiss.fu-berlin.de/suhl/bizer/rdfapi/

- http://kaon.semanticweb.org/

- http://sesame.aidministrator.nl

The choice was subjectively given to the Open-Source project "Jena Semantic Web Toolkit"[33] meaning that no evaluation framework or case study was carried out to strengthen the decision. Jena is a Java API providing

- A core RDF API

- Readers and writers for RDF/XML

- N-Triples and N3 together with RDQL

- Ontology API together with rule-based reasoners for RDFS and OWL

The fact that a Javadoc and a documented tutorial existed were convincing enough to choose Jena.

---

[33]See [56] and http://sourceforge.net/projects/jena/

```
public String getLP()
{
String output="";
try
{
String inputFileName = "http://131.130.139.248:8080/axis/DKE_libs/TomcatAx
isRDFwebservice/resources/lo_lp_1.rdf";
Model model = ModelFactory.createDefaultModel();
model.read(inputFileName);

StmtIterator iter = model.listStatements();
while (iter.hasNext())
{
Statement stmt      = (Statement) iter.next();
     Resource  subject   = stmt.getSubject();
     Property  predicate = stmt.getPredicate();
     RDFNode   object    = stmt.getObject();
     if ((predicate.toString().equals("http://www.w3.org/2001/vcard-rdf/3.0
#FN")))
     {
     output=output+subject.toString()+";";
}
}
output=output.substring(0,output.length()-1);
}
catch(Exception e)

<...>

return output;
}
```

Code-Example 6.3: Code fragment of **getLP**

The Jena API was included in the classpath of Tomcat with Axis SOAP engine and needs to provide the following Web-Services methods according to the Web-Services workflow from Figure 6.12:

- List all LPs from the RDF resource file (**getLP**, see Code-Example 6.3)

- Return properties of resources (**returnProperties**, see Code-Example 6.4)

- List all LOs that the student has already applied for and all LOs that are still missing in his curriculum (**returnUnassignedLOs**, see Code-Example 6.5)

To lift the provided Web-Services to their full interoperability potential, two scenarios are considered for the Service Requestor:

```
public String returnProperties(String URI)
{
String output="";
try
{
String inputFileName = "http://131.130.139.248:8080/axis/DKE_libs/TomcatAx
isRDFwebservice/resources/lo_lp_1.rdf";
Model model = ModelFactory.createDefaultModel();
model.read(inputFileName);
Resource ResourceURI = model.getResource(URI);
StmtIterator iter = model.listStatements(new SimpleSelector (ResourceURI,
VCARD.FN, (RDFNode) null));
while (iter.hasNext())
{
output=output+"Full Name: " + iter.nextStatement().getString() + "; ";
}
iter = model.listStatements(new SimpleSelector (ResourceURI, VCARD.BDAY,
(RDFNode) null));
while (iter.hasNext())
{
output=output+"Birthdate: " + iter.nextStatement().getString() + "; ";
}

<...>

}
catch(Exception e)
{

<...>

}
return output;
}
```

Code-Example 6.4: Code fragment of returnProperties

```java
public String returnUnassignedLOs(String URI)
{
String output="";
Vector allSubjectsOfLOs = new Vector();
Vector allSubjectsOfStudent = new Vector();
try
{
<...>
StmtIterator iterAllLOs = model.listStatements();
while (iterAllLOs.hasNext())
{
Statement stmt      = (Statement) iterAllLOs.next();
Resource  subject   = stmt.getSubject();
Property  predicate = stmt.getPredicate();
RDFNode   object    = stmt.getObject();
if ((predicate.toString().equals("http://purl.org/dc/elements/1.1/format")
) && (object.toString().equals("www-Site")))
{
allSubjectsOfLOs.addElement(subject.toString());
}
}
StmtIterator iter = model.listStatements(new SimpleSelector (ResourceURI,
DC.relation, (RDFNode) null));
while (iter.hasNext())
{
allSubjectsOfStudent.addElement(iter.nextStatement().getObject().toString(
));
}
for (int i=0;i<allSubjectsOfLOs.size();i++)
{
for (int j=0;j<allSubjectsOfStudent.size();j++)
{
if (allSubjectsOfLOs.elementAt(i)!=allSubjectsOfStudent.elementAt(j))
{
output=output+allSubjectsOfLOs.elementAt(i)+";";
}
}
}
<...>
output=output.substring(0,output.length()-1);
}
catch(Exception e)
{
<...>
}
return output;
}
```

Code-Example 6.5: Code fragment of `returnUnassignedLOs`

- A .NET Web Application client deploying the Jena API within the Tomcat Axis environment via a SOAP call

- A mobile application also deploying the Jena API within the Tomcat Axis environment via a SOAP call with the help of Java 2 Platform, Micro Edition (J2ME) and kSOAP[34]

The following test-beds do not claim to be secure fault-tolerant or programmatically efficient; they only show the feasibility of the application scenario.

6.3.1.1 The RDF Web-Services

According to Figure 6.13, the RDF Web-Services reside in a Tomcat 4.1.24 with AXIS SOAP Engine container within the Service Provider tier. The Web-Services methods are:

- `getLP` returns all resources (LOs and LPs) that are listed in the resource pool

- `returnProperties` returns the properties of a selected resource for a specified URI

- `returnUnassignedLOs` returns not yet assigned LOs for students for a specified URI

These services can be invoked from the namespace `http://131.130.139.248:8080/axis/services/RDFWebService` with the WSDL description at `http://131.130.139.248:8080/axis/services/RDFWebService?wsdl`[35]. All services return an unstructured String-output.

6.3.1.2 The .NET Visual Basic Client

According to Figure 6.13, the .NET client resides in a .NET Windows 2003 server engine within the Service Requestor tier.

The development platform for the .NET Client is the Visual Studio .NET using the Visual Basic programming language. Web-Services may easily be integrated with the function "Add Web Reference". The browser interface is depicted in Figure 6.15.

Depending on the RDF resource-pool (the file lo_lp_1.rdf residing in the Tomcat Axis environment) and after pressing the `Get Resources` button all resources are displayed in the ListBox `Available Resources`. Choosing a resource and pressing the `Properties of`

---

[34]See [269] and [86]; the Java Specification Request JSR-000172 J2ME Web Services Specification (see [270]) from Sun is still in the works (see [268]). The Sun J2ME Wireless Toolkit 2.0 (`http://java.sun.com/products/j2mewtoolkit/download-2_0.html`) is the basis for developing Java Mobile applications. Each vendor may also extend the basic J2ME with proprietary functionality, e.g. the SonyEricsson J2ME SDK at [256]

[35]Note that all services, servers and client applications run temporarily.

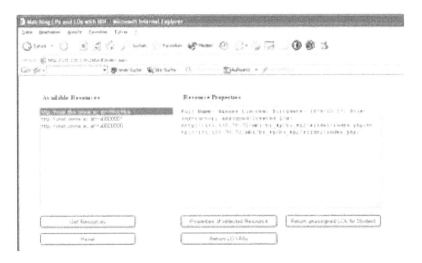

Figure 6.15: VB .NET User Interface

`selected Resource` button assigned properties will be listed. In this case, the instructor "Hannes Lischka" is shown in the TextBox `Resource Properties` with a specific birthday and with URIs of LOs that he created. Pressing the `Return LO URIs` extracts URIs from the Resource Properties and lists them in the ListBox. After pressing `Properties of selected Resource` the details of the LO are displayed.

Selecting a student resource and pressing the `Return unassigned LOs for Student` lists the not yet assigned LOs. Possible results are URIs of LOs or an information text "No LO assigned so far".

6.3.1.3   The Sony Ericsson J2ME Client

According to Figure 6.13, the J2ME client resides in the Service Requestor tier. Figure 6.16 depicts the mobile interface.

Due to the limited display capabilities of a mobile phone only a very basic functionality was implemented. The mobile application returns the properties of the instructor "Hannes Lischka" invoking the same Web-Service as the .NET Client. The application was tested with the Sony Ericsson J2ME SDK but should run on any mobile device supporting J2ME.

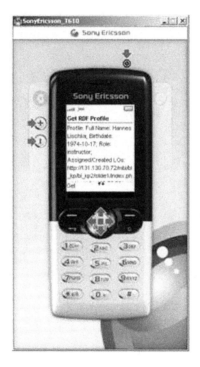

Figure 6.16: J2ME User Interface

6.4 Summary

This Chapter described one concrete instance of an E-Learning Engineering Framework with a focus on Resource-driven Learning. The main advantages of interoperability and networked LOs and the adoption of new learning paradigms that see the student as the central role in learning make this effort worth exploring.

As sketched in Chapter 3, Resource-driven Learning is the precursor of envisioned life-long learning and future learning scenarios.

Chapter 7

Conclusion and Future Outlook

To start with the conclusion and a future outlook of this thesis let's review the delivered ideas:

- E-Learning has become one of the most dominant technologies in computer sciences. The term life-long learning has diffused into a great variety disciplines like Knowledge Management, Business Process Management and of course E-Learning itself, to name but a few.

- In order to define and specify E-Learning scenarios an E-Learning Framework consisting of four Dimensions was presented.

- Based on this Framework, an E-Learning Engineering Framework with support from generic visual modeling methods instantiates actual learning scenarios.

With the help of the E-Learning Framework and the E-Learning Engineering Framework, this thesis envisions a Roadmap on the way to life-long learning in four steps:

1. Traditional Learning

2. Technology-driven Learning in a Document-centric way

3. Technology-driven Learning in a Resource-driven way

4. Life-long Learning

Figure 7.1 shows this Roadmap aligned to the structure of this thesis together with the published papers.

Before stepping in medias res of the discipline of E-Learning, this thesis begins with a glance at philosophical aspects and scientific methods to be used in the discipline "Business Informatics"; it chooses the method "Business Engineering" to formulate and construct a theory. Business Engineering can be compared to the tasks an architect has to

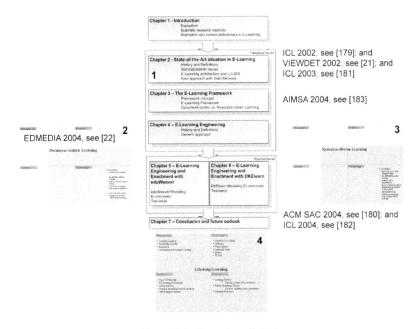

Figure 7.1: Overview of thesis

fulfill when building a house: model, manage, coordinate and plan the actions that are needed in order to provide his customer with a long lasting and enjoyable piece of work. Business Engineering therefore defines a generic methodology and methods for the construction of an organizational memory for a customer. Not only aspects of how to run the business have to be modeled but also techniques of how to implement these business processes technically. The Business Engineering paradigm is strongly using processes for constructing complex scenarios and has to rely on technologies such as Knowledge Management to define the surrounding knowledge structure. Emerging technologies coming from the Semantic Web and Web-Services communities leverage great potential to support Business Engineering with technological support especially when thinking of Business-to-Business contracts integrating business and supply-chain flows between several businesses. The theoretical part of this thesis deals with E-Learning as a scientific discipline outlining historical developments, specifications and standards specifically designed to fit learning goals. Revealing another aspect to the isolated E-Learning discipline, an introduction into Knowledge Management and a service-oriented framework to describe knowledge intensive processes shifts E-Learning into a greater picture bringing it closer to an engineering discipline. The next theoretical topic deals with a new technology concerning service-orientation being able to support Knowledge Management on a technical level: Web-Services become the new means of integrating business logic in a process-oriented way bridging the gap between different platforms and programming languages.

As outlined in the first paragraphs, this thesis takes Business Engineering into the domain of E-Learning presenting an E-Learning Engineering Framework. Two different instances of this Framework make up the practical part of this thesis. Document-centric method eduWeaver focuses on exchange of LOs, DKElearn focuses on passing model information in the Semantic Web technology RDF. DKElearn sets the basis so that standard Web-Services are able to process learning resources with the highest degree of interoperability and extensibility for other parties or platforms.

As outlined in the first paragraphs, this thesis takes Business Engineering into the domain of E-Learning presenting an E-Learning Engineering Framework. Two different instances of this Framework make up the practical part of this thesis. Document-centric method eduWeaver focuses on exchange of LOs, DKElearn focuses on passing model information in the Semantic Web technology RDF. DKElearn sets the basis so that standard Web-Services are able to process learning resources with the highest degree of interoperability and extensibility for other parties or platforms.

For the reason of being able to pick the right tools and methods for defining a Business Engineering language for E-Learning, a taxonomy of Knowledge Representation Formalisms gives a historic and technological overview on how to describe knowledge formally. Taking all findings into account, a formal generic approach towards E-Learning Business Engineering is presented. Taking the method "Engineering", the historical evolution and the standards and specifications into account, an abstract model of the "learning world" - the so called E-Learning Framework - is introduced in order to be able to categorize learning scenarios.

In order to show the feasibility of this approach, some test-beds are introduced which means that not all Business Engineering levels are dealt with: i.e. using methodologies, the description of business processes and the technical architecture to enact Web-Services workflows are neglected in favor of the ability to model RDF learning resources for deployment by Web-Services.

According to the E-Learning Framework, the presented Roadmap is shown with the help of two examples:

1. A Document-centric test-bed

2. A Resource-driven test-bed

The test-beds show partial instantiation of the E-Learning Engineering Framework approach in the following way:

- The first step addresses engineering learning resources with specific modeling methods.

- Second, the engineered models are transformed into XML-files and Semantic Web compliant RDF resources.

- Third, a Run-Time environment is able to understand these resources and manages the enactment.

- Finally, the enactment is shown prototypically by an Import/Export- and a Backl-loading scenario (Document-centric Learning) on the one hand and by Java implemented Web-Services that handle RDF resources that are deployed by both a .NET Client and a J2ME Client via the SOAP protocol (Resource-driven Learning) on the other hand.

Future improvements therefore will focus on two different aspects: First, to enhance the existing environment, and second, to cope with the "neglected" topics as discussed in the former paragraph. The following enumeration lists some of these future improvements depending on the learning paradigm:

- General issues

  - More integration for information coming from different domains like KM, Strategic Management, etc.

  - Reach a more semantic scenario by adding information to all dimensions of the E-Learning Framework

  - Using Web-Services workflow containers to automatically execute modeled workflows. This includes discussion of technological requirements concerning the modeling method and the way of passing parameters between services. It is considered reasonable to pass information in the syntax of RDF Result vocabularies as already defined in the Jena Semantic Web Toolkit.

  - Extending the test-beds from static information-display interfaces to dynamic RDF-based agents.

  - Further scrutinize mobile scenarios, especially deploying Web-Services over handheld devices (e.g. including mobile positioning services such as `http://ww`

w.ericsson.com/mobilityworld/sub/open/technologies/mobile_positio
ning/tools/mps_60_tool).

- Always work according to standards developments meaning that all RDFS related transformation routines should be validated by independent tools like the
W3C RDF Validator or the WS-I interoperability tools (http://www.webservi
ces.org/index.php/article/view/1007/). In this context the developments
of the LOM and Content Package RDF-bindings are of extreme importance.
The use of "flat" Dublin Core RDF for the E-Learning scenario is sufficient to
prove feasibility of the use of RDF and Web-Services in E-Learning but still
lacks the full potential that an ontology language like RDF, DAML+OIL or
OWL would be able to provide.

- Document-centric Learning

  - Include more semantics into the eduWeaver Modeling Methods (e.g. relation
  to a calendar, general notes concerning a course, information about roles, etc.;
  currently research is done in creation of modeling methods to describe standards compliant Exams and Tests)

  - Include more transformation scenarios (currently a Flash-to-IMS is being developed)

  - Enhance Backloading with "intelligent" transformation of Powerpoint slides
  into de-contextualized chunks of information (extract text from slide title, from
  memos, etc.)

  - Include more formats for the concept of Backloading (all Microsoft Office products, other formats, etc.; currently research efforts are carried out in this field
  trying to extract more relevant semantic information out of MS Powerpoint
  slides)

  - Automate meta-data extraction (*"Kill forms"* is the main slogan of Erik Duval
  from the Catholic University of Leuven)

- Resource-driven Learning

  - Actual integration of DKElearn into a KM modeling framework like PRO-
  MOTE and designing a standard example as a reference.

  - Integration of UDDI directories to serve as learning pools and semantic service
  registries.

- B2B integration scenarios: Show integration of modeled environment into an ERP system (mysap.com, community platform, SCORM or IMS Run-Time). Current approaches regarding B2B integration are:

  * `http://www-106.ibm.com/developerworks/webservices/edu/ws-dw-bp eltut-i.html`

  * `http://www.alphaworks.ibm.com/tech/bpws4j`

  * `http://www.collaxa.com/developer.download.html`

  * `http://www.microsoft.com/biztalk/beta/`

- Enhance import and output parameters: change the simple String format to RDF messages

- Current research efforts focus on the adaption of actual LOM compliant RDF resources, in describing learning scenarios like curricula in OWL and testing RDF compliant application frameworks like Mozilla

Finally, what will the real impact be for the future of E-Learning? E-Learning will adapt to Semantic Web standards for sure, but it is not clear, when this is going to happen. The contemporary situation on the commercial market for vendors of L(C)MS is still dynamic and real key players may not have been installed. At the moment, the solutions are quite proprietary supporting XML standards only basically. The vision can already be seen in scientific projects that rely solely on Peer-to-Peer technologies and RDF as representation formalism. These projects provide pools of learning resources that may be consumed by anyone or any Web-Service capable of understanding meta-data annotated learning resources.

Let's see what the future of E-Learning will bring ...

Appendix A

Web-Services Standards and Architectures

This Chapter is dedicated to the new software programming paradigm Web-Services. As one part of the technological solution of the DKElearn test-beds a theoretical discussion about the main ideas of this topic is considered suitable.

A.1 Chapter Outline

This Chapter is divided into two parts as shown in Figure A.1. First, definitions and the three major specifications in the context of Web-Services are outlined. Second, different architectures are presented that implement these technologies.

A.2 Definitions

Let us start this Chapter with some definitions given by respected authors and organizations concerning Web-Services:

- *"A Web-Service is any service that is available over the Internet, uses standardized XML messaging system, and is not tied to any one operating system or programming language"*[1].

- *"Web Services is an emerging technology driven by the will to securely expose business logic beyond the firewall. Through Web services companies can encapsulate existing business processes, publish them as services, search for and subscribe to other*

---

[1][47], p. 3

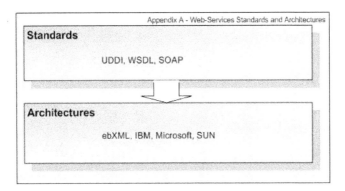

Figure A.1: Overview

services, and exchange information throughout and beyond the enterprise. Web services will enable application-to-application e-marketplace interaction, removing the inefficiencies of human intervention"[2].

- *"A Web service is a software system identified by a URI, whose public interfaces and bindings are defined and described using XML. Its definition can be discovered by other software systems. These systems may then interact with the Web service in a manner prescribed by its definition, using XML based messages conveyed by internet protocols"[3].*

The definitions are straight forward supposing the internet as exchange medium for standardized XML documents to transfer services. This directly leads to the enumeration of standards and the organizations that are involved in their creation. There are no recommendations to use a specific specification or standard, but there are two main approaches, one coming from Business Process automation (ebXML, BPMI, etc.) and the other coming from the Semantic Web Community (DARPA, W3C, OASIS, etc.).
The standards or specifications these organizations - according to WebServices.org[4] - build on are

- SOAP

- WSDL

- UDDI

---

[2][317]
[3][292]
[4][318]

Discovery	**UDDI**
Description	**WSDL**
Messaging	XML-RPC, **SOAP**
Transport	**HTTP**, SMTP, FTP

Table A.1: Web-Services stack

- WS-Transactions

- WS-Inspection

- Security

- WS-Coordination

- BPEL4WS

- WSCL

- WSIA/WSRP

- WS-Interoperability

- GXA

There are some other efforts going into the Web-Services standards direction, i.e. Web Services Conversation Language (WSCL) by Hewlett-Packard, Web Services Flow Language (WSFL) by IBM or the Web Services Experience Language (WSXL).

These standards or specifications alone are of little use. Therefore, the concept of the so-called Web-Services stack introduces relations between them. The Web-Services stack - like the ISO OSI architecture model for distributed systems - separates different Web-Service functionalities on several levels. The stack deals with physical connection, quality of service, security, messaging, describing, finding and arranging services. The W3C introduces a very detailed stack[5], but it can be broken down to the following table[6]:

The bold faced standards in Table A.1 "implement" the most common stack and are discussed in the following Chapter A.3. A brief description of these three will be sufficient to have enough information for the concluding scenario. Chapter A.4 continues with

---

[5]See [293]

[6][47], pp. 9. This basic simple stack is also known as the Basic Profile of the WS-I, see [329], p. 6. A profile in this context is the specific assembly of several technologies for a certain application scenario. Besides this Basic-Profile, extensions exist to include technologies for orchestration, security, etc.; see [284], p. 41

industry architectures that take the stack into account to provide Web-Services.

A normal Web-Service usage lifecycle[7] from a client's point of view is mapped to this stack:

- In order to employ a Web-Service, it has to be found or discovered via UDDI description.

- In order to really use a service, the public interface has to be retrieved via WSDL.

- Finally, a message request has to be formulated, that invokes a certain method via SOAP.

The same process has to be reversed when seeing it from a provider's point of view.

- The first step is to program the service in a desired platform and programming language.

- For this service, a SOAP wrapper has to be added, together with a WSDL service description.

- Finally, the service has to be registered in an UDDI repository.

A.3 Standards

UDDI, WSDL and SOAP are the most popular standards in Web-Services. They enable people to find a Web-Service according to their requirements, describe the services' interfaces and invoke remote procedure calls over the HTTP protocol. This all sounds very promising for distributed application building and also covers all aspects of the later to be discussed scenario. But using merely these standards will cover test implementations, because main issues are not addressed: security, semantically rich descriptions of Web-Services for better automation, quality of service, authentication to name but a few.

A great part of these insufficiencies arise because strategic issues and mapping the technology into a business plan are not sufficiently considered. For now, a brief overview of the mentioned Web-Services stack will be enough to explain the concept of Web-Services[8]. Figure A.2 shows the relations between UDDI, WSDL and SOAP.

---

[7][47], pp. 23

[8]This Chapter shall only give general information on the discussed standards and specifications. Historical overview, detailed descriptions and examples can be found in the following sources (non-taxative) and would go beyond the scope of this thesis: [285], [47], [319], [202]

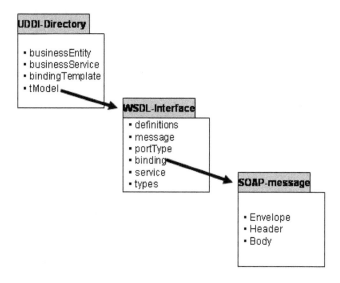

Figure A.2: Interdependence between UDDI, WSDL and SOAP

A.3.1 Discovery - UDDI

If someone wants to buy, use or employ some kind of product or service, the desired item has to be found in a central repository in the first place. In Software Engineering's history there have been a lot of efforts in this field, mostly associated with the term software reuse. The "Standard Template Library"[9] is an example. The aim is to introduce a further layer of abstraction to encapsulate the physical service-endpoint within an entry in the UDDI.

This role in Web-Services is undertaken by the Universal Description, Discovery and Integration of Web-Services (UDDI). *"UDDI creates a standard interoperable platform that enables companies and applications to quickly, easily, and dynamically find and use Web services over the Internet"*[10].

Several key players for the UDDI development process exist. They are responsible for specification, quality assurance and dissemination of UDDI. The most important players are UDDI.org and OASIS.

OASIS[11] is a non-profit organization that was founded under the name of "SGML Open" to introduce and address interoperability issues in the context of the Standard Generalized

---

[9]See [250]
[10][286]
[11]See [203]

Markup Language (SGML). With the rise and success of the XML, SGML Open decided to change its name to reflect this development. OASIS produces standards in the fields of security, Web-Services, XML conformance, business transactions, electronic publishing, topic maps and interoperability within and between marketplaces and also jointly sponsor ebXML[12] together with the United Nations. As a reflection of the XML-focused work, OASIS operates XML.org, a community that addresses schemas, vocabularies and related documents. Finally, among other networks like cgmopen.org, legalxml.oasis-open.org and pkiforum.org, OASIS hosts and manages UDDI.org within its network.

UDDI.org[13] is a cross-country driven platform within the OASIS network to address and engage discussion and specification of UDDI-driven matters. It also focuses deeply on XML and tries to provide a link to other Web-Services standards like SOAP enforced by the W3C.org. Although UDDI does not specify special invocation methods (CORBA, RMI, etc.), it has to be pointed out that SOAP will play a key role within Semantic Web-Services, because it is HTTP-based. Within UDDI.org, the UDDI Specification Technical Committee focuses on Web-Services needs, producing UDDI specifications, best practices and technical notes.

Critics of UDDI argue[14] that the description of services by UDDI is insufficient to be really able to implement Web-Services. It is quite clear, that these critical voices bear truth, but at this point, it is not quite clear, how to overcome these insufficiencies. In that context, the Semantic Web community has introduced several concepts for better description of these services and coined the name Semantic Web-Services, inheriting ideas from the Semantic Web, i.e. ontological descriptions, Topic Maps, etc.

A.3.1.1 Technical Specifications

UDDI is an XML format for describing Web-Service directories. Recently, UDDI version 3 was released[15]. In principle, the UDDI technical architecture consists of[16]

- **UDDI data model**:
  The UDDI data model (see Figure A.3[17]) combines several XML schemas for describing Web-Services. UDDI lists four different types of information that shall

---

[12]See Chapter A.4.1 for more information on ebXML.

[13]See [289]

[14]See [290], p. 4, and [54]

[15]Historical development and comparison to former UDDI versions can be found in [287] and [288]. Furthermore, UDDI will not be part of the application scenario, therefore a general overview will be sufficient for this Chapter.

[16]See [47], pp. 161

[17]taken from [288], p. 30

be annotated: `businessEntity`, `businessService`, `bindingTemplate` and `tModel`. Figure A.3[18] shows the interdependencies between these information types: in order to register a service in a UDDI directory, the businessEntity has to provide description about itself ("White pages"). After registering, it is uniquely identified by a businessKey value, contact information and other general data. A businessEntity provides businessServices. A businessService is a single Web-Service or a group of Web-Services. Each businessService is identified again by a unique serviceKey ("Yellow pages"). The bindingTemplate provides information or reference how and where to access a businessService ("Green pages"). Finally technical models, called tModels, round up the UDDI data model. bindingTemplates only address the location of a businessService but contain no information about its interface. This is solved by pointing to an actual WSDL file.

- **UDDI API**:
  In order to apply Web-Services according to UDDI annotation, it has to be published first, so it can be discovered in a second step. Both processes can be done in two ways: first, renowned providers like IBM or Microsoft provide a web interface at http://www-3.ibm.com/services/uddi and http://uddi.microsoft.com. And second, businesses can directly access the UDDI Inquiry and Publishing API. The Inquiry API offers methods for finding and retrieving Web-Services (`find-xxx` and `get-xxx` functions); the Publishing API offers functions to update and maintain Web-Services (authentication, save-xxx and delete-xxx functions).

- **UDDI cloud services**:
  For global availability, several UDDI-servers shall give access to Web-Services. The data between these servers needs to be replicated in order to provide valid information globally. The "UDDI cloud" refers to this transparent server pool.

A.3.2 Description - WSDL

After having found a Web-Service with the help of a UDDI directory service, you still do not know, how it looks like. Like a Java interface, publicly available functions have to be declared, data type information of input and output data has to be given, binding information about the used transport protocol and an address information of the service have to be provided; it can be said, that the Web-Services Description Language

---

[18]taken from [288], p. 3

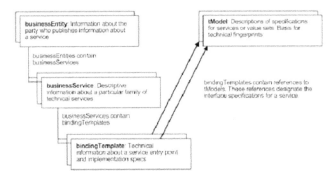

Figure A.3: UDDI data model

(WSDL) *"represents a contract between the service requestor and the service provider"*[19]. As mentioned in Chapter A.3.1, UDDI's tModels point to such a WSDL resource.

A.3.2.1 Technical Specifications

The latest WSDL working draft is 1.2, released by the W3C in July 2002 (Working Draft)[20]. WSDL is an XML format for describing Web-Services[21] that was invented by Ariba, IBM and Microsoft and applied as standard to the W3C[22]. WSDL separates the abstract description of a service's interface from the concrete details of offered functionalities[23].

As shown in Figure A.4, the WSDL Specification has got six main elements:

- **definitions**:

  The definitions-element must be the root-element of the WSDL-file. It defines the name and namespaces of the to-be described service.

- **message**:

  The message-element defines a one-way input or output message. Each message consists of zero or more part-elements, that have a specific data-type, defined in the types-element.

- **portType**:

  The portType-element combines several messages to a logical unit, defining either

---

[19]See [47], p. 119
[20]Same to the treatment of UDDI, WSDL also is only looked at on a general level.
[21]See [302]
[22]See [224], p. 316
[23]See [302]

one-way, request-response, solicit-response or notification operations.

- **binding**:
  The binding-element defines, how a portType will be implemented with a specific protocol. Again, WSDL is open to all protocols (HTTP, MIME), but offers built-in extensions for SOAP.

- **service**:
  The service-element adds the network-sink to a binding, in form of a network-address (URL).

- **types**:
  The types-element defines the data-types used within the WSDL-file. For reason of interoperability, XML-Schema data-types are preferred, but also existing XML-Schema documents can be referenced via the import-element.

These six elements are related to each other in the following way[24]: a service is identified by the definition-element together with the used namespaces. Each service can be seen as a set of network-nodes exchanging input and output messages with each other. The data-types used within the WSDL file are declared in the types-element. The portType-element specifies the interface of operations a service has to offer. So far, no information about a network protocol has been given; this is done by the binding-element - WSDL offers built-in extensions for defining SOAP-services. Finally, the service-element defines the address (a URL in most cases) of the invoked service.

A.3.3 Messaging - SOAP

The Simple Object Access Protocol (SOAP) originated as large companies' ideas, including IBM, Microsoft and Ariba, and was submitted to the W3C. Unlike other frameworks, such as CORBA, DCOM or Java RMI, SOAP is totally platform independent, because messages are written in standard XML format. Although intended independent of any sub-protocol, SOAP enforces the idea of the Semantic Web, using the internet and its HTTP protocol as a means for messaging. Besides the aspects of platform interdependence, this offers another advantage: message delivery is possible over the HTTP standard-port and therefore overcomes the limits of firewalls that CORBA's IIOP has to face[25].

---

[24]See [224], pp. 316, and [47], pp. 120
[25]See [224], p. 299

Figure A.4: WSDL Specification

A.3.3.1 Technical Specifications

The latest SOAP specification is 1.2, released by the W3C in December 2002 as a Candidate Recommendation. SOAP is an XML format for *"a lightweight protocol intended for exchanging structured information in a decentralized, distributed environment ... designed to be independent of any particular programming model and other implementation specific semantics"*[26], but again emphasizes message delivery over HTTP-protocol.

Figure A.5 shows the SOAP specification, consisting of three parts:

- **Envelope**:
  The Envelope-element is the root element of a SOAP message, containing information about target namespaces and coding information[27] and extensions[28] such as

---

[26]See [305]

[27]Standard serialization is provided by XML-Schema. This includes simple data-types as string or integer, and complex data-types such as array.

[28]See [224], p. 300

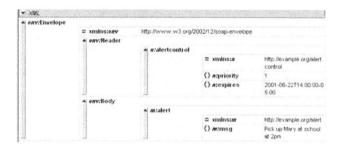

Figure A.5: SOAP Specification

authentication, transaction management, etc.

- **Header (optional)**[29]:

  The SOAP-Header may carry information about the Processing model and application level requirements. The Processing model implies that there is one originating sender, one receiver and zero or more intermediaries (SOAP sender, ultimate SOAP receiver, SOAP intermediary). Such meta-information about the SOAP message itself may be information about expiration, priority, etc. The SOAP-Header may attract some attention in the future as a bearer for solutions concerning encryption, authentication, etc.

- **Body**:

  The ultimate SOAP receiver must process the Body of a SOAP message. The SOAP messaging process is the same as in client-server structures: a client sends a request to a server and receives a response. Both messages, the request and the response, are SOAP messages.

A.3.4 Transport - HTTP

The Hypertext Transfer Protocol (HTTP) is in use by the World-Wide Web global information initiative since 1990. It is the foundation of the internet and is defined as *"an application-level protocol for distributed, collaborative, hypermedia information systems"*[30].

Although Web-Services - as mentioned already - do not pre-suppose or favor specific technologies, but, mainly as part of the Semantic Web vision, suggest the use of the internet

---

[29]See [305]
[30]See [135]

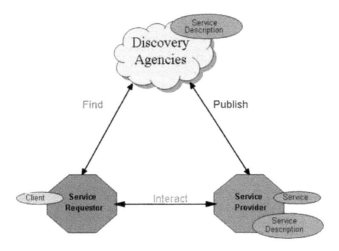

Figure A.6: (Basic) Web-Service architecture

for building distributed applications. Hence, HTTP is the means for message passing on the "physical" level, where SOAP messages build upon.

A.4 Architectures

Having discussed the main standards and specifications of Web-Services, we talk about implementing the Web-Service stack on concrete platforms. According to the W3C, a (basic) architecture is depicted in Figure A.6[31].

This (basic) architecture also shows three main roles that have to be incorporated[32]:

- Service Registry or Discovery Agencies

- Service Requestor

- Service Provider

This reflects the Basic Web-Services stack published by the WS-I.org, where the Service Registry contains a UDDI directory, the Service Provider publishes the interfaces of his services via WSDL, and the Service Requestor exploits these services via SOAP messages[33].

---

[31]taken from [292]
[32]See [47], p. 9
[33]The W3C calls this process Message Exchange Pattern (MEP), see [292]

Another dimension has yet to be discussed, namely strategic concerns for using Web-Services. The described Web-Service architecture is purely looked at from a technological point of view: it provides mechanisms to use and share programming code described in standard XML. But what about a greater scope: e.g. how to deploy these Web-Services within a B2B context?

The W3C addresses this matter only slightly, because it represents the ICT view. In other words: *"Web-Services can be used alone or in conjunction with other Web-Services to carry out a complex aggregation or a business transaction"*[34]. Conceptually speaking, there are two main occurrences for the use of Web-Services:

1. **ICT-driven**:

   Like the W3C, providing mechanisms for the use of Web-Services. This is more a bottom-up approach, reflecting only on services, resources and their relation, without respect to business goals[35].

2. **E-Business driven**:

   This view is rather top-down, because it starts from business strategies, business processes and organizational structure, without any respect to technical implementations in the first place. Today, through the extensive use of ICT and the need for it to stay competitive, Web-Services also play an important role in E-Business. Historically speaking, this approach has been using Electronic Data Interchange (EDI) and EDIFACT on the ICT-side already.

Therefore, these two occurrences still have to be distinguished. The ICT-driven approach is provided by software vendors that will be discussed in the following, and the E-Business-driven approach exists more on a conceptual view, using underlying Web-Services technologies. The approach taken in this thesis is a top-down approach in this sense.

In the following, a short overview of one E-Business-driven approach, namely ebXML, and the main ICT-driven platforms by IBM, Microsoft and Sun is given.

A.4.1   ebXML

ebXML (Electronic-Business using XML) *"sponsored by UN/CEFACT*[36] *and OASIS*[37], *is a modular suite of specifications that enables enterprises of any size and in any geographical location to conduct business over the Internet. Using ebXML, companies now have a*

---

[34][292]
[35]strongly simplified!
[36]See http://www.unece.org/cefact
[37]See http://www.oasis-open.org

standard method to exchange business messages, conduct trading relationships, communicate data in common terms and define and register business processes[38].

ebXML therefore is the E-Business-driven representative in this context: it is business-process-driven and therefore is business-process-oriented, which implies inclusion of roles and human resources[39].

Historically speaking, ebXML has its own roots, and the relation to the Web-Services stack referred to in this thesis is not really clear. There are only few hints to be found concerning UDDI[40], WSDL and SOAP[41]. Generally speaking, the Business Process Specification Schema (BPSS)[42] is a framework for Business Process specification with the goal to create interoperable Business Processes to allow business partners to collaborate. BPSS is available in either in UML or in XML representation. As a methodology UN/CEFACT Modeling Methodology (UMM) is recommended. UMM describes Business Processes, roles and Business Information Objects coming from the UMM Business Library.

Historically speaking, ebXML has its own roots, and the relation to the Web-Services stack referred to in this thesis is not really clear. There are only few hints to be found concerning UDDI[43], WSDL and SOAP[44]. Generally speaking, the Business Process Specification Schema (BPSS)[45] is a framework for Business Process specification with the goal to create interoperable Business Processes to allow business partners to collaborate. BPSS is available in either in UML or in XML representation. As a methodology UN/CEFACT Modeling Methodology (UMM) is recommended. UMM describes Business Processes, roles and Business Information Objects coming from the UMM Business Library.

The future will surely bring convergence to common Web-Service standards to ebXML, but at the moment, no clear statement can be made about this relationship.

A.4.2   IBM Web-Services

IBM strongly participated in the standard efforts for UDDI, WSDL and SOAP[46] and has got a very "E-Business"-driven point of view. Although ICT-driven primarily, IBM can

---

[38][81]

[39]See [27], p. 278.

[40]See [279]

[41]See [82]

[42]See [278] for complete information on BPSS

[43]See [279]

[44]See [82]

[45]See [278] for complete information on BPSS

[46]Even IBM's definition of Web-Services says: Web-Services *"are self-contained, modular business process applications, which are based on open, Internet standards. Using the technologies of WSDL (to describe), UDDI (to advertise and syndicate), and SOAP (to communicate), Web services can be mixed and matched to create innovative applications, processes, and value chains"*, see [114]

be viewed as E-Business driven, concerning its Web-Services approach. IBM even coined a new name for this conjunction, namely "dynamic E-Business"[47]: *"It is the dynamic adaptation of E-Business processes and associated systems to support changing business strategies and tactics. It is our initiative to be the leader in delivering the standards-based platform you need in order to build, run and manage Web Services applications"*. In order to deploy Web-Services, IBM offers a suite of applications and servers[48]:

- **IBM WebSphere Application Server**[49]:
  WebSphere is a Java 2 Enterprise Edition (J2EE) compliant application server enabling the creation of enterprise applications built out of standard modular components. WebSphere also supports seamless integration of Web-Services with interfaces for WSDL and SOAP. For application development, WebSphere provides integrated tools for WebSphere Studio Application Developer[50].

- **WebSphere Studio Application Developer**[51]:
  WebSphere Studio Application development is a development environment to build Java, Web and Web-Services applications.

- **Web-Services Toolkit**[52]:
  The Web-Services Toolkit provides an entry point to IBM's Web-Services for developers. Besides a great load of example files and applications, the Toolkit offers a client Run-Time environment, UDDI, WSDL and SOAP annotating tools, demos and documentation.

In this context, another IBM specification and concept should be mentioned, namely the Web-Services Flow Language (WSFL)[53]. For describing WSFL, the "simple" proposed Web-Services stack of Chapter A.3 has to be extended: on top, a layer for Business Process Orchestration (also known as flow composition or choreography) has to be added. WSFL provides the link from Business Processes to a workflow-like execution sequencing of modular services.

---

[47]See [114]
[48]See [121] and [115], pp. 9
[49]See [116]
[50]For further information see [119].
[51]See [117]
[52]See [120]
[53]See [175], pp. 6

A.4.3 Microsoft - .NET

Like IBM, Microsoft is one of the main contributors to Web-Services standards efforts. With the .NET platform, Microsoft introduces a totally new concept of the Windows operating system culture. .NET builds the technical foundation for *"small discrete building block applications"*[54] to run on servers and clients.

.NET is also the only platform that defines Web-Services as means of communication between applications: *".NET is infused into the products that make up the Microsoft platform, providing the ability to quickly and reliably build, host, deploy, and utilize connected solutions using XML Web-Services, all with the protection of industry-standard security technologies"*[55].

The .NET architecture consists of the following components:

- Servers

- Smart Clients

- XML Web-Services

- Developer tools

As already mentioned, Web-Services are the building blocks for Microsoft's operating systems as well. This enables Smart Clients, being PCs, PDAs or other portable devices, to act as receivers as well. Furthermore, seamless integration of Web-Services and Office products will be reached, making it possible to call services out of Office documents[56].

The presentation of Web-Services as foundation of .NET as a distributed (operating) system, makes Microsoft a very promising partner, in particular as being de-facto supplier for operating systems and Office tools globally. Believing the Microsoft statements, the non-computer experts' dreams seem reachable.

A.4.4 Sun ONE

The third global key player in Web-Services is Sun. Sun's Java platform and programming language are the role model for bringing the idea of platform independence to the internet-public. With the success of Java and the emerging J2EE, programmers are capable of building complex web-applications, including all key issues like security, transaction, authentication, remote repositories, etc. Sun Web-Services start on top of J2EE architecture,

---

[54]See [194]
[55]See [194]
[56]See [195]

leveraging the momentum from existing B2B applications to create Web-Services without "radical Re-Engineering"[57]. The Sun ONE platform includes the following applications and servers:

- Sun ONE Directory Server

- Sun ONE Portal Server

- Sun ONE Integration Server

- Sun ONE Application and Web Server

Besides the Sun ONE platform and architecture, it offers a methodology or checklist to bring existing assets to Services on Demand or Web-Services, called Data, Applications, Reports, Transactions (DART)[58]. The DART model implies data, that has to be suited for aggregation and other partners. With the help of Java based objects, the data are represented on the mandatory Sun ONE Application and Web Server. Reports and transactions round up the functional requirements for an architecture to represent Web-Services.

Besides the Sun ONE architecture, Sun offers developing tools for Web-Services, called Java Web-Services Developer Pack 1.0 (WSDP)[59]. With WSDP, developers can build XML based applications and Servlets, JavaBeans and JavaServer Pages and deploy Web-Services via UDDI, WSDL, SOAP and ebXML interfaces.

Real (physical) interdependence between Sun ONE and WSDP could not be found in the literature of Sun's web sites.

A.4.5   Comparison of Architectures

All of the above mentioned architectures build a solid foundation for executing and publishing Web-Services. They were looked at specifically against the "basic" Web-Services stack's specifications UDDI, WSDL and SOAP. All other specifications that build on these "basic" ones are out of scope for this thesis. It also has to be mentioned, that the information given is very brief and gathered from the companies' internet sites, presenting a very biased and superficial view. For deeper consideration of requirements and specifications, future work will include scrutinizing Microsoft's .NET architecture and open-source platform Apache-Tomcat that both were chosen as platforms for the (theoretically presented)

---

[57]See [151]
[58]See [272]
[59]See [271]

	Discovery	Description	Messaging	Transport
ebXML	UDDI (existing efforts)	BPSS	SOAP (probably possible in future)	HTTP(S) (when SOAP is used)
IBM Web-Services	UDDI	WSDL	SOAP	HTTP(S)
Microsoft .NET	UDDI	WSDL	SOAP	HTTP(S)
Sun ONE	UDDI[61]	WSDL	SOAP[62]	HTTP(S)
W3C	UDDI	WSDL	SOAP	HTTP(S)

Table A.2: Comparison of Web-Service architectures

scenario in Chapter 6.3.

Table A.2[60] shows the discussed platforms and approaches and their convergence to UDDI, WSDL and SOAP, as "basic" implementation of Web-Services, except where noted, if not or only partly existing. The conclusion of this table is the fact that standards consortia as the W3C and the industry have accepted UDDI, WSDL and SOAP as de-facto standards and will continue their future work in this direction. Additionally, this basic Web-Services stack will be extended by proprietary specifications for matters of security, trust, authentication, etc. and especially for matters of Business-to-Business issues. This includes efforts by OASIS, ebXML, IBM (see WSFL) and others to formally specify the so called Business Process Orchestration.

A.5 Summary

This Chapter gave an overview on the topic of Web-Services. Web-Services are to be considered one main focus of current software developments. The main advantage - interoperability - will be clearly shown by the DKElearn test-beds.

---

[60]See Framework from Turner et al. and DKE-Web-Services Study carried out in the winter term 2003/2004, see http://www.gigaweb.com.

Appendix B

Knowledge Representation Formalisms

This Chapter is dedicated to Knowledge Representation Formalisms. Knowledge Representation Formalisms make up the foundation of the Modeling Methods of Chapters 5 and 6 and are therefore discussed. Before being able to create an E-Learning meta-modeling method that has the power to describe competency Just-in-Time learning, Knowledge Representation Formalisms - the munition of describing knowledge structures - have to be evaluated.

B.1 Chapter Outline

This Chapter is divided into three parts as shown in Figure B.1. First, a historical overview is presented, because especially in this discipline research and solutions date back until ancient times and vital conclusions can be drawn from these findings for current technologies. Second, technologies to treat the statically described knowledge are discussed. Third, a list of tools that implement both the static and dynamic part round up this Chapter.

B.2 Describing knowledge: Knowledge Representation Formalisms

There are numerous aspects that have to be considered before being able to tell, define and talk about ways of describing knowledge in a formal and mathematical way to best transform human neural structures. In general, this Chapter tries to explain Knowledge

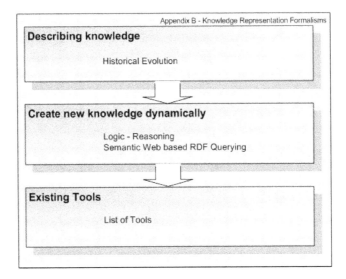

Figure B.1: Overview

Representation Formalisms according to their historical evolution. There are several other taxonomies that could have been deployed, e.g. clustering the Formalisms in respect to their properties. The deeper sense of using the historical overview as an introduction is to show, that Knowledge Representation Formalisms are by far not an invention of the Semantic Web. Knowledge has been represented since the beginning of mankind.

In order to place Knowledge Representation into an understandable context, a framework of KM is essential, because Knowledge Representation is only a technical aspect within the discipline KM[1].

KM can be seen as the paradigm in this context, targeting on finding, describing, managing and using knowledge assets[2]. Figure B.2 shows KM on different levels. Knowledge Representation as cognitive formulation of human thoughts can be put on the "Human Level", but Knowledge Representation Formalisms focus on technological aspects of transforming this cognitive knowledge into a formal description and thus can be assigned to the "ICT Level". This thesis focuses on technical aspects of Knowledge Representation. Still, Figure B.3 shows a risk of starting application development from the "ICT Level". Because of focusing merely on technical aspects, business requirements are neglected and therefore the ICT-driven Application faces functional deficiencies and a "vicious circle"

---

[1]See [41], p. 21-29
[2]See [219]

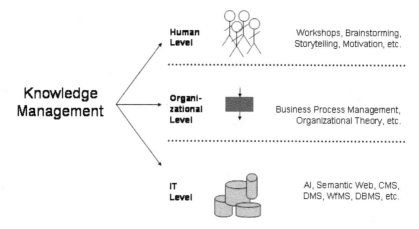

Figure B.2: Taxonomy of Knowledge Management

may start due to ignorance towards the application, stray over inconsistent data management and end with costs that never get a positive ROI.

After having introduced Knowledge Representation Formalisms in Chapter B.2, techniques to infer to new knowledge from the static representations will be introduced in Chapter B.3. Based on the introductory Chapters B.2 and B.3 that express requirements for implementing Knowledge Representation Formalisms, Chapter B.4 presents tools that are able to manipulate, store and infer knowledge on basis of existing Knowledge Representation Formalisms. With the help of the theoretical findings from Appendix A requirements for a representation meta-model will be presented, that enforces standards deployment and integration of LOs. First steps for the integration of the modeled LOs through Web-Services round up this thesis and take Knowledge Representation Formalisms into a practical surrounding.

Before jumping into the historical overview, some definitions and related terms shall be discussed.

When looking into AI literature[3], the term Knowledge Representation always appears in the index as a general concept and is further discussed with a variety of technologies. Chapter B.2.2 will deal with that in detail. Generally speaking, Knowledge Representation is the formalized approach of describing a condition or state that is part of the real world in order to be machine-processable[4]. Therefore the real world has to be encoded in

---

[3]See [101], [155], [225], [231], [257]
[4]See [231], p. 157

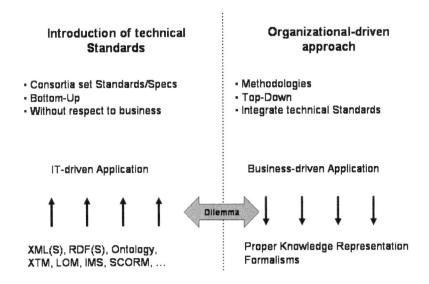

Figure B.3: Top-Down and Bottom-Up Dilemma

some way. The action of encoding is also called modeling the real world with the help of standard tools called Knowledge Representation Formalisms. There are three main areas, which have to be dealt with in order to be able to create such a model[5]:

- Knowledge Acquisition

- Knowledge Representation

  - Declarative description

  - Procedural description

- Knowledge Inference (Chapter B.3).

Besides this classification, languages or formalisms have to be provided for a systematic description of knowledge[6]. One problem of AI probably was the lacking of a general theory or standard for describing knowledge; only "recipes" can be derived that give hints how to create Knowledge Representation Formalisms; these hints are[7]:

- Which part of the world will be modeled

---

[5][172], p. 53
[6]See [314], p. 5
[7]See [155], p. 54

- Which level of detail needs to be expressed

- What kind of semantic primitives are used

- Use a modular way of modeling

- Use efficient and user-friendly processing mechanisms

- Usability is a main goal

Furthermore, the following principles about Knowledge Representations[8] have to be acknowledged:

- An existing entity is described by a symbol (surrogate)

- These entities have got complex relationships and domains (ontological commitment)

- Static representation builds the foundation for dynamic behavior and interactions (theory of intelligent reasoning)

- The represented entities and relationships have to be processable in a reasonable amount of time (medium for efficient computation)

- The represented entities should be human and machine readable and should especially serve as an interface between knowledge engineers and domain experts (medium of human expression)

The conclusion of these two enumerations is, that Knowledge Representation needs to grasp two things[9]

- Syntax

- Semantics

Syntax alone is useless, as it gives no hint for the interpretation of the originator and therefore meaning is not provided and thus a machine is not able to act "intelligently" on the basis of the represented knowledge.

Within today's Semantic Web, the lacking of standard Knowledge Representation Formalisms have a good chance to be overcome: the use of XML as "alphabet" for formalisms

---

[8]See [257], p. 134
[9]See [231], p. 157

and the possible establishment of RDF and technologies building on RDF as "vocabulary"-language are quite promising at the moment.

As already mentioned, Knowledge Representation has been input to scientific research in nearly every period of mankind. Still, there are no real interdependencies of interchange between results from one period to the next. There are almost no references in AI literature to Aristotle's findings, and the Semantic Web community nearly never refers to AI techniques. Only few authors[10] take the approach to explain the development on a historical basis. The structure of this Chapter therefore reflects the development in three main periods:

- "The days before yesterday"

- "Yesterday"

- "Today"

B.2.1 "The days before yesterday"

In many ways, philosophy is very much connected to the research area Knowledge Representation. In order to be able to find knowledge, it is necessary to represent the world in a structured manner. Although the use of Knowledge Representation in philosophy is different to the use in computer sciences, it helps to understand concepts in one scientific field by relating them to another. Almost all contemporary literature reviewing the history of Knowledge Representation starts in ancient Greece with the three philosophers Socrates[11], Plato[12] and Aristotle[13]. This short overview will also concentrate on this approach, although it is biased by an occidental point of view.

These three men can be seen as the inventors of KM, Knowledge Representation and many other scientific fields. Their scientific heritage includes the field of epistemology (the study of what knowledge is) and knowledge inference through syllogisms (deduction). A syllogism is a logical deduction to combine premises to a conclusion. In Aristotle's words this sounds like:

> "A deduction is speech (logos) in which, certain things having been supposed, something different from those supposed results of necessity because of their being so". (Prior Analytics I.2, 24b18-20)

---

[10]See [257] and [231]
[11]See [188], pp. 9-43
[12]See [252] and [37], pp. 44-83
[13]See [255] and [291], pp. 84-128

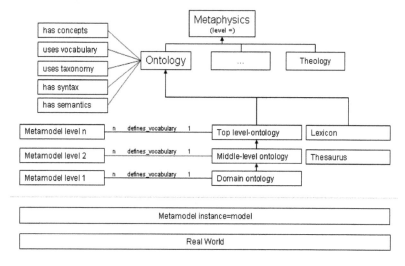

Figure B.4: Relationships in Knowledge Representation

Aristotelian logic was recaptured in the medieval times by so called Scholastic Logic and its prominent representative Saint Thomas Aquinas[14]. In the course of time until present days, many other philosophical disciplines tried to explain how to gain knowledge or reach cognition (gnosis). These include materialism, empirism, positivism and rationalism to name but a few[15].

Besides the historical evolution of Knowledge Representation as a scientific discipline, some other technical terms have to be mentioned in this context. Many of them are so general that an assignment to any of the presented periods is possible. Moreover, they are commonly used in other disciplines like philosophy. In this section, these terms are looked at from the philosophical point of view. The following Chapters will give the context to computer sciences. The terms therefore can be seen as basic vocabulary of Knowledge Representation. They are:

- **Meta-data**:

  Translated from Greek meta-data has the meaning of *"after (more than) data"*. The term meta-data is commonly used in computer sciences to express that a piece of data has got some extra data associated (*"data about data"*[16]). Meta-data and meta-data management in the past is strongly related to libraries and also set foundations

---

[14]See [193] and [165], pp. 177-220
[15]See [231], pp. 8
[16][65]

for the Semantic Web context. Meta-data is the basis for the vocabulary of meta-models.

- **Meta-model/metaphysics**:

  It is not quite clear, where the term meta-model originates. So far it seems that the term meta-model has been defined by the field of computer sciences. In terms of "meta", philosophical literature only speaks of metaphysics (from Greek "meta ta physika" beyond/behind the physical, Latin "trans naturam"). A causal connection between these two terms therefore does not exist. Metaphysics hereby is the basic philosophical science, from which all other sciences can be derived; sub sciences are ontology, cosmology, anthropology and theology[17].

  Figure B.4 tries to put metaphysics, meta-models and ontologies into order, depicting the relationships of these terms using its own generic method of representation, where directed arcs can be compared to inheritance and undirected arcs can be compared to relationships in object-orientation. Meta-models use ontological vocabularies on different levels of abstraction. Modeling the real world per se is independent of constructs or a semantic schema. Only in connection with formal ontological vocabularies (semantics), a meta-model can be deduced from a model[18].

- **Ontology/Concept**:

  The word ontology can be translated from Greek as "doctrine of the being"[19]. This translation already points out the highly philosophical touch and can be related to religious beliefs, metaphysics, meta-models and related fields. The term "ontology" originated in Aristotelian times but was coined as a scientific discipline in the 17th century[20].

  In ancient Greece, philosophy could be defined as getting rid of chaos to get to see things as they really (Greek ontos "being, becoming") are. An ontology tries to seek for the explanation[21]. In many ways, an ontology can be seen as the top-level concept for describing things or entities and their relationships. E.g. a taxonomy only represents concepts (=taxons) in a subclass-manner. A thesaurus is a "lightweight" ontology, expressing only a level of similarity of terms. Ontologies go far beyond this static representation function; they also capture the dimension measures, composite objects, time, space, change, events and processes, physical objects, substances and

---

[17]See [238], p. 478
[18]See [211], p. 16
[19]See [78], p. 551
[20]See [281], p. 13
[21]See [73], p. 12

beliefs[22].

- **Syntax and Semantics/Grammar**:

  *"The first step in defining a grammar is to define a lexicon, or a list of allowable vo-
  cabulary words. These words are grouped into categories ...: nouns ..., pronouns ...,
  verbs ..., adjectives ..., adverbs ..., articles ..., prepositions ... and conjunctions."*[23]
  The terms syntax and semantics strongly relate to linguistics. The syntax of a sentence defines the way a sentence can be structured, whereas the semantics places the
  correct sentence into a given context, giving meaning to the (vocabulary) words[24].
  An English speaking person may be able to put together a Chinese sentence using a
  rule book, but will never understand the meaning of the sentence[25]. In terms of XML
  for example, syntax and semantics can be compared to the concepts well-formed and
  valid.

- **Taxonomy**:

  A taxonomy (from Greek "taxon" class, strain, category, concept; "nomos" law,
  order. Taxonomy can be translated as "classification"[26]) or taxonomic hierarchy is a
  set of controlled vocabulary terms placed in hierarchical order. Objects with similar
  properties are merged to classes/concepts/taxons, which have a kind of subclass
  relationship with each other. This relationship includes the concept of inheritance[27].

- **Thesaurus**:

  *"A thesaurus, for the purposes of this standard, is a controlled vocabulary of terms in
  natural language that are designed for post-coordination"*[28]. A thesaurus is a complex
  type of a vocabulary, where the hierarchical relationships have special meaning,
  expressing the level of similarity of terms (homonyms, polynyms, and synonyms).

- **Vocabulary/Lexicon**:

  A vocabulary is a list of preferred terms, an index of words[29]. In natural language,
  the vocabulary for the English language consists of all existing known English words.

---

[22]See [231], p. 228

[23][231], p. 664

[24][78], p. 709, defines semantics as branch of linguistics that concentrates on the meaning of characters
and sequence of characters and [78], p. 761, as doctrine of structure of a sentence.

[25]Compare this example with the "Chinese Room" experiment in AI.

[26]See [78], p.768

[27]Exactly the same approach can be found in computer science when talking about the object-oriented
paradigm.

[28][13], p. 1

[29]See [78], p.817

A lexicon, being the pool of all vocabulary words, can be seen as taxonomy with alphabetical order. A vocabulary gives meaning to syntactically correct sentences.

B.2.2 "Yesterday": (Classic) Artificial Intelligence

In order to fully understand Knowledge Representation from the Artificial Intelligence (AI) point of view, it is quite useful to produce a taxonomy of technologies in a bibliographical kind of way. Table B.1 shows the Knowledge Representation Formalisms mentioned in literature.

[31]	<ul><li>Associative Networks</li><li>Frames</li><li>Images</li><li>Logic (Higher, Horn, Modal, Predicate, Sort)</li><li>Natural Language</li><li>Neural Networks</li><li>Production systems</li></ul>
[39][30]	<ul><li>Frames</li><li>Inheritance</li><li>Logic</li><li>Rules</li></ul>

---

[30]The Knowledge Representation Formalisms of [39] were distilled from all articles.

[50]	• Logic (Predicate) • Indexing • Inheritance (ISA relations)
[84]	• Logic (Inference machine IM2 with logic-based Knowledge Representation Formalism) • Rules (proprietary system)
[101]	• Logic (Predicate, First Order)
[155]	• Frames • Logic • Rules • Semantic Networks
[211]	• Logic

[225]	• Conceptual dependency • Frames • Logic (Propositional, Predicate) • Procedures • Rules • Scripts • Semantic Networks
[231]	• Logic (First Order)
[241]	• Logic (Propositional, Predicate)[31]
[257]	• Frames • Logic • Object-oriented systems • Ontology • Natural Language Semantics • Rules

---

[31]Note, that [241] only refers to Logic in his book

[277]	• Concept hierarchies • Frames • Logic (Propositional, Predicate) • Relational databases • Rules • Semantic Networks
[327]	• Frames • Inheritance (ISA relations) • Logic

Table B.1: Bibliographical order of Knowledge Representation Formalisms

Table B.1 already shows that Logic has a predominant position - a least common denominator[32] - within Knowledge Representation Formalisms. This can easily be explained, because nearly all techniques can somehow be transformed into a logical expression[33]. Figure B.5 is a good example showing the equivalence between (Predicate) Logic and Semantic Networks. In many ways, other techniques like Semantic Networks try to add a visual interface to Logic, but eventually failed because of the lack of standards[34]. Other concepts like object-oriented features (inheritance) can also enrich Logic in order to become an ontology language[35].

---

[32]Logic has long been seen as the means of representing intelligence. Its predominant position goes back to the use of logic, mathematics and algebra by nearly all important scientists, including Gottfried Wilhelm Leibniz, born on July 1st 1646, [239], pp. 139-175.

[33]See [155], p. 67

[34]See [155], p. 67: a major disadvantage of Knowledge Representation Formalisms is the lack of profound theories. Logic is the only exception.

[35]The Semantic Web (Chapter B.2.3.1) provides standard languages for ontology engineering.

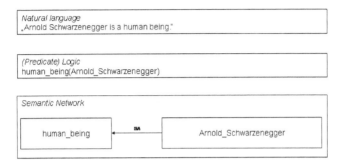

Figure B.5: Relations between (Predicate) Logic and Semantic Networks

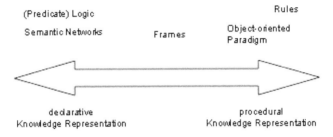

Figure B.6: Distinction between declarative and procedural Knowledge Representation Formalisms

Table B.2 aggregates the formalisms from Table B.1 and gives a short description about each one of them.

Each of these (hopefully) taxatively listed Knowledge Representation Formalisms[40] can be further clustered into declarative ("know that") and procedural ("know how") Formalisms (Figure B.6[41]), meaning that some Formalisms only present static information and others represent dynamic information[42]. It is clear, that only a combination of both Formalisms is reasonable, especially when representing ontological interdependencies.

---

[40]The mentioned Representation Formalisms are part of symbolic AI; sub-symbolic AI and its Representation Formalisms will not be discussed at all. For further interest, please consider [77], pp. 217 and equivalent literature.

[41]See [155], p. 56

[42]Figure B.6 pushes all Formalisms into either the declarative or the procedural category. Some properties of Formalisms overlap and therefore Figure B.6 has to be looked at carefully. E.g. the object-oriented paradigm is declarative as well, because you have to declare the schema of classes first.

Logic	Formal Logic explores how to concatenate assertions and how to introduce formal reasoning[36]. *"Formal Logic indicates that ... deduction is created only on the syntactical level. ... it therefore is independent from semantics"*[37]
Frames	*"Here is the essence of the frame theory: When one encounters a new situation (or makes a substantial change in one's view of the present problem), one selects from memory a structure called a frame. This is a remembered framework to be adapted to fit reality by changing details as necessary."*[38]
Object-oriented Paradigm	Some concepts can be aggregated to reach object-oriented status, because historically speaking object-orientation was not yet an existing paradigm. These concepts are hierarchies, scripts, inheritance, procedures (ISA relations). Frames can be seen as predecessor of object-orientation, but are still viewed at separately, because they own a dominant status in AI.
Semantic Networks	Semantic Networks originated in psychology to model the complex structure of the human memory. They can also be seen as visual representation for Predicate Logic and Frames.[39]
Rules	Rules are simple but powerful means to express if-then statements on top of a knowledge base.
Others	Formalisms like Images, Natural Language, Neural Networks and Indexing are not part of this thesis.

Table B.2: Knowledge Representation Formalisms; ordered by technologies and frequency

B.2.2.1 Declarative Knowledge Representation

Declarative Knowledge Representation Formalisms present a static snapshot model of the real world. They are Logic, Frames and Semantic Networks.

Logic: As already mentioned, Logic is by far the most important Knowledge Representation Formalism. The two reasons have been already given (nearly all other Formalisms can be represented in Logic; Logic is the best explored field in Knowledge Representation[43]) in Chapter B.2.2.

Two main research areas

- Propositional Logic

- First-order Logic (First-order predicate calculus with equality)

and several others[44]

---

[43]Logic dates back to the early stages of occidental philosophy (Aristotelian Logic, see Chapter B.2.1)

[44]Only Propositional and First-order Logic are covered in this thesis. For further information please consider relevant literature, i.e. [231], [31]

- Modal Logic

- Fuzzy Logic

- Higher-order Logic

- Logic of questions and answers

- Frame Logic (F-Logic)

- Temporal Logic

- Description Logic

- etc.

exist.

(Formal) Propositional Logic concentrates on analyses of sentences[45]. In Propositional Logic, symbols[46]

- Represent facts, i.e. A="Arnold Schwarzenegger is a human being"

- Hold the propositional value true or false

- May be combined with the connectives ¬ (not), ⇒ (implies), ⇔ (equivalent), ∧ (and), ∨ (or), () (parentheses)

- Can be concatenated syntactically to sentences

Each sentence can be depicted by a truth table that maps the Boolean values true and false to the given sentence. Different sentences may have the same Boolean values. An example is A⇒B ⇔ A¬B.

Propositional Logic is very simple but lacks expressiveness in certain situations[47]. To overcome these obstacles, First-order Logic adds several features[48]:

- Predicates/Properties

- Literals/Objects

---

[45]See [155], p. 68

[46]See [231], p.166

[47]The symbol A="Arnold Schwarzenegger is a human being" can not be divided into further sub-parts and represents an atomic value. If there is another symbol B="All human beings are bodybuilders", the deduction "Arnold Schwarzenegger is a bodybuilder" cannot be made.

[48]See [155], p. 73, and [231], p. 185; the example from Footer 47 can now be solved: (∀x) (human_being(x)⇒bodybuilder(x)) ⇒ human_being(Arnold_Schwarzenegger) deduces bodybuilder(Arnold_Schwarzenegger).

- Functions

- Relations

- Quantifiers: ∃ (existential), ∀ (universal)

One drawback in Logic is the complex interpretation of semantic interdependencies[49]. There is no mechanism to create a domain vocabulary with the intention of making it machine-readable. Concepts in Logic exist, that state a need for a mapping of internal (formal) representation and meaning in the real world[50]. But this vocabulary definition (=interpretation) by the writer himself has to be provided[51]. Logic therefore can describe knowledge syntactically but misses the semantic interpretation. Another notable problem about (classic formal) Logic is its two-valued character (tertium non datur).

Frames: Frames are on the edge of declarative and procedural Knowledge Representation Formalisms. Frames were invented by M. Minsky and can be seen as predecessor of complex data-types and object-orientation. The definition[52] implies the existence of objects that have a certain schema (declarative) and procedures/methods (procedural) in order to change the objects' status. The basic idea of frames lies in the nature of modeling the real world: new situations are mapped to existing and similar ones. Therefore, an existing frame is evoked and filled with details from the new situation[53]. Drawback: the more complex the situations get, the harder is the representation with frames[54].

Most of the concepts of frames are equivalent to Logic and can be represented: procedures may be represented by functions or sub-class properties by relations.

Semantic Networks: Semantic Net(work)s are also referred to as Associative Networks[55]. They consist of literals modeled with squares or circles and directed arcs[56]. The arcs may have different semantics, according to the literature[57]: Charniak/McDermott[58] allow all kinds of properties (color, supported-by, etc.), whereas Collins/Quillian[59] only refer to certain basic elements (HAS, ISA, etc.). This Knowledge Representation Formalism can easily be mapped to Logic and can be seen as graphical representation of

---

[49]See [327], p. 228
[50]See [225], p. 136
[51]See [231], pp. 162
[52]See [196], p. 246
[53]See [225], p. 229
[54]See [196], p. 255
[55]See [50], p. 22
[56]See [101], p. 257
[57]The various interpretations already show, that there has never been a standard visualization technique for Semantic Networks.
[58]See [50], p. 23
[59]See [222], pp. 216-270

First-order Logic[60]. An example of this equivalence was shown in Figure B.5.

B.2.2.2 Procedural Knowledge Representation

Procedural Knowledge Representation Formalisms represent knowledge in a dynamic way, using rules or procedures that change the state of a knowledge base. They are the object-oriented Paradigm and rules.

Object-oriented Paradigm: The object-oriented paradigm is a scientific field in Software Engineering and includes the concepts inheritance, polymorphism, unique objects and abstract data-types. It therefore is the most complex Knowledge Representation Formalism, because all concepts can be programmed as they should be. An object-oriented programming system also incorporates declarative and procedural forms of Knowledge Representation and rules and frames can easily be mapped[61].

A combination of several approaches with an object-oriented front-end is to be considered very reasonable, depending on the application.

Rules: Rules can be compared to heuristic thinking. Rules are represented as sentences consisting of one or more concatenated premises (left-hand side) and one or more conclusions (right-hand side): `if <premise(s)> then <conclusion(s)>`[62]. Rule based systems are often implemented as expert-systems and rely on storage of data in the existential-subset of logic[63] and use the same inference rules (modus ponens, modus tollens)[64]. The strength of rules lies in the combination of atomic rules using mechanisms forward and backward chaining within the recognize-select-act cycle, that dynamically decides which rule to take (conflict-resolution); rule-based systems consist of a working memory (facts), a production memory (rules) and a rule interpreter (inference engine)[65].

B.2.2.3 Others

All other found Knowledge Representation Formalisms are not considered in this thesis.

---

[60]See [155], p. 79
[61]See [257], p. 169
[62]See [155], p. 56
[63]Equivalence to Logic:
```
IF (Arnold_Schwarzenegger has muscles) THEN
(Arnold_Schwarzenegger is human_being)
⇔ muscles(Arnold_Schwarzenegger)
⇒human_being(Arnold_Schwarzenegger)
```
[64]See [257], p. 156
[65]See [50], p. 438

B.2.3 "Today": Semantic Web

The term "Semantic Web"[66] was coined by Tim Berners-Lee to express the need for more semantics in the current world-wide web (WWW). The Semantic Web makes use of some key technologies and protocols pushed by the W3C - RDF(S)[67], XML[68], HTTP[69] - that make the idea a promising one to be realized and used. Basically speaking, the Semantic Web uses known Knowledge Representation mechanisms based on First-order Logic with an XML- or RDF-binding, where resources are uniquely identified by Uniform Resource Identifiers (URI) to transform the WWW into a "Web of Trust"[70]. The fact, that also graphical representations are evolving and the status of ontology languages like RDF, DAML+OIL[71] or OWL[72] is in a state of constant evolution to get a standard soon, make the Semantic Web almost reality. One drawback is the difficulty of bringing experts and users to annotate their resources with ontology meta-data, which makes the Semantic Web dependent on the will of moderately motivated human beings[73]. This makes the "pure" Semantic Web a potential candidate for scientific research only.

Even more promising is an extension of the Semantic Web, namely Web-Services[74]. Whereas the Semantic Web provides only declarative information, Web-Services promise to bring procedural information and dynamics into B2B workflows. Figure B.7 sketches the interdependence between Semantic Web and Web-Services, with quite similar categories to those used in Chapter B.2.2 (declarative-static; procedural-dynamic). To reach the goal of Intelligent or Semantic Web-Services, a great number of basic steps still have to be taken. Figure B.9[75] shows the State-of-the-Art situation in Semantic Web and takes a closer look at requirements for a modeling method in E-Learning using an ontology repository enabled by Web-Services.

One example to illustrate the desired power of the Semantic Web is the TAP - An Application Framework for Building the Semantic Web - that can be found at `http://www.w3.org/2002/05/tap/`.

---

[66]See [29]

[67]See [307]

[68]See [304]

[69]See [135]

[70]See [308]; "Web of Trust" does not imply that the Web will be trustworthy per se. But authentication, digital signatures and assigning levels of reliability via meta-data will support to perceive the trustworthiness of a resource.

[71]See [58]

[72]See [305]

[73]This problem is underlined by statements like "A Crying Need for RDF" by people like Tim Berners-Lee, see [28]

[74]See [309], [320], [47], etc.

[75]See [94]

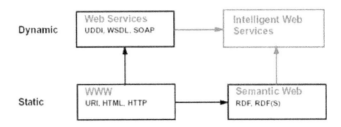

Figure B.7: Semantic Web and Web-Services

Ontologies in the computer scientific sense are believed to be the *"key-enabling technolo-gies"*[76] to set the foundation for the Semantic Web, building up the structure of global internet resources that can be queried to get the ultimate result. The next Chapter is dedicated to ontologies and the instances that are used in the Semantic Web.

B.2.3.1 Ontologies and Meta-modeling

Whereas the AI community has at least acknowledged the ideas and concepts about Knowledge Representation Formalisms of antique or medieval times, the young Semantic Web community only cites them occasionally. This is quite interesting to mention, be-cause - unlike the AI community - Greek terms like ontologies or taxonomies are quite popular in the Semantic Web community. One problem of ontologies not being accepted in their original sense may lie in the fact, that clear definitions are missing, or that the existing definitions are vacuous to many listeners. Whatever the causes of inacceptance may be, ontologies are the basic concept in the Semantic Web to represent knowledge and that is why they are scrutinized in this Chapter.

Again[77] "number 1", ontology is defined as the "doctrine of the being". This means according to Willard Van Ormen Quine, that the question to pose when building an on-tology is *"What is there?"* with the corresponding answer *"Everything!"*[78]. Again "number 2" (see Figure B.1), an ontology is the means of describing things as a sub-concept for meta-physics. Therefore, the broadly used definition *"An ontology is a formal, explicit specification of a shared conceptualization"*[79] in the Semantic Web community is a reason-able one, but without explanation, these few words are pretty hard to grasp and bear much more complexity. Is the Semantic Network in Figure B.5 an ontology, respectively, what

---

[76][60], p. 4
[77]See Chapter B.2.1
[78]See [104], p. 1
[79][92], p. 11, referring to the definition of Gruber, 1993

does it miss to become one? The answer: No, it is not an ontology, because "everything" is missing, meaning, that nothing about the following[80] is said

- concepts

- dimension measures

- composite objects

- time

- space

- change

- events and processes

- physical objects

- substances

- beliefs

A concept(ualization) is something that exists in the real world, like a class in the object-oriented paradigm, also called type or domain[81], which has schema information as well as instances. A concept is language independent, which makes it kind of objective, whereas an ontology is language dependent[82], giving room for certain subjective interpretations. The question arises, whether there is an ontological (semantic) construct to represent a concept and if so, is it complete[83]? Figure B.8[84] depicts these interdependencies in the so called "meaning triangle".

The meaning triangle has to be scrutinized from every corner:

- It is possible, that the same object can exist for different concepts: Arnold Schwarzenegger as an actor and as a politician?

---

[80]See [231], p. 228

[81]See [257], p. 51

[82]See [106]

[83]See [316], p. 93. This need to map two different worlds brings up the need for managing ontologies, which can be found under the name ontology engineering in literature. The management of these ontological resources is closely related to KM and can be clustered into several phases: Knowledge Acquisition, Knowledge Representation, Knowledge Maintenance and Knowledge Use (see [60]). Ontology engineering is not part of this thesis.

[84]See [257], pp. 191. Compare the "meaning triangle" with the levels of abstracting knowledge: knowledge exists on a cognitive, representational and implementation level (see [226], pp. 8) or on the implementational, logical, epistemological, conceptual and linguistic level (Brachman (1979), in [257], p. 187).

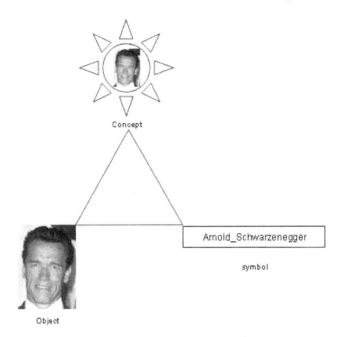

Figure B.8: The meaning triangle, concepts and ontologies

- The concept itself is language- and context independent. Arnold Schwarzenegger is perceived as such all over the world.

- The symbol is language dependent.

The other properties like time or space need to be defined as well, so information about the whereabouts and the life of `Arnold_Schwarzenegger`, his relations etc. are missing (again example from Figure B.5). Providing these additional "things", we are getting nearer to an ontology.

Ontologies also exist on three different levels[85]:

- **Top-level (general purpose) ontologies**:
  description of domain-independent knowledge[86] representing the top-down approach (philosophy)

- **Middle-level ontologies**:
  contain concepts of medium specialization

---

[85]See [240]
[86]An example are Aristotle's categories, cited in [257], p. 57

- **Domain ontologies**:

  contain highly specialized concepts, representing the bottom-up approach (computer sciences)[87]

And this is the point, where philosophy and computer sciences take different paths. Whereas philosophy takes a top-down approach starting with grand conceptions ("being"), computer sciences only describe so called micro-worlds in a bottom-up approach[88], because ontological information in their context is only the information that can be processed by a computer system[89]; the set of described objects and the relations - the schema information of an ontology - is called vocabulary[90].

A concept also represents an abstraction of the real world, which brings up the discussion about the terms meta-model and model, because models also are defined as simplified views of the real world (conceptualization of knowledge[91]).

Meta-models in computer sciences are a common means to describe modeling methods[92], an abstraction of models themselves. The concept of meta-modeling is primarily used in process management as a means to abstract different kinds of process modeling methods. This so-called "meta-ization"[93] - abstractions of meta-models are meta-meta-models, etc. - can be repeated infinitely. Especially in process-management, this leads to the discussion of better re-use and extensibility of existing concepts from a higher level meta-model to a lower level meta-model[94]. The same holds true for top-level ontologies that define a basic vocabulary that serves as concept for lower level ontologies.

As depicted in Figure B.5, the different levels of meta-ization correspond to different levels of ontologies. The coherence between ontologies and meta-models therefore is more than just the fact, that meta-ization has to overcome the ontological question which vocabulary[95] to use. E.g. Kaschek argues that process-ontologies and meta-models use the same vocabulary[96].

This short discussion will return in Chapter 6.2, where different ontologies (learning resources, Learner Profiles, etc.) have to be transformed into meta-models to serve as a modeling environment for E-Learning.

---

[87] An example is the vCard specification, [306]

[88] See [257], p. 52

[89] One can also say that ontologies in computer sciences only emerge together with economical value.

[90] See [104], p.1, and Chapter B.2.1

[91] See [246]. A debate about the term model can also be found in [243] and [263], pp. 19, especially language as a modeling method. This debate is not part of this thesis.

[92] See [263], p. 10

[93] See [263], p. 24

[94] See [159]

[95] Discussed in [95], p. 23, taken from Klein/Lyytinen, 1992

[96] See [159]

The following sub-Chapters are concerned with ontology description languages that will have high chances to be used as Knowledge Representation Formalisms in the Semantic Web[97].

Topic Maps: The term "Topic Map" is not very often used in the Semantic Web community, nevertheless it is worth mentioning. Interesting is the fact, that a standard already exists, confirmed by ISO JTC1/SC34/WG3 (ISO 13250)[98] since 1999, which makes it per se worth watching, because standards enable interoperability, being a major subject in B2B integration with Web-Services.

A Topic Map can be defined as a semantic network of knowledge, where a topic is the smallest chunk of knowledge. Topic Maps *"enable multiple, concurrent views of sets of information objects"*[99]. A topic, the fundamental subject uniquely defined by an identity-attribute, may be any entity in a given context that may have an arbitrary number of links to external resources, called occurrences; associations define the relations among the topics, where association roles may further define the type of relationship; the problem of homonymic topics is solved by scopes, so that topics within a scope are unique[100].

The basic notation of the ISO standard 13250 is defined by the Standard Generalized Markup Language (SGML), which is opposed to the XML Topic Maps (XTM) specification[101]. XTM is derived from the ISO 13250 and has the advantage - besides minor additions - that the binding language is the Semantic Web lingua franca XML. Furthermore, XTM dissolved into Organization for Advancement of Structured Information Standards (OASIS)[102] that is heavily concerned with Web-Services and the B2B integration.

Generally speaking, Topic Maps are a well explored field, as research started in the beginning of the 1990-ies. Especially when looking at XTM, applications, graphical representation and API like TM4J.org exist. Still, the future is not clear, because the connection to the Semantic Web and the power of other ontological languages is missing (see next Chapter). Merely a simple semantic schema to provide sub-class relationships exist, comparable to a simple RDFS[103], where a "topic" is nearly the only meta-concept[104] The adoption of expressiveness of an ontology language is also not quite clear. Topic Maps

---

[97]Meta-modeling and ontology language concepts like the Meta Object Facility (MOF) and the Unified Modeling Language (UML), for both see [208], and Simple HTML Ontology Extensions (SHOE), see [280], are not considered, because either the domain is improper (UML and MOF for Software Engineering) or the project was terminated (SHOE).
[98]See [145]
[99]See [147], p.1
[100]See [322], pp. 7-14
[101]See [330]
[102]See [212], p. 55
[103][212], p. 283-325, talks about Topic Maps and RDF, showing similarities and an example of an RDF graph in XTM syntax.
[104]except from additions in the XTM Processing Model (XTMP), see [331].

were used to merge large indexes and only are a representation method for ontologies[105]. The future will show, whether Topic Maps will play a role in the Semantic Web.

RDF (revisited), RDFS, DAML+OIL, OWL: One may wonder why the three Knowledge Representation Formalisms Resource Description Framework (RDF), DARPA Agent Markup Language plus Ontology Inference Layer (DAML+OIL) and Web Ontology Language (OWL) are mixed together in one Chapter. Each of them deserves a PhD thesis alone.

The explanation is threefold:

- RDF(S) can be seen as the basic framework. It is enforced by the W3C, hence the Semantic Web Community.

- The WebOnt Working Group[106] of the W3C specifies OWL as a revision of DAML+OIL[107]. DAML+OIL itself is a successor of DAML-ONT[108] and OIL[109].

- All three use the XML for serialization as a uniform data-exchange format.

First, as a little excursion, Figure B.9[110] shows the main picture that is associated with the Semantic Web compared to natural languages, that also points out the function of RDF as a basic concept for ontology languages DAML+OIL and OWL. Compared to natural language, the evolution of the Semantic Web can be seen in some historic period of mankind, where language was invented (ignoring the fact of the written language and the knowledge of an alphabet). All levels above either still do not exist or are still in the state of scientific exploration. Second, Figure B.9 also clearly draws the lines of this Chapter, coping only with the technologies below the "today"-line.

RDF[111], a W3C recommendation, is a foundation for processing meta-data. Similar to First-order Logic, RDF consists of properties and property-values that - in concatenation with other properties and property-values (literals or other properties that represent resources) form statements, similar to sentences in natural language. The difference or the essence of RDF lies in the use of URIs that represent unique references to resources.

RDF has three different representations:

- A labeled graph with directed arcs (properties), rectangles (literals) and resources (oval)

---

[105]See [212], p. 129
[106]See [313]
[107]See [311]
[108]See [59]
[109]See [206]
[110]rearranged from [308]
[111]See [307]

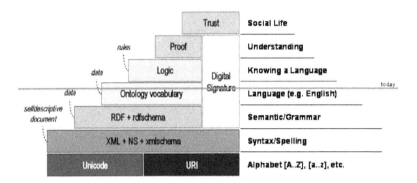

Figure B.9: Levels of the Semantic Web compared to natural language

- A (natural language) sentence with subjects (resources), predicates (properties) and objects (literals or resources)[112]

- and the XML Schema (XMLS) notation[113], a basic serialization syntax and an abbreviated serialization syntax.

RDF also provides containers that are able to subsume several resources or literals. Types of containers are bag, sequence and alternative.

An important feature of RDF is the so-called reification to be able to make statements about statements (meta-statements). It is an easy concept but hard to grasp. The following definitions are for clarification:

- "Any RDF statement can be the object or value of a triple, which means graphs can be nested as well as chained" [114]

- The RDF specification calls reified statements higher order statements. Syntactically, the reified statement needs to be modeled as a resource with four properties, namely `type`, `subject`, `predicate` and `object` with an additional property, that points to the object asserting something about the original statement. The original and the reified statement both exist independently[115].

---

[112]a more Logic kind of representation in the form of an object-attribute-value triple Attribute(Object, Value) is possible as well. See [93], p. 13.

[113]RDF does not force XML as serialization syntax, but the W3C and the fact, that XML has become the lingua franca of the internet, strongly recommends it.

[114]See [93], p. 14

[115]See [307]

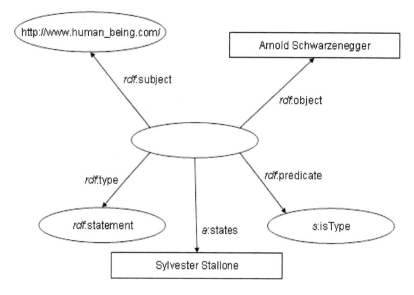

Figure B.10: Reified RDF-statement

- *"Reification is the process of turning a predicate or function into an object in the language"*[116]

- *"The act of creating a topic is called reification. When anything is reified it becomes the subject of the topic thus created; to reify something is therefore to create a topic of which that thing is the subject. Reification of a subject allows topic characteristics to be assigned to the topic that reifies it: In other words, it makes it possible to discourse about that subject within the terms of the topic map paradigm"*[117]

The simple Schwarzenegger example can be represented like sketched in Figure B.10[118] as a graphical representation, when his colleague "Sylvester Stallone states, that Arnold Schwarzenegger is a human being":

---

[116]See [231], p. 230
[117]See [330]
[118]This example probably is not perfect. But the sentence "Arnold Schwarzenegger is a human being" should also apply, therefore the predicate isType was chosen and the subject's URI was chosen without respect to a taxonomy.

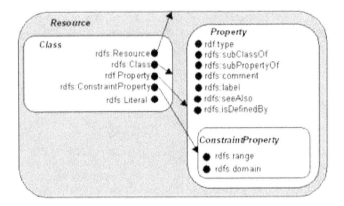

Figure B.11: RDFS classes and resources

Because of its "primitive" and limited functions, RDF is not quite sufficient to serve as an ontology description language[119]. The vocabulary description language RDF-Schema (RDFS) addresses these insufficiencies by providing a formal vocabulary for RDF graphs giving meaning (semantics) to RDF[120]. The vocabulary consists of a simple model for properties and property values, where properties are either attributes of resources or relationships among resources; RDFS does not define a vocabulary as such but gives "a mechanism to define such elements" of vocabularies[121]. The RDFS basic type-system is shown in Figure B.11[122]. Of course it is possible to reuse[123] other standard vocabularies in combination with RDFS, e.g. the Dublin Core Element Set from the Dublin Core Meta-data Initiative (DCMI)[124], the Learning Objects Meta-data (LOM)[125] or the RDF Site Summary (RSS)[126].

Still, the level of expressiveness is too limited for an ontology language, and this is where DAML+OIL[127] and OWL step in, extending RDFS coming from a frame-based Knowledge Representation Formalism. For pragmatic reasons, only OWL will be glanced

---

[119]Remember the "everything" from Chapter B.2.3.1. As always, the advantage in "primitivity" lies in the better understanding and being able to use it with primitive devices like Personal Digital Assistants (PDA) or mobile phones with limited processing power (see [113]).

[120]This is the point, where Logic ended, because it did not provide mechanisms for describing standard vocabularies. See also [93], p. 14. RDF and RDFS can be said to be Logic+semantic.

[121]See [312]

[122]See [312]

[123]See [113], p. 114

[124]See [72]

[125]See [133] and Chapter 4.3 for details.

[126]See [220]

[127]See [310] for reference description .

at because of the explanation item 2 in the beginning of this Chapter. OWL[128] provides three different levels of abstraction[129]:

- **OWL Lite**:
  language near to RDF(S), with light extensions for cardinalities.

- **OWL DL (description logics)**:
  full expressiveness and guaranteed computability

- **OWL Full**:
  full expressiveness with no guaranteed computability and maximum freedom from RDF.

As a last comment some critical statements about the use of URIs in RDF (and therefore all related ontology languages): any resource in RDF has to be named by a URI[130]. Problems arise, because the usage of creating and managing URIs is not clearly defined; misuse can lead to the loss of the two main properties of resource identifiers: unique identification and retrievability; one suggestion is to introduce Unified Resource Names (URN) as naming concept[131].

B.2.4 Taxonomy of Knowledge Representation Formalisms

Concluding the topic Knowledge Representation Formalisms, a taxonomy of (static or declarative) Knowledge Representation Formalisms is given, with respect to the contemporary situation of the Semantic Web and the need for an ontology description language within a Semantic Web. One property of the Formalisms is not given, namely the status of maturity. Historically speaking, above all Logic stands on solid mathematical grounds, whereas emerging languages DAML+OIL and OWL are still in the state of scientific research and not as tested as XML(S) and RDF(S). The question therefore remains, whether they will be the ones to make the race as established ontology languages.

Table B.3 shows the taxonomy.

---

[128]OWL is based on Description Logics. Description Logics is *"unifying and giving a logical basis to the well known traditions of Frame-based systems, Semantic Networks and KL-ONE-like languages, Object-Oriented representations, Semantic data models, and Type systems"*, see [184].

[129]See [311]

[130]See [307]

[131]See [49] and [48] for information about the critical use of URIs and [303] for general information about addressing schemas.

	Declarative Procedural	Syntax	Semantics	Other ontological commitments
DAML+OIL, OWL	D	Yes	Yes	Hierarchy, inheritance, predicates, relations, unique identity, object-orientation, datatypes, cardinality, XOR and AND relationships
First-order Logic	D	Yes	No	Predicates, relations, unique identity
Frames	D/P	Yes	No	No (at least no standard way of defining a semantic vocabulary)
Object-oriented Paradigm	D/P	Yes	Yes (by manual programming)	No (everything has to be programmed from scratch. The object-oriented paradigm in Software Engineering per se is not specified to serve for providing ontology languages and reasoning)
Propositional Logic	D	Yes	No	No (at least no standard way of defining a semantic vocabulary)
RDF(S)	D	Yes	Yes (RDFS)	Hierarchy, inheritance, predicates, relations, unique identity, object-orientation
Topic Maps	D	Yes	Yes (simple)	No

Table B.3: Taxonomy of Knowledge Representation Formalisms

B.3 Create new knowledge dynamically: Querying Knowledge Representation Formalisms

On top of Knowledge Representation Formalisms that make knowledge readable by machines because of their transparent semantic information, intelligent machine agents should be able to create and process knowledge. One of the main ideas of human intelligence and AI is the ability to induce, deduce, query or infer the knowledge base in order to find new coherences. Philosophically speaking, the following methods can be used:

- Induction (from Latin in "into" and ducere "lead"): philosophical and scientific method that infers from a special case to generality; inductions are correct, until one case is found that proves them wrong[132].

- Deduction (from Latin de "from" and ducere "lead"): philosophical and scientific method that infers from generality to a special case; deductive methods are only plausible in natural sciences and mathematics[133].

- Abduction (from Latin ab "from" and ducere "lead"): philosophical and scientific method that infers from the result, given the rule, towards the premise, from the effect towards the cause[134].

Induction and Abduction process rules from right to left, Deduction from left to right[135]. In classic AI, the concept of blind or heuristic searching first tackled the finding of new intelligence; in fact, almost every problem can be mapped to some kind of search query[136]. Whether to find a satisfying result or not depends on

- The quality of the modeled knowledge base

- The expressiveness of the latter

- The reasonability of the posed question

- The power of the querying technology

One point has to be added to the quality of the modeled knowledge base: so far - and this has been one of the major problems of AI - we are dealing with models that are limited by

---

[132]See [238], p. 333
[133]See [238], p. 121
[134]See [238], p. 2
[135]See [31], p. 18
[136]See [155], p. 40

the *"closed world assumption"*[137], because reality is by far more complex to be modeled. Until now, there has not been any chance of overcoming this. But given the tera-bytes of information from the internet, what potential would there be in a Semantic Web?

In the sub-sequent Chapters, querying technologies are discussed in general. Logic was chosen because of the fact that nearly all other Knowledge Representation Formalisms can be mapped to it[138], and Semantic Web based RDF Querying was chosen because of the State-of-the-Art importance and the fact, that nearly all technologies are based on RDF somehow.

B.3.1 Logic - Reasoning

The most prominent rules[139] in logical reasoning are

- Modus ponens: If an assertion A is true and A⇒B then B also is true.

- Modus tollens: If an assertion B is false and A⇒B then also A is false.

- And-Elimination: from a conjunction you can infer any of the conjuncts.

- Or-Introduction: from a sentence you can infer its disjunction with anything.

- Double-Negation-Elimination: from a doubly negated sentence you can infer a positive sentence.

- Unit resolution: from a disjunction, if one of the disjuncts is false, you can infer that the other one is true.

- Resolution: is the most complex rule. Resolution can also be called "proof by contradiction", because the posed question onto the knowledge base is negated. If the resolution process results in a contradiction, the negated statement is false and hence the question is true. In order to use resolution, first, everything has to be transformed into logic clauses. Then, the negated question clause is added to the knowledge base. Recursively clauses are resolved using substitution[140] and unification[141]. If a contradiction is reached, the compared clauses can be eliminated,

---

[137]See [31], p. 114

[138]See Chapter B.2.2.1

[139]Rules are classes of inference, established to reach soundness of querying results. Rules are patterns of inference that infer without the tedious process of building truth tables, see [231], p. 171

[140]The process of substituting variables with literals.

[141]In order to determine contradictions, predicates literals have to be matched. Unification is the recursive process that compares predicates together with arguments beginning from the left side until there is no remaining element resulting in a contradiction or not. See [225], p.154.

because a statement cannot be true and false at the same time. The process ends, when there is nothing left to unify or substitute, no progress can be made or a canceling criterion is reached.

Reasoning in Logic has tremendous advantages from the view of existing and tested implementations, e.g. PROgramming in Logic[142] (PROLOG) and a GNU public license API SWI-PROLOG (http://www.swi-prolog.org/).

B.3.2 Semantic Web based RDF Querying

Querying ontological knowledge bases in the Semantic Web is even more in the beginnings than ontology engineering itself. It is to be considered positive, that RDF is based on First-order Logic, Description Logics or F-Logic[143] (DAML+OIL, OWL), which already brings up interesting tools to combine RDF and logic reasoning[144]. Other approaches include:

- **RDF Query and Sesame[145]:**
  RDF documents may be queried at three different levels:

  - Syntactic level: the RDF document is queried with an XML query language (e.g. XQuery). Drawback: only XML tree-structured information can be retrieved, RDF-model information cannot.

  - Structure level: the RDF document is syntactically queried according to RDF structure (predicate calculus, triples). No semantic information can be retrieved.

  - Semantic level: not the document itself but the RDF(S) graph is queried, including automatic inference of new statements during querying. RDF Query Language (RQL)[146] is used for this purpose.
    Querying the knowledge base with RQL is made possible by the Sesame[147] architecture - a generic architecture for storing, managing and querying RDF based data. All data storage functions are encapsulated in the Storage and Inference Layer (SAIL), that consists of an RQL query engine, an RDF admin module and an RDF export module.

---

[142]Note that PROLOG does not fully conform to formal Logic.
[143]F-Logic is based on declarative concepts and object-oriented taxonomies.
[144]See [323]
[145]See [40], pp. 71-91
[146]See [158]
[147]See [12]

- QuizRDF[148]:

  is a search engine, that combines free-text and RDF-based queries. RDFS is used
  as an indexing technology for the web interface, that searches for ontological information from the RDFS information together with well-known functionalities from
  classic search engines (case matches, match words exactly, etc.).

- RDF Query Exchange Language (RDF-QEL-i):

  is a key technology within the Edutella project (http://edutella.jxta.org/)
  that is dealing with meta-data for Peer-to-Peer networks, focusing on E-Learning
  technologies. *"The Edutella Query Exchange Language and the Edutella common
  data model provide the syntax and semantics for an overall standard query interface
  across heterogeneous peer repositories for any kind of RDF meta-data. The Edutella
  network uses the query exchange language family RDF-QEL-i (based on Datalog semantics and subsets thereof) as standardized query exchange language format which
  is transmitted in an RDF/XML-format"*. Design criteria for RDF QEL-i include
  Standard Semantics, Expressiveness, Adaptability and Transformability. In terms
  of expressiveness, RDF-QEL-i exists on five different levels, where level 1 is the
  simplest and level 5 supports highest expressiveness.

B.3.3   Querying methods in a nutshell

Chapter B.3.1 very briefly introduced the main concepts in Logic-based reasoning presenting the main rules needed. Chapter B.3.2 showed the current approaches[149] in Semantic
Web, clearly pointing out the non-maturity of the field. What can be stated though is,
that the Semantic Web techniques will rely on two things:

- Logic as the basis for reasoning

- RDF and RDFS as the main elements for the technological infrastructure

So far, no real standard querying language has been proposed and it will still take some
time, until agents process data on the internet intelligently.

---

[148]See [61], pp. 133-145

[149]The presented technologies and approaches are not exhaustive. Several others exist. Hence, it is only
a demonstrative and selective list.

B.4 Existing Tools

A vast number of tools provide features to represent and query a knowledge base in form
of ontological descriptions. The focus of the list given lies on incorporation of Semantic
Web technologies and is to be seen as a demonstrative enumeration. Table B.4 captures
this list.

The tools in Table B.4 are considered to be the most important ones. Other tools can be
found in the following surveys:

- `http://xml.coverpages.org/Denny-OntologyEditorSurveyTable20021111.htm l`

- `http://www.daml.org/tools`

- `http://www.daml.org/tools/`

- `http://139.91.183.30:9090/RDF/references.html#query`

- Tools according to Hjelm[150]

- XML authoring tools like Altova XMLSPY (`http://www.altova.com/products_id e.html`) or upcoming MS Infopath (`http://msdn.microsoft.com/library/defaul t.asp?url=/library/en-us/odc_ip2003_ta/html/odc_intechov.asp`) do not provide RDF(S) interfaces and are therefore not mentioned here.

ADONIS meta-modeling platform; ADVISOR	`http://www.boc-eu.com/english/adonis/adonis.shtml` The ADONIS meta-modeling platform is based on a meta-model compiler that enables online creation of modeling methods from a meta2-model. These modeling methods can be mapped to any ontology that can be represented in a graph-based style. ADONIS has got a proprietary interface called ADONIS Definition language (ADL). ADONIS is a commercial product.

---

[150]See [113], Chapter 10

Amaya and Annotea	http://www.w3.org/Amaya/ and http://www.w3.org/2001/Annotea/ Amaya and Annotea are both projects launched by the W3C to enforce the creation of the Semantic Web. Amaya is a Web editor to create and update documents on the web. Furthermore, Amaya includes Annotea, a collaborative application environment that is based on RDF in order to annotate the created documents with meta-data. Both Amaya and Annotea are free and open source products.
IMS Content Packaging editors	The Semantic Web ideas and the concept of ontologies have yet not been adapted by E-Learning. Still, standards and specifications with XML bindings exist. Some of them are supported by annotation tools. The IMS Global Consortium (http://www.imsglobal.org) recommends three tools for the IMS Content Packaging specifications: Sun LOM-IMS XML Toolkit http://www.imsglobal.org/tools/LOM-IMSXMLToolkit1_0.zip), Microsoft LRN Toolkit 3.0 (http://www.microsoft.com/eLearn/), Educational Content Packager or EC-Pac (http://www.met.ed.ac.uk/pac-man/editor/). The RELOAD Package Editor (http://www.reload.ac.uk/editor.html) is an open source meta-data editor in the field of E-Learning. All editors are available free.
Jena Semantic Web Toolkit	http://www.hpl.hp.com/semweb/index.htm Hewlett-Packard is very engaged in creating Semantic Web compliant tools. Core applications are provided by the Jena Semantic Web toolkit, Joseki, an experimental WebAPI for the Jena RDF framework, and Brown-Sauce RDF Browser, an experimental generic RDF browser. Jena is a Java-based API that supports statement-centric processing of RDF documents. Semantic support for RDFS or DAML is currently under development; DAML ontologies may be imported and stored in a Jena compliant model. Jena is an open-source project.

KAON	http://kaon.semanticweb.org/ "KAON is an open-source ontology management infrastructure targeted for business applications. It includes a comprehensive tool suite allowing easy ontology creation and management, as well as building ontology-based applications". Tools include an engineering server, KAON API, KAON portal, KAON Query, KAON server, KAON views, OI-modeler, ontology registry, ON-TOMAT SOEP, RDF API, RDF server and TEXT-TO-ONTO. KAON is an open-source project.
LOOM	http://www.isi.edu/isd/LOOM/LOOM-HOME.html LOOM is a model-based knowledge representation system and was developed by the University of Southern California (http://www.usc.edu/). Representation and reasoning technology is based on description logic and is named after the project itself LOOM. LOOM is related to the Knowledge Interchange Format (KIF) (http://logic.stanford.edu/kif/specification.html). LOOM tools are available for free.
Mewforge	Mewforge is an RDF annotation tool created at the Vienna University of Economics and Business Administration (http://www.wu-wien.ac.at/). Mewforge is based on the script language XOTcl (http://www.xotcl.org) and is a web forms prototype for editing RDF data on the basis of a provided RDF data model. Download is not available.
OntoBroker	http://www.ontoprise.de/ OntoBroker is the main element in an architecture that enables ontology management, engineering and reasoning by processing knowledge models. Other tools that belong to the architecture are OntoEdit, for creating ontologies on the basis of Semantic Web technologies, OntoAnnotate, an intuitive document annotation tool, SemanticMiner, a knowledge retrieving component, and OntoOffice. OntoBroker tools and related research were developed at the University of Karlsruhe (http://ontoweb.aifb.uni-karlsruhe.de). OntoEdit is available for free (limited concepts).

OntoBuilder	http://www.cs.msstate.edu/ gmodica/Education/OntoBuilder OntoBuilder is a browser-based Java-Applet for creating and editing ontologies. OntoBuilder uses a proprietary XML (XML++) format to manage ontologies. Future works include the import and export of DAML+OIL compliant ontologies. OntoBuilder was developed at the Michigan State University. OntoBuilder is available free.
Ontolingua	http://www.ksl.stanford.edu/software/ontolingua/ and http://www.ksl.stanford.edu/software/chimaera/ Ontolingua was developed by the Stanford University and serves as a distributed collaborative environment to browse, create, edit, modify, and use ontologies. On top of Ontolingua, Chimaera supports users in creating and maintaining distributed ontologies on the web, which includes functionalities like loading knowledge bases in differing formats, reorganizing taxonomies, resolving name conflicts, browsing ontologies, editing terms, etc. Ontolingua and Chimaera are Web-based systems for editing ontologies. Download is not available.
PROTÉGÉ	http://protege.stanford.edu/index.html PROTÉGÉ is a tool developed by the University of Stanford, which allows the user to construct a domain ontology, customize knowledge-acquisition forms, enter domain knowledge, a platform, which can be extended with graphical widgets for tables, diagrams, animation components to access other knowledge-based systems embedded applications, and a library, which other applications can use to access and display knowledge bases. PROTÉGÉ is available free.
VUE	http://at.tccs.tufts.edu/publications/current-online-edition/16/ Visual Understanding Environment (VUE) is being developed at Tufts University (http://www.tufts.edu). It provides a visual interface to gather and organize Tufts digital library information into learning content maps. Download or additional information is not available.

Table B.4: List of tools for representing and querying
ontologies

B.5 Summary

This Chapter was dedicated to presenting a historical evolution of Knowledge Representation Formalisms. Dating back to ancient philosophers, the technique of describing artifacts with standard languages gets of great importance in the ages of the Semantic Web, where humans and machines have to communicate to a mutual benefit. Furthermore, the concepts of describing knowledge build the foundation for the Modeling Methods eduWeaver and DKElearn.

Appendix C

Backloading

This Chapter is dedicated to the concept of Backloading in detail that has already been briefly discussed in Chapter 5.3.2.

C.1 Chapter Outline

This Chapter is dedicated to a special focus on a concept and an accompanying Test-Bed in the context of a Document-centric Learning scenario as depicted in Figure C.1.

It starts out with general statements about Blended Learning and embeds an actual scenario taken from the University of Vienna to show the contemporary relevance of Backloading. In the following, the concept of Backloading is scrutinized and concrete added value arguments are given to show the urgency for such a concept in today's European Educational Institutions. Eventually, the concept and the embedded University scenario are demonstrated with the help of a Test-Bed with the help of a Transformation Tool for MS PowerPoint slides.

C.2 Blended Learning Scenarios

A historical overview of the developments surrounding Learning supported with Educational Technologies has already been given in Chapter 2.2. This Chapter has shown the diversity and the multitute of existing approaches and definitions of electronically supported Learning. Chapter 2.2.4 defined E-Learning as an analogy to the definition of E-Business: *"E-Learning is the support or combination of 'normal learning' with the help of electronic means, especially with the use of internet technologies"*. This very general - almost superficial - definition shall be sufficient in this context.

One other "popular" technical terminus has to be defined though as well, and that is

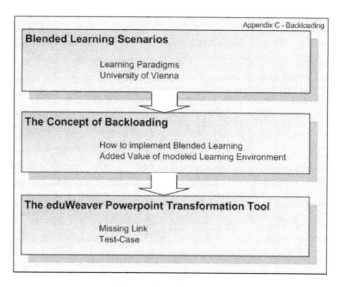

Figure C.1: Overview

the term Blended Learning. Blended Learning can be defined as *Learning and Teaching concepts that combine reasonable didactical scenarios as a concatenation of traditional classroom learning with virtual or online learning based on ICT"*[1].

Especially in an academic context and existing Universities pure E-Learning courses do and will not exist in the near future, whereas Universities definitely will have to look after their Blended Learning support as they are competing with numerous other Universities in the context of *e*Europe[2]. The situation of the University of Vienna is taken as an example in this context and will be further discussed in Chapter C.2.2.

In a way, this methodology reflects a Blended Learning Paradigm, because actual classroom lectures can be planned beforehand and additional and existing resources have to be added during the course of the mentioned lecture.

C.2.1 Learning vs. E-Learning vs. Blended Learning vs. Lifelong Learning

A lot of different aspects and dimensions have been already presented in this thesis that define a Learning scenario with the help of Educational Technologies. An E-Learning

---

[1]See [249], p. 23
[2]See Chapter 3.4

Framework merged and compiled these dimensions into a coherent conceptual approach from which many scenarios and a Roadmap to future Semantic Learning have been outlined. The two intermediate steps on the way have been defined as Document-centric and Resource-driven Learning where Document-centric Learning has a management and planning focus and Resource-driven Learning copes with Learning Pools and interdependencies between LOs. Actually, these paradigms have to be mixed into Blended Learning especially in the context of the requirements of the University of Vienna. Backloading can be seen as a missing link to merge these approaches. On the one hand, management decisions and support for better evaluation have to be provided from the top-level management, and on the other hand professional domain experts like professors and instructors have to be supported in a way that their existing resources can easily be combined and reused in an E-Learning context. The added value emerges in the "collision" of these both paradigms and make up a holistic Learning scenario that also offers several by-products. The "Normal" methodology of the Document-centric instance eduWeaver as depicted in Figure 5.3 follows a Top-Down approach first defining Lectures and Modules and gradually refining them until the granularity of LOs is reached. Unfortunately, such a methodology often cannot be accomplished, because legacy applications and/or resources have to be considered as they form the organizational memory of an institutiont to a great extent. Therefore this knowledge arising from a Resource-driven approach has to be tackled in the first place with the help of a Bottom-Up integration support so that Top-Down strategies and learning processes are able to plug-into this environment on a certain level forming a coherent overall picture.

With such a hybrid approach, nearly all paradigms can be integrated: Learning and E-Learning take respective parts of a Blended Learning approach on the way to future or Life-long Learning filling all dimensions of the E-Learning Framework.

C.2.2 The situation at the University of Vienna

Taking these restrictions into account, a concrete scenario coming from the University of Vienna shall illustrate the problem dimensions. The encountered situation comprises of the following:

- 17 Faculties ranging from theological faculty, faculty of physics to faculty of informatics[3]

- Different Peers with different interests

---

[3]See http://www.univie.ac.at/implementierung/fakultaeten.html

- Complex organizational structure (organizational management, academic management, organizational staff, academic staff, etc.)

- About 4800 employees (academic staff) and 63000 students to manage[4]

These statistical figures have to be well considered when the University of Vienna suddenly is confronted with New Media and Educational Technologies. It is in the eye of the author that a generic approach for support of the Technology Dimension is the only way of bridging the gap between organizational needs and motivation for the employees to use the new mechanisms and see them as a benefit and not as an instrument to control someone.

In this context, eduWeaver and the Backloading concept are presented in order to provide this generic language to integrate different and multiple views. It was tested prototypically in various domains like Theoretical Chemistry, Business Administration and of course Business Informatics to show the feasibility and the generic design potential.

C.3 The Concept of Backloading

The concept of Backloading was borrowed digital archiving from the task of scanning large amounts of documents into an electronic form with one specific difference: Backloading in an educational context not only has the task of digitizing analog documents but transforming existing digital documents into a generic format so that different learning scenarios can be produced together with some by-products. Backloading can be defined as the structured transformation of digital documents (especially MS PowerPoint slides) into a generic information format with preserving as much semantics as possible.

As already mentioned, Backloading is the borderline between Top-Down driven Document-centric Learning with focus on management and design and Bottom-Up Resource-driven Learning that encourages domain experts to incorporate their PowerPoint slides into an organizational memory with the obvious added-value of an automatic and "two-click" transformation into an LMS.

C.3.1 How to implement Blended Learning

Many unexperienced domain experts are suddenly facing new technologies and buzzword like E-Learning. But they cannot be forced to adapt their teaching based long term experiences without being given motivation and added value and sense for using

---

[4]See http://www.univie.ac.at/organisationshandbuch/Allgemeines/vorstellung.html

new technologies. The question therefore is how to actually implement the Backloading concept.

Two possible ways can be identified:

1. Directly backload transformed PowerPoint slides into a target learning system

2. Backload the transformed PowerPoint slides into a generic format so that re-context-ualization is still possible

Given the two enumerations, one looks like a quick win, because the problem is easy to implement as only the method of transformating the slides is the bottleneck; re-contextualizing it into an XML application like an IMS Content Package is a matter of easy programming and XSLT. But a number of drawbacks arise from this approach, as the following Chapter clearly points out. The second way - also identifying the slide-transformation as the hard part - seems tedious because an intermediary step is needed, but in the end proves to be the better choice.

C.3.2 Added Value of modeled Learning Environment - By-Products

In the context of Backloading, the discussion of sense and added-value in order to motivate such a scenario is indispensable.

	Direct Backloading	Generic Backloading
Inter-operability	Content and structure reside in an XML application. The semantics of this application is defined according to E-Learning standards and specifications and therefore is dependent on them. In course of (likely) changes interoperability cannot be served.	Content and structure are described generically by the visual design modeling methods (like eduWeaver). The information is independent of standards and specifications; the semantics of the application is defined according to domain requirements. In case of changes in standards and specifications, re-contextualization is possible, therefore interoperability is guaranteed.

Possibility to re-context-ualize	Re-contextualization is possible on the basis of a new PowerPoint Transformation algorithm or in ways of transforming the XML application. Concerning both of these arguments, new code has to be written and the resulting application again is not interoperable. Note, that information is likely to be lost due to many transformation steps.	Re-contextualization is possible. All information given by the domain defined structure is maintained in the visually designed models. In case of re-contextualization transformation algorithms have to be changed without loss of information.
Flexibility through generic structure	The structure of the XML application is not generic but pre-defined by non domain-experts. Flexibility is low.	The structure of the transformed information into generic models semantically maps to the domain requirements. Flexibility is high.
By-Products	By-Products only in the course of programming with the drawback mentioned in "Possibility to re-contextualize.	The generic model-information can be basis for re-contextualization as is in many different scenarios: basis for Knowledge Balance, basis for didactical transformations, basis for quality assurance like ISO 900x, basis for documentation like automatically created schedules or comments for students, etc.

Table C.1: Direct vs. Generic Backloading

Arguments for pros and cons resulting from the described ways in the latter Chapter can be summarized in Table C.1.

Backloading not only represents a missing link technologically as described in Chapter C.4.1 but also in the context of the E-Learning Framework as described in Chapter 3. Thinking of the By-Products like a Knowledge Balance, the Technology Dimension servers as data provider for the Management Dimension of the E-Learning Framework and thus enriches the Framework to become more powerful on the way to future learning according to the E-Learning Roadmap.

Added values for participating roles like instructors, managers and administrators were already mentioned in Chapter 5.3.2.

C.4 The eduWeaver Powerpoint Transformation Tool

Having talked about Blended Learning scenarios especially in the context of the University of Vienna and the concept of Backloading, this Chapter is dedicated to the subsumption yielding into the actual implementation, the so called PowerPoint Transformation Tool. Prerequisites for the PowerPoint Transformation Tool are:

- MS Windows operating system (tested on MS Windows XP)

- MS PowerPoint (tested with MS Office 2002)

- MS .NET Framework 1.1 (or higher)

- Print Driver from `http://www.print-diver.com`

- "normal" PC desktop

The architecture of the Tool is depicted in Figure C.2 and represents a prototypical approach. Other external references to add information except from the DKElearn resources and the Amazon Web-Service are likely to be implemented in the future.

The architecture according to Figure C.2 is technologically made up of the following components:

- **PPT (Office)**: At the moment, only PowerPoint slides are supported as they are the prime medium of presenting teaching material in classic classroom education. In the future, MS Office products are likely to be integrated with the help of Backloading as well in a first step, and follow up materials may be of arbitrary format.

- **PowerPoint Transformation Tool**: The Transformation Tool works as described in this Chapter[5].

---

[5] The print.driver.com utilities provide a print driver that enables printing of pages into images.

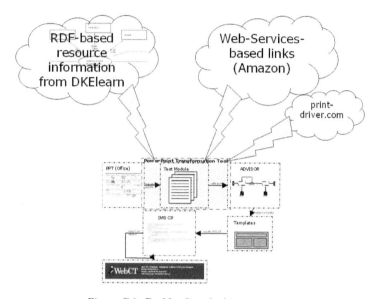

Figure C.2: Backloading Architecture

- **ADVISOR eduWeaver**: The visual modeling tool eduWeaver receives all information from the transformed PowerPoint slides in structure as well as the actual created LOs and visualizes the results. The imported models have to be linked to Modules. Re-engineering in eduWeaver may be done.

- **Templates**: The templates serve as basis for re-contextualization. At the moment, only an export to IMS Content Packages is available. Other templates are discussed in this Chapter.

    - **IMS Content Package**: IMS Content Packaging is a popular exchange format for LOs. Most of current LMS have implemented an IMS Content Package API.

- **WebCT LMS**: Any LMS with an IMS Content Packaging API is relevant for the final part of Backloading. The given scenario with focus at the University of Vienna defines WebCT as LMS.

Some drawbacks of the eduWeaver solution (i.e. impossibility of multiple numeric naming of LOs) and the IMS Content Package information model (i.e. parallel processes modeled in eduWeaver cannot be semantically expressed) were engaged in workaround solutions. The following enumeration lists these together with the functionality of the PowerPoint Transformation Tool.

- The creation of Text Modules was prototypically implemented with the semantically poor method of making a figure out of each slide

- An easy step-by-step wizard guides the user through the process of Backloading

  - Step 1: Choose PowerPoint File
  - Step 2: Specify Target Directory (with optional Semantic Web enrichment)
  - Step 3: LO Transformation
    * Creation of HTML files with the figures embedded
    * Creation of an eduWeaver compliant import file grasping the information and the structure as well as the actual resources

- eduWeaver steps

  - Import models
  - The renaming of the LO Usage and LO Pool models was chosen deliberately, because automatically created IDs would not have been sufficient in order to correctly semantically contextualize these two models into an actual course
  - The imported models can be fit into the given context by referencing the imported models

- Drawbacks for the resulting IMS-Content Package export

  - Unique GUIDs were chosen for LOs
  - Complex eduWeaver processes are transformed into simple hierarchic structure

C.4.1 Missing Link between Document-centric and Resource-driven Learning

As already mentioned, Document-centric and Resource-driven Learning collide methodology-wise with the use of a Backloading concept. The Transformation Tool goes one step further and also shows integration of both aspects technology-wise adding RDF-based resource-information from the DKElearn Modeling Environment from Chapter 6 and Web-Services-based links coming from existing Amazon Web-Services[6] to the IMS Content Package compliant eduWeaver models.

The Transformation Tool enables the user with the two mentioned add-ons to enrich the eduWeaver models with additional information coming from the

---

[6]See http://www.amazon.com/gp/aws/download_sdk.html/

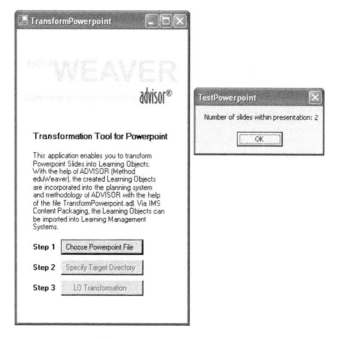

Figure C.3: Step 1: Choose PowerPoint File

- **Semantic Web**: Resources modeled in a DKElearn environment can be included together with semantic information about the creator of the resource. Such a scenario can be seen as a reasonable Semantic Web implementation, because not only the resource itself can be retrieved but also information about the resource.

- **Amazon Web-Services**: It can also be reasonabel to add information about literature to given resources. Therefore, the Amazon Web-Service was included to add information about related books.

C.4.2 Test Case

For the actual Test-Case an arbitrary PowerPoint File with two slides was created (`test.ppt`). The file was also uploaded to a web server and included in the DKElearn environment as a resource in order to be used as additional information for the Transformation Tool. Figure C.3 shows the Transformation Tool with the already mentioned buttons representing the three steps "Choose PowerPoint File", "Specify Target Directory" and "LO Transformation".

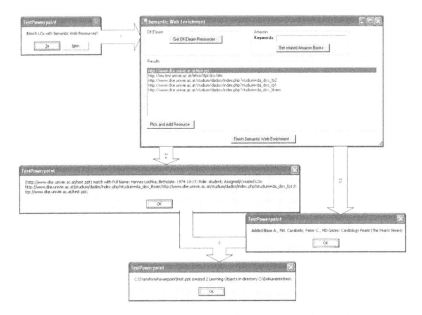

Figure C.4: Steps 2 and 3: Specify Target Directory and LO Transformation

At the end of Step 1, a messagebox displays the number of slides that are to be processed.

Figure C.4 depicts Step 2 after having chosen the target directory. The user now has the possibility either to continue without adding information or to enrich the LOs with information. The arrow marked with "1" depicts this step together with showing the interface. With the help of the two buttons "Get DKElearn Resources" or "Get related Amazon Books" the user may add additional information, that will be displayed in the Listbox below. By pressing the button "Pick and Add Resource" the chosen resources are added to a third html-file. Messageboxes marked with the arrows 2 a and 2 b display the results respectively. After pressing "Finish Semantic Web Enrichment", the third step "LO Transformation" rounds up the transformation process.

The messagebox informs the user on the created LOs and that an eduWeaver compliant *.adl file were created.

Figure C.5 displays the transformed and imported eduWeaver models, where two LOs result from the two PowerPoint slides and the third resource marks the LO with the additional information (note also the uniquely created names coming from the use of the mentioned GUIDs). The two models are concatenated via model references.

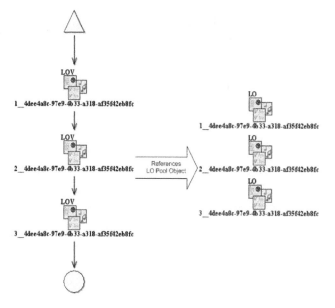

Figure C.5: Transformed LOs in eduWeaver

Figure C.5 displays the transformed and imported eduWeaver models, where two LOs result from the two PowerPoint slides and the third resource marks the LO with the additional information (note also the uniquely created names coming from the use of the mentioned GUIDs). The two models are concatenated via model references.

After creating IMS Content Packages with the export module of eduWeaver, Figure C.6 shows the result of the WebCT import process that is initiated with the command line API with the instruction

`cp_api.pl -action=import -course=Modul_M -pkgloc=IMS_root.zip`.

Finally, Figure C.7 shows the result in the LMS WebCT. The arrow marked 1 displays the relationship between the two transformed eduWeaver models, and arrow 3 displays

Figure C.6: WebCT Command Line Import API

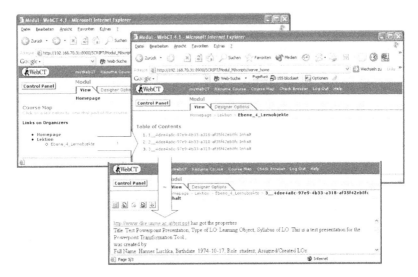

Figure C.7: The transformed LOs rendered in the WebCT template

the html-file of LO 3 representing the additional Semantic Web information coming from the DKElearn environment.

C.5 Summary

This Chapter presented the concept of Backloading as part of the Blended Learning paradigm. Furthermore, Backloading can be seen as a missing link on the way to a future learning paradigm according to the E-Learning Framework that was presented in this thesis both technologically and with respect to domain requirements.

Future efforts and developments concerning the Backloading concept and the PowerPoint Transformation Tool will focus on:

- Seamless integration of eduWeaver, the Transformation Tool and LMS like WebCT

- Use of semantically intelligent algorithms to extract relevant information into the LO transformation process

- Include more external Semantic Web applications to enrich the Backloading information

- Improve message and information exchange on the basis of XML or RDF and not on the basis of simple String-formats

- Find out about potential for mobile applications as both the DKElearn and the Amazon resources are executed via interoperable Web-Services

Bibliography

[1] S. D. Achtemeier, L. V. Morris, and C. L. Finnegan. Considerations for Developing Evaluations of Online Courses. *In: Journal of Asynchronous Learning Networks, vol. 7*, 2003.

[2] R. Ackoff. *Scientific Method*. John Wiley and Sons Ltd., 1962.

[3] S. Adkins. The Brave new World of Learning.
http://www.samadico.com/images/Adkins_TDmag_Workflow_June6.pdf, 2003/Aug/19th.

[4] ADL. Advanced Distributed Learning Network (ADLNet) - ADL Overview.
http://www.adlnet.org/index.cfm?fuseaction=abtadl, 2002/May/25th.

[5] ADL. The SCORM Content Aggregation Model.
http://www.adlnet.org/ADLDOCS/Document/SCORM_1.2_CAM.pdf, 2002/May/25th.

[6] ADL. The SCORM Overview.
http://www.adlnet.org/ADLDOCS/Document/SCORM_1.2_Overview.pdf, 2002/May/25th.

[7] ADL-Net. Advanced Distributed Learning - Home.
http://www.adlnet.org/, 2004/May/9th.

[8] D. Affeld. *Mit Best Practice im Supply Chain Management (SCM) zur Optimierung der Wertschöpfungskette*. In: Voegele, A. R. and Zeuch, M. P. (Eds.), Supply Network Management, Gabler Verlag, 2002.

[9] AICC. AICC FAQ.
http://www.aicc.org/pages/aicc_faq.htm, 2002/May/25th.

[10] AICC. CMI status.
http://www.aicc.org/docs/meetings/29jan2001/cmi.zip, 2002/May/25th.

[11] AICC. Types of AICC Publications.
http://www.aicc.org/pages/aicc3.htm#PUB1, 2002/May/25th.

[12] aidministrator nederland. aidministrator: Sesame.
http://sesame.aidministrator.nl/, 2003/Jul/14th.

[13] ANSI/NISO. Guidelines for the Construction, Format, and Management of Mono-
lingual Thesauri.
http://www.niso.org/standards/resources/Z39-19.pdf, 2003/Jun/22nd.

[14] ARIADNE. Presentation of the ARIADNE Foundation.
http://www.ariadne-eu.org/1_AF/1.1_Presentation/main.html#Top,
2002/May/25th.

[15] ARIADNE. The two ARIADNE Projects: A brief description.
http://www.ariadne-eu.org/4_AP/4.1_project/main.html, 2002/May/25th.

[16] ASTD. Achieving Interoperability in e-Learning.
http://www.learningcircuits.org/mar2000/singh.html, 2002/May/25th.

[17] ASTD. An Intro to Metadata Tagging.
http://www.learningcircuits.org/dec2000/dec2000_ttools.html#standards,
2002/May/25th.

[18] ASTD. E-Learning Glossary.
http://www.learningcircuits.org/glossary.html, 2002/May/25th.

[19] ASTD. Standards: The Vision and the Hype.
http://www.learningcircuits.org/nov2000/standards.html, 2002/May/25th.

[20] Andrea Back, Oliver Bendel, and Damiel Stoller-Schai. *E-Learning im Unternehmen.* orell füssli; Zürich, 2001.

[21] J. Bajnai, D. Chalaris, G.and Karagiannis, and J. Lischka. The Virtual Global
University: A Case Study. *In: RiedlIng, E. (Ed.): Proceedings of VIEWDET 2002,
Vienna International Working Conference - eLearning and eCulture, published by
OCG*, 2002.

[22] J. Bajnai and J. Lischka. Planning and Simulation in an E-Learning Engineering
Framework. *Proceedings of the EDMEDIA 2004*, 2004.

[23] J. Bajnai and C. Steinberger. eduWeaver The web-based Courseware Design Tool. *Proceedings of WWW/Internet 2003*, pages 659–666, 2003.

[24] P. Baumgartner. Informations - und Kommunikationstechnologien und Schulentwicklung in der Wissensgesellschaft.
http://www.peter.baumgartner.name/Filer/filetree/peter/articles/esslingen-oecd.pdf, 2004/Jul/06th.

[25] J. Becker and G. Vossen. *Geschäftsprozeßmodellierung und Workflow-Management: Eine Einführung.* In: Vossen, G. and Becker, J.; Geschäftsprozeßmodellierung und Workflow Management; International Thomson Publishing, 1996.

[26] D. Beckett, E. Miller, and D. Brickley. Expressing Simple Dublin Core in RDF/XML.
http://www.dublincore.org/documents/dcmes-xml/, 2004/Jul/13rd.

[27] D. Beimborn, S. Minert, and T. Weitzel. Web Services und ebXML. *In: Wirtschaftsinformatik, 44. Jahrgang, Heft 3/2002*, 2002.

[28] T. Berners-Lee. *Foreword.* In: Fensel, D. and Hendler, J. and Lieberman, H. and Wahlster, W.; Spinning the Semantic Web; MIT Press, Cambridge (MA), 2003.

[29] T. Berners-Lee, J. Hendler, and O. Lassila. The Semantic Web - A new form of Web content that is meaningful to computers will unleash a revolution of new possibilities.
http://www.sciam.com/article.cfm?articleID=00048144-10D2-1C70-84A9809EC588EF21, 2002/Dec/17th.

[30] P. Bernus and L. Nemes. A Framework to Define a Generic Enterprise Reference Architecture and Methodology.
http://www.cit.gu.edu.au/ bernus/taskforce/geram/report.v1/report/report.html, 2004/May/9th.

[31] W. Bibel, S. Hölldobler, and T. Schaub. *Wissensrepräsentation und Inferenz.* vieweg, 1993.

[32] Blackboard. Course and Portal Solutions.
http://products.blackboard.com/cp/bb5/access/faqs.cgi, 2002/May/25th.

[33] BM:BWK. Bundesgesetz über die Organisation der Universitäten und ihre Studien (Universitätsgesetz 2002).

http://www.bmbwk.gv.at/universitaeten/recht/gesetze/ug02/Universitaetsgesetz_2
0027724.xml, 2004/Jul/13rd.

[34] BOC. ADVISOR.
http://www.boc-eu.com/advisor/start.html, 2002/May/25th.

[35] BOC. PROMOTE.
http://www.boc-eu.com/promote, 2003/Jan/10th.

[36] BOC. BOC Information Technologies Consulting.
http://www.boc-eu.com/english/index.shtml/adonis.shtml, 2003/Jan/20th.

[37] K. Bormann. *Platon: Die Idee.* In: Speck, J.; Grundprobleme der großen
Philosophen - Philosophie des Altertums und des Mittelalters; UTB Vandenhoeck,
2nd edition, 1978.

[38] J. Bortz and N. Döring. *Forschungmethoden und Evaluation.* 3rd. edition, Springer,
2002.

[39] R. J. Brachman and H. J. Levesque. *Readings in Knowledge Representation.* In:
Brachman, R. J. and Levesque, H. J.; Readings in Knowledge Representation; Morgan Kaufmann Publishers Inc., 1985.

[40] J. Broekstra, A. Kampman, and F. van Harmelen. *Sesame: A Generic Architecture
for Storing and Querying RDF and RDF Schema.* In: Davies, J. and Fensel, D.
and van Harmelen, F.; Towards the Semantic Web - Ontology-Driven Knowledge
Management; John Wiley and Sons Ltd., 2003.

[41] H.-J. Bullinger, K. Wörner, and Prieto J. *Wissensmanagement. Modelle und Strate-
gien für die Praxis.* In Bürgel, H.-D. (Ed.), Wissensmanagement. Schritte zum
intelligenten Unternehmen. Berlin, 1998.

[42] W. Büttemeyer. *Wissenschaftstheorie für Informatik.* Spektrum akademischer Verlag, 1995.

[43] F. Cardinali. Keynote address held at E-Learning Results 2004.
http://www.elearningresults.com/ppt/OPENING/2, 2004/May/24th.

[44] CEN. Learning Technologies Workshop homepage.
http://www.cenorm.be/isss/Workshop/lt/, 2002/May/25th.

[45] CEN. Objectives and principles of CEN.
http://www.cenorm.be/aboutcen/whatis/objectives.htm, 2002/May/25th.

[46] CEN. Organization.
http://www.cenorm.be/isss/About_ISSS/organization.htm, 2002/May/25th.

[47] E. Cerami. *Web Service Essentials.* O'Reilly; USA, 2002.

[48] P.-A. Champin. RDF Tutorial.
http://www710.univ-lyon1.fr/~champin/rdf-tutorial/rdf-tutorial.pdf,
2003/Jul/30th.

[49] P.-A. Champin, J. Euzenat, and A. Mille. Why URLs are good URIs, and why they are not.
http://www710.univ-lyon1.fr/ champin/urls, 2003/Jul/30th.

[50] E. Charniak and D. McDermott. *Introduction to Artificial Intelligence.* Addison-Wesley Publishing Company, 1985.

[51] K. Chmielewicz. *Forschungskonzeption der Wirtschaftswissenschaft.* C. E. Poeschel Verlag, Stuttgart, 1979.

[52] CIMOSA-Association. CIMSOA.
http://www.cimosa.de/About_us.htm, 2004/May/9th.

[53] J. Clement. Learning via Model Construction and Criticism: Protocol Evidence on Sources of Creativity in Science. *In: J. A. Glover, R. R. Ronning, and C. R. Reynolds (eds), Handbook of Creativity: Assessment, Theory and Research (New York: Plenum Press), 341-381,* 1989.

[54] DAML Services Coalition. DAML-S: Web Service Description for the Semantic Web.
http://www.daml.org/services/ISWC2002-DAMLS.pdf, 2003/Jan/4th.

[55] Edward J. Cohen. The Emerging Standards Effort in E-Learning.
http://www.elearningmag.com/elearning/article/articleDetail.jsp?id=6787,
2002/May/25th.

[56] Hewlett-Packard Company. Jena Semantic Web Toolkit.
http://www.hpl.hp.com/semweb/jena.htm, 2003/Aug/19th.

[57] MASIE E-Learning Consortium. Making Sense of Learning Specifications and Standards: A Decision Maker's Guide to their Adoption.
http://www.masie.com/standards/S3_Guide.pdf, 2002/May/25th.

[58] DAML. DAML Language.
http://www.daml.org/language/, 2003/Jul/4th.

[59] DAML. DAML-ONT Initial Release.
http://www.daml.org/2000/10/daml-ont.html, 2003/Jul/9th.

[60] J. Davies, D. Fensel, and F. van Harmelen. *Introduction.* In: Davies, J. and Fensel, D. and van Harmelen, F.; Towards the Semantic Web - Ontology-Driven Knowledge Management; John Wiley and Sons Ltd., 2003.

[61] J. Davies, R. Weeks, and U. Krohn. *QuizRDF: Search Technology for the Semantic Web.* In: Davies, J. and Fensel, D. and van Harmelen, F.; Towards the Semantic Web - Ontology-Driven Knowledge Management; John Wiley and Sons Ltd., 2003.

[62] DCMI. About the Dublin Core Metadata Initiative (DCMI).
http://dublincore.org/about/, 2002/May/25th.

[63] DCMI. DCMI Organization.
http://dublincore.org/about/organization/, 2002/May/25th.

[64] DCMI. Dublin Core Metadata Initiative (DCMI) Frequently Asked Questions (FAQ).
http://dublincore.org/resources/faq/#whatismetadata, 2002/May/25th.

[65] DCMI. Dublin Core Metadata Initiative (DCMI) Frequently Asked Questions (FAQ).
http://dublincore.org/resources/faq/#whatismetadata, 2002/May/25th.

[66] DCMI. Dublin Core Qualifiers.
http://dublincore.org/documents/2000/07/11/dcmes-qualifiers/, 2002/May/25th.

[67] DCMI. Glossary.
http://dublincore.org/documents/2001/04/12/usageguide/glossary.shtml#Q, 2002/May/25th.

[68] DCMI. Expressing Qualified Dublin Core in RDF / XML.
http://www.dublincore.org/documents/dcq-rdf-xml/, 2003/Aug/19th.

[69] DCMI. Expressing Simple Dublin Core in RDF/XML.
http://www.dublincore.org/documents/2002/07/31/dcmes-xml/, 2003/Aug/19th.

[70] DCMI. Expressing Qualified Dublin Core in RDF / XML.
http://dublincore.org/documents/2002/04/14/dcq-rdf-xml/, 2003/Jul/30th.

[71] DCMI. Memorandum of Understanding between the Dublin Core Metadata Initiative and the IEEE Learning Technology Standards Committee.
http://dublincore.org/documents/2000/12/06/dcmi-ieee-mou/, 2003/Jul/30th.

[72] DCMI. Dublin Core Metadata Initiative (DCMI).
http://dublincore.org/, 2003/Jul/9th.

[73] L. M. DeRijk. *Aristotle - Semantics and Ontology (Volume 1)*. Brill, 2002.

[74] DigitalThink. DigitalThink: Solutions: Products and Services: Enterprise Gateway.
http://www.digitalthink.com/solutions/products/platform/, 2002/May/25th.

[75] Prof. Dr. Ullrich (Hrsg.) Dittler. *E-Learning*. Oldenbourg, 2002.

[76] J. J. Donovan. *Business Re-Engineering with Information Technology*. Prentice Hall, Englewood Cliffs, New Jersey, 1994.

[77] G. Dorffner. *Konnektionismus*. Teubner, 1. edition, Stuttgart, 1991.

[78] M. Dose. *DUDEN - Das Fremdwörterbuch*, volume 5. Meyers Lexikonverlag, Mannheim-Leipzig-Wien-Zürich, 5th edition edition, 1990.

[79] Erik Duval. Learning Technology Standardization: Too Many? Too Few?
http://www.rz.uni-frankfurt.de/neue_medien/standardisierung/duval_text.pdf,
2002/May/25th.

[80] Engineering E-Learning. Engineering E-Learning.
http://www.elearning-engineering.com/learning/e-learning/engineering-elearning.htm, 2003/Nov/14th.

[81] ebXML.org. ebXML - Enabling A Global Electronic Market - General Information.
http://www.ebxml.org/geninfo.htm, 2003/Jan/6th.

[82] ebXML.org. ebXML Integrates SOAP Into Messaging Services Specification.
http://www.ebxml.org/news/pr_20010222.htm, 2003/Jan/7th.

[83] EducaNext. The EducaNext Portal for Learning Resources.
http://www.educanext.org/ubp, 2004/Jul/13rd.

[84] W. Emde. *Modellbildung, Wissensrevision und Wissensrepräsentation im Maschinellen Lernen.* Springer Verlag Berlin, 1991.

[85] Thomas Engelmann. *Business process reengineering: Grundlagen - Gestaltungsempfehlungen - Vorgehensmodell.* Wiesbaden, 1995.

[86] Enhydra.org. The home of kSOAP at Enhydra.org.
http://ksoap.enhydra.org/, 2003/Aug/19th.

[87] European-Commission. Knowledge Society - Homepage.
http://europa.eu.int/comm/employment_social/knowledge_society/index_en.htm,
2004/Jul/13rd.

[88] European-Commission. Making a European Area of Lifelong Learning a Reality.
http://europa.eu.int/comm/education/policies/lll/life/communication/com_en.pdf,
2004/Jul/13rd.

[89] European-Commission. The eLearning Action Plan.
http://europa.eu.int/eur-lex/en/com/cnc/2001/com2001_0172en01.pdf,
2004/May/16th.

[90] European-Union. ECTS - European Credit Transfer System.
http://europa.eu.int/comm/education/programmes/socrates/ects_en.html,
2004/Jul/12th.

[91] European-Union. The Bologna Declaration on the European space for higher
education: an explanation.
http://europa.eu.int/comm/education/policies/educ/bologna/bologna.pdf,
2004/Jul/12th.

[92] D. Fensel, J. Hendler, H. Lieberman, and W. Wahlster. *Introduction.* In: Fensel, D.
and Hendler, J. and Lieberman, H. and Wahlster, W.; Spinning the Semantic Web;
MIT Press, Cambridge (MA), 2003.

[93] D. Fensel, F. van Harmelen, and I. Horrocks. *OIL and DAML+OIL: Ontology
Languages for the Semantic Web.* In: Davies, J. and Fensel, D. and van Harmelen,
F.; Towards the Semantic Web - Ontology-Driven Knowledge Management; John
Wiley and Sons Ltd., 2003.

[94] D. Fensel, F. van Harmelen, and H. Stuckenschmidt. The Semantic Web (Slides). http://informatik.uibk.ac.at/users/c70385/ftp/slides/kcap.pdf, 2003/Jul/9th.

[95] C. Floyd and R. Klischewski. *Modellierung - ein Handgriff zur Wirklichkeit.* In: Pohl, K. and Schürr, A. and Vossen, G.; Modellierung '98 - Proceedings; Universität Münster, Bericht # 6/98, S. 21-26, 1998.

[96] Robert Gagné. *The conditions of Learning and Theory of Instruction.* Holt, Rinehart and Winston, 1985.

[97] N. Génieux and D. Montel. *The Continuity between Design and Implementation.* In: Fischer, L.; Workflow Handbook 2003; Future Strategies Inc. and Book Division, Lighthouse Point, Florida, 2003.

[98] G. M. Giaglis. Integrated Design and Evaluation of Business Processes and Information Systems. *In: Communications of AIS Volume 2, Article 5*, 1999.

[99] A. S. Gibbons and E. Brewer. Elementary Principles of Design Languages and Design Notation Systems for Instructional Design. *In: Innovations to Instructional Technology: Essays in Honor of M. David Merrill, M. Spector and D. Wiley, Eds., New Jersey: Lawrence Erlbaum,* 2004.

[100] A. S. Gibbons, J. Nelson, and R. Richards. The Architecture of Instructional Simulation: A Design for Tool Construction. *Idaho National Engineering & Environmental Laboratory, Idaho Falls, Center for Human-System Simulation Technical Report,* 2000.

[101] M. Ginsberg. *Essentials of Artificial Intelligence.* Morgan Kaufmann Publishers, San Fransisco, 1993.

[102] KMR Group. RDF binding of IMS content packaging. http://kmr.nada.kth.se/el/ims/cp.html, 2003/Jul/28th.

[103] KMR Group. RDF binding of LOM metadata. http://kmr.nada.kth.se/el/ims/metadata.html, 2003/Jul/28th.

[104] T. R. Gruber. A translation approach to portable ontologies. http://ksl-web.stanford.edu/KSL_Abstracts/KSL-92-71.html; Knowledge Acquisition, 5(2):199-220, 1993, 2003/Jul/4th.

[105] I. Gruetzner, N. Niniek Angkasaputra, and D. Pfahl. A systematic approach to produce small courseware modules for combined learning and knowledge management environments. *In Proceedings of the 14th International conference on Software engineering and knowledge engineering, Ischia, Italy*, 2002.

[106] N. Guarino. *Formal Ontology and Information Systems*. In: Guarino, N.; Proceedings of FOIS '98; IOS Press, Amsterdam, pp. 3-15, 1998.

[107] M. Gutierrez-Diaz. Putting Results First: From Technical Innovation to European Strategies for wider eLearning, eContent & eKnowledge Adoption & Convergence towards the Knowledge Society (Keynote address held at E-Learning Results 2004). http://www.elearningresults.com/ppt/OPENING%20PLENARY/Maruja%20Gutie rrez%20Diaz/eLearning%20Results%202004%20mg%203.ppt, 2004/May/24th.

[108] Brandon Hall. *Six Steps to Developing a Successful E-Learning Initiative: Excerpts from the E-Learning Guidebook*. McGraw-Hill, 2002.

[109] Marion E. Haynes. *Project management: from idea to implementation*. London, 1995.

[110] M. Heidelberger. *Was erklärt uns die Informatik*. In: Schefe, P, Hastedt, H. and Dittrich, Y. and Keil, G;Informatik und Philosophie; BI Wissenschaftsverlag, 1994.

[111] Lutz J. Heinrich. Entwickeln von Informatik-Strategien - Vorgehensmodell und Fallstudien. http://www.swe.uni-linz.ac.at/publications/pdf/TR-SE-99.17.pdf, 2002/May/25th.

[112] Diane Hillman. Using Dublin Core. http://dublincore.org/documents/2001/04/12/usageguide/, 2002/May/25th.

[113] J. Hjelm. *Creating the Semantic Web with RDF*. John Wiley and Sons Ltd., 2001.

[114] IBM. Web services by IBM. http://www-3.ibm.com/software/solutions/webservices/overview.html, 2003/Jan/7th.

[115] IBM. Building Web Services the right way using IBM® WebSphere Studio. http://www-3.ibm.com/software/solutions/webservices/pdf/therightway.pdf, 2003/Jan/8th.

[116] IBM. WebSphere Application Server - Add-on Overview - IBM Software. http://www-3.ibm.com/software/webservers/appserv/was/, 2003/Jan/8th.

[117] IBM. WebSphere Studio Site Developer - Product Overview - IBM Software. http://www-3.ibm.com/software/ad/studiositedev/, 2003/Jan/8th.

[118] IBM. Slides to address the Session "Governmental & Public Authorities eLearning" at the E-Learning Results 2004. http://www.elearningresults.com/pdf/agenda.pdf, 2004/May/16th.

[119] S. IBM Caruso and J. Reser. Supporting open standards for Web services and the Java 2 Platform, Enterprise Edition (J2EE). ftp://ftp.software.ibm.com/software/webserver/appserv/library/g325-1971-00.pdf, 2003/Jan/8th.

[120] J. IBM Feller. IBM Web Services ToolKit 60812 characters, 6153 words, 3464 lines-A showcase for emerging web services technologies. http://www-3.ibm.com/software/solutions/webservices/wstk-info.html, 2003/Jan/8th.

[121] S. IBM Holbrook. Web Services Architecture - Technical Overview of the Pieces. ftp://ftp.software.ibm.com/software/websphere/webservices/wsa-tech-overview.pdf, 2003/Jan/8th.

[122] IEEE. About the IEEE. http://www.ieee.org/about/, 2002/May/25th.

[123] IEEE. Draft Standard for Learning Object Metadata. http://ltsc.ieee.org/doc/wg12/LOM_WD6_4.pdf, 2002/May/25th.

[124] IEEE. Draft Standard for Learning Technology - Public and Private Information (PAPI) for Learners (PAPI Learner). http://ltsc.ieee.org/wg2/papi_learner_07_main.pdf, 2002/May/25th.

[125] IEEE. IEEE 1484.11.1, Working Draft 10 - Draft Standard for Data Model for Content to Learning Management System Communication. http://ltsc.ieee.org/doc/wg11/IEEE_1484_11_1-WD10.zip, 2002/May/25th.

[126] IEEE. IEEE Learning Technology Standards Committee. http://grouper.ieee.org/LTSC/, 2002/May/25th.

[127] IEEE. IEEE LTSC Learning Objects Metadata WG Home.
http://ltsc.ieee.org/wg12/index.html, 2002/May/25th.

[128] IEEE. IEEE P1484.12 Learning Object Metadata Working Group - Scope and Purpose.
http://ltsc.ieee.org/wg12/s_p.html, 2002/May/25th.

[129] IEEE. IEEE P1484.1/D9, 2001-11-30; Draft Standard for Learning Technology-Learning Technology Systems Architecture (LTSA).
http://ltsc.ieee.org/doc/wg1/IEEE_1484_01_D09_LTSA.pdf, 2002/May/25th.

[130] IEEE. IEEE Standards Process-at-a-Glance.
http://standards.ieee.org/resources/glance.html, 2002/May/25th.

[131] IEEE. Draft Standard for Learning Object Metadata.
http://ltsc.ieee.org/doc/wg12/LOM_1484_12_1_v1_Final_Draft.pdf, 2003/Jul/28th.

[132] IEEE. IEEE P1484.17 Content Packaging Working Group.
http://grouper.ieee.org/LTSC/wg17/, 2003/Jul/28th.

[133] IEEE. IEEE LTSC Learning Objects Metadata WG Home.
http://ltsc.ieee.org/wg12/index.html, 2003/Jul/9th.

[134] IEEE. IEEE LTSC.
http://ltsc.ieee.org, 2004/May/9th.

[135] IETF. Hypertext Transfer Protocol – HTTP/1.1.
http://www.ietf.org/rfc/rfc2616.txt, 2003/Jan/4th.

[136] IMS. About IMS Global Learning Consortium, Inc.
http://www.imsglobal.org/aboutims.html, 2002/May/25th.

[137] IMS. IMS Learning Resource Meta-Data Information Model.
http://www.imsglobal.org/metadata/imsmdv1p2p1/imsmd_infov1p2p1.html, 2002/May/25th.

[138] IMS. Welcome to IMS Global Learning Consortium, Inc.
http://www.imsglobal.org/, 2002/May/25th.

[139] IMS. IMS Content Packaging Specification.
http://www.imsglobal.org/content/packaging/index.cfm, 2003/Jul/28th.

[140] IMS. IMS Resource Description Framework(RDF) Bindings.
http://www.imsglobal.org/rdf/index.cfm, 2003/Jul/28th.

[141] IMS. IMS Global Consortium Inc.
http://www.imsglobal.org, 2004/May/9th.

[142] ISO. Introduction.
http://www.iso.org/iso/en/aboutiso/introduction/whatisISO.html,
2002/May/25th.

[143] ISO. ISO - International Organization for Standardization.
http://www.iso.org/iso/en/faqs/faq-general.html, 2002/May/25th.

[144] ISO. What are Standards?
http://www.iso.org/iso/en/aboutiso/introduction/index.html, 2002/May/25th.

[145] ISO. ISO/IEC SC 34/WG 3.
http://www.isotopicmaps.org/, 2003/Jul/9th.

[146] ISO. JTC 1/SC36.
http://www.iso.ch/iso/en/stdsdevelopment/tc/tclist/TechnicalCommitteeDetailPa
ge.TechnicalCommitteeDetail?COMMID=4997, 2004/May/9th.

[147] ISO/IEC. ISO/IEC 13250 Topic Maps.
http://www.y12.doe.gov/sgml/sc34/document/0322_files/iso13250-2nd-ed-v2.pdf,
2003/Jul/9th.

[148] IST. IST program 1999, Key activity 2, Overview of the program.
http://www.cordis.lu/ist/overview.html, 2001/May/18.

[149] Thomas Jechle. *Tele-Lernen in der wissenschaftlichen Weiterbildung.* Oldenbourg,
2002.

[150] S. Junginger. *Workflowbasierte Umsetzung von Geschäftsprozessen.* Dissertation,
Wien, 2001.

[151] J. Kao. Developer's Guide to Building XML-based Web Services with the Java 2
Platform, Enterprise Edition (J2EE).
http://www2.theserverside.com/resources/article.jsp?l=WebServices-Dev-Guide,
2003/Jan/9th.

[152] R. Kaplan and D. Norton. *The Balanced Scorecard: Measures That Drive Performance.* Havard Business Review, Heft 70, Nr. 1, S. 71-79, 1992.

[153] R. S. Kaplan and D. P. Norton. *The Balanced Scorecard: Translating Strategy into Action.* Harvard Business School Press, 1996.

[154] D Karagiannis, G. Stefanidis, and R. Woitsch. The PROMOTE approach: ModellIng Knowledge Management Processes to describe organisational knowledge systems. *In proceedings of OKLC 2002 Athens,* 2002.

[155] D. Karagiannis and R. Telesko. *Wissensmanagement. Konzepte der künstlichen Intelligenz und des Softcomputing.* Oldenbourg. München Wien, 2001.

[156] Dimitris Karagiannis, Junginger, and Robert Stefan, Strobl. *Introduction to Business Process Management Systems Concepts.* Springer, Berlin, 1996.

[157] Dimitris Karagiannis, Rainer Telesko, and Robert Woitsch. *Knowledge management concepts and tools: The PROMOTE project.* Shaker Verlag, 2001.

[158] G. Karvounarakis, V. Christophides, and D. Plexousakis. Querying Semistructured (Meta) Data and Schemas on the Web: The case of RDF and RDFS. ftp://ftp.ics.forth.gr/tech-reports/2000/2000.TR269.RDF.Querying.ps.gz, 2003/Jul/14th.

[159] R. Kaschek. *Prozeßontologie als Faktor der Geschäftsprozeßmodellierung.* In: Pohl, K. and Schürr, A. and Vossen, G.; Modellierung '98 - Proceedings; Universität Münster, 1998.

[160] G. Kearsley. *Developments in Learning.* in Adelsberger, H. and Collis, B. and Pawlowski, J. M.; Handbook on Information Technologies for Education and Training; Springer, Berlin, 2002.

[161] B. Khan. A Framework for E-Learning. http://www.bookstoread.com/framework/, 2004/May/10th.

[162] M. Klein, Y. Ding, D. Fensel, and B. Omelayenko. *Ontology Management: Storing, Aligning and Maintaining Ontologies.* In: Davies, J. and Fensel, D. and van Harmelen, F.; Towards the Semantic Web - Ontology-Driven Knowledge Management; John Wiley and Sons Ltd., 2003.

[163] Müge Klein and Wolffried Stucky. *Ein Vorgehensmodell zur Erstellung virtueller Bildungsinhalte.* vieweg, Wiesbaden, 2001.

[164] Klein-Kretzschmar and Volker Jörg, Zimmermann. *Vom Wissensbedarf zum Web-based Training*. Gabler Verlag, 2001.

[165] W. Kluxen. *Thomas von Aquin: Das Seiende und seine Prinzipien*. In: Speck, J.; Grundprobleme der großen Philosophen - Philosophie des Altertums und des Mittelalters; UTB Vandenhoeck, 2nd edition, 1978.

[166] KMRG. RDF binding of LOM metadata.
http://kmr.nada.kth.se/el/ims/metadata.html, 2004/Jul/13rd.

[167] A. Kotok. Web services standards are good, but a Web services vision is better.
http://www.webservices.org/index.php/article/articleview/826/1/7/,
2003/Jan/13rd.

[168] H. Kreger. *Web Services Conceptual Architecture*. www-4.ibm.com/software/solutions/webservices/pdf/WSCA.pdf, 2003/Jul/24th.

[169] R. (Ed.) Kristöfl. Österreichische Metadatenspezifikation für elektronische Lehrma-terialien.
Mail from Bernd Simon; Metadaten WG Neue Version 1.3 des Metadaten-Modells;
June 16th, 2003, 2003/Mar/12.

[170] C. Kugler, R. Brühl, and C. Wachter. Optimierung von Ausbildungsprozessen durch den EInsatz eInes LearnIng Content Management Systems. *In: LearnIng Manage-ment; 18. Jahrgang, Februar 2003; www.IM-Fachzeitschrift.de*, 2003.

[171] H. Kühn, S. Junginger, F. Bayer, and A. Petzmann. *The E-BPMS Framework - Managing Complexity in E-Business*. In: Proceedings of the 8th European Concur-rent Engineering Conference 2001 (ECEC'2001), April 18-20, 2001, Valencia, Spain. Society of Computer Simulation, 2001.

[172] K. Kurbel. *Entwicklung und Einsatz von Expertensystemen*. Springer, Berlin, 2. Auflage, 1992.

[173] F. Lehner. *Theoriebildung in der Wirtschaftsinformatik*. In: Becker, J. and König, W. and Schütte, R. and Wendt, O. and Zelewski, S.; Wirtschaftsinformatik und Wissenschaftstheorie; Gabler, 1999.

[174] F. Leymann. Web-Services. *In: Datenbank Spektrum; Heft 6; Juni; dpunkt.verlag*, 2003.

[175] F. Leymann. Web Services Flow Language (WSFL 1.0).
http://www-3.ibm.com/software/solutions/webservices/pdf/WSFL.pdf,
2003/Jan/8th.

[176] F. Leymann and D. Roller. *Business Process Management with FlowMark*. In Proc.
39th IEEE Computer Society Int'l Conf. (CompCon), 1994.

[177] H. Lienhard. *Web Services and Workflow - a Unified Approach*. In: Fischer, L.;
Workflow Handbook 2003; Future Strategies Inc. and Book Division, Lighthouse
Point, Florida, 2003.

[178] A. Lischka. Wissensmanagement und E-Learning clever kombiniert. *Praxis Wissensmanagement*, 5(04):14, 2004.

[179] H. Lischka, J. Bajnai, D. Karagiannis, and G. Chalaris. *The Virtual Global University: The Realization of a fully Virtual University - Concept and Experiences*. In
Auer, M. E. and Auer, U. (Eds.): Proceedings of the workshop ICL, 2002.

[180] H. Lischka and D. Karagiannis. Modeling and Execution of E-Learning Resources.
In: Proceedings of the 2004 ACM Symposium on Applied Computing, ACM Press,
2004.

[181] H. Lischka and R. Woitsch. Knowledge Management and E-Learning - Integration
of both disciplines in a top-down approach. *In: Auer, M. E., Auer, U. (Eds.):
Proceedings of the workshop ICL*, 2003.

[182] J. Lischka and et al. Roadmap for Reaching Semantic E-Learning - Test Cases.
Auer, M. E., Auer, U. (Eds.): Proceedings of the workshop ICL, 2004.

[183] J. Lischka and D. Karagiannis. A generic E-Learning Engineering Framework embracing the Semantic Web. *To appear in: in Proceedings of AIMSA 2004, Springer*,
2004.

[184] C. Lutz. Description Logics.
http://dl.kr.org/, 2003/Jul/22nd.

[185] M. D. Lytras. Semantics for E-learning: An advanced Knowledge Management
oriented metadata schema for learning purposes.
http://www.aace.org/dl/search/files/paper_3009_2526.pdf, 2002/May/25th.

[186] M. D. Lytras and N. Pouloudi. Expanding e-learning effectiveness. The shift from content orientation to knowledge management utilization. http://www.aace.org/dl/search/files/EdMedia2001p1184.pdf, 2002/May/25th.

[187] D. Malks and M. Sum. Developing Web Services with ebXML and SOAP: An Overview. http://www.webservices.org/index.php/article/view/1015/, 2003/Jul/24th.

[188] G. Martin. *Sokrates: Das Allgemeine*. In: Speck, J.; Grundprobleme der großen Philosophen - Philosophie des Altertums und des Mittelalters; UTB Vandenhoeck, 2nd edition, 1978.

[189] H. Maurer and M. Sapper. E-Learning Has to be Seen as Part of General Knowledge Management. http://www.aace.org/dl/search/files/EdMedia2001p1249.pdf, 2002/Nov/09.

[190] E. Mayberry. Fail to Plan - Plan to Fail. http://www.learningcircuits.org/2004/jul2004/mayberry.htm, 2004/Jul/12th.

[191] C. McGarel. Building Enterprise-class Web Services using Messaging-oriented Middleware. http://www.webservices.org/index.php/article/view/1024/, 2003/Jul/24th.

[192] Rory McGreal. A Primer on Metadata for Learning Objects. http://www.elearningmag.com/elearning/article/articleDetail.jsp?id=2031, 2002/May/25th.

[193] Ralph McInerny. Saint Thomas Aquinas, The Stanford Encyclopedia of Philosophy, Spring 2002 Edition, Edward N. Zalta. http://plato.stanford.edu/archives/spr2002/entries/aquinas/, 2003/Jun/22nd.

[194] Microsoft. Defining the Basic Elements of .NET. http://www.microsoft.com/net/basics/whatis.asp, 2003/Jan/10th.

[195] Microsoft. New Toolkit Lets You Share Information Between Office Documents and Web Services. http://msdn.microsoft.com/webservices/building/office/default.aspx, 2003/Jan/10th.

[196] M. Minsky. *A Framework for Representing Knowledge.* In: Brachman, R. J. and Levesque, H. J.; Readings in Knowledge Representation; Morgan Kaufmann Pubilshers Inc., 1985.

[197] W. Nejdl, S. Decker, and W. Siberski. Project: edutella. http://edutella.jxta.org/, 2004/Jul/13rd.

[198] M. Nilsson. Semantic issues with the LOM RDF binding. http://kmr.nada.kth.se/el/ims/md-lom-semantics.html, 2003/Jul/30th.

[199] M. Nilsson. The Edutella P2P Network. http://kmr.nada.kth.se/papers/SemanticWeb/Edutella-chapter.pdf, 2003/Jul/30th.

[200] M. Nilsson. The semantic web: How RDF will change learning technology standards. http://www.cetis.ac.uk/content/20010927172953, 2003/Jul/30th.

[201] M. (Ed.) Nilsson. IEEE Learning Object Metadata RDF binding. http://kmr.nada.kth.se/el/ims/md-lomrdf.html, 2003/Jul/30th.

[202] OASIS.org. OASIS. http://www.oasis-open.org/, 2002/Dec/17th.

[203] OASIS.org. OASIS - Who We Are - Mission. http://www.oasis-open.org/who/, 2003/Jan/4th.

[204] New Zealand Ministry of Education. Interim Tertiary e-Learning Framework. http://www.steo.govt.nz/download/Interim%20Tertiary%20e-Learning%20Framework%20-%20web.pdf, 2004/May/10th.

[205] University of Vienna-Rectorate. Aufgabenbereiche - Rektorat der Universität Wien. http://www.univie.ac.at/rektorenteam/aufgaben.html, 2004/Jul/13rd.

[206] OIL. Welcome to the OIL-Page. http://www.ontoknowledge.org/oil/, 2003/Jul/9th.

[207] Universität Oldenburg. E-Learning Engineering. http://www-is.informatik.uni-oldenburg.de/forschung/forschung_elearning_inhalt.htm, 2003/Nov/14th.

[208] OMG. Catalog of OMG Modeling and Metadata Specifications.
http://www.omg.org/technology/documents/modeling_spec_catalog.htm,
2003/Jul/4th.

[209] OMG. OMG Unified Modeling Language Specification, Version 1.5, March 2003.
http://www.omg.org/cgi-bin/doc?formal/03-03-01, 2004/May/12th.

[210] H. Österle, C. Brenner, C. Gaßner, T. Gutzwiller, and T. Hess. *Business Engineering
- Prozeß- und Systementwicklung*. 1. verbesserte Auflage, Springer, 1996.

[211] B. Owsnicki-Klewe, K. v. Luck, and B. Nebel. *Wissensrepräsentation und Logik*.
In: Görz, G.; Einführung in die künstliche Intelligenz; Addison-Wesley; 2. Auflage,
1995.

[212] J. Park and S. Hunting. *XML Topic Maps*. Addison-Wesley Publishing Company,
2003.

[213] Jan Pawlowski and Heimo Adelsberger. *Standardisierung von Lerntechnologien*.
vieweg, Wiesbaden, 2001.

[214] J. Peppard and P. Rowland. *The essence of Business Process Re-Engineering*. Prentice Hall, 1995.

[215] J. Phelps and M. Papaefthimiou. Embedding the use of Information and Communication Technology into teaching and learning activities: An E-Learning
Framework.
http://www.rdg.ac.uk/cdotl/learning_techs/docs/elearning_framework.pdf,
2004/July/13rd.

[216] G. PiccInelli and E. Stammers. From E-Processes to E-Networks: an EService-oriented approach. *Hewlett-Packard Laboratories, Bristol*, 2001.

[217] L. Praml. *Die Integration von Wissensmanagement und E-Learning mit speziellem
Fokus auf die Skill-Ebene am Beispiel von PROMOTE® und ADVISOR®*. Thesis
approved by the University of Vienna, Vienna University Library, 2003.

[218] C. Prior. *Workflow and Process Management*. In: Fischer, L.; Workflow Handbook
2003; Future Strategies Inc. and Book Division, Lighthouse Point, Florida, 2003.

[219] Gilbert Probst. Bausteine des Wissensmanagements.
http://www.cck.uni-kl.de/wmk/papers/public/Bausteine/, 2002/May/15th.

[220] Purl.org. RDF Site Summary (RSS) 1.0.
http://www.purl.org/rss/, 2003/Jul/9th.

[221] J. Pyke. *Emerging Technologies - Where the Market is headed.* In: Fischer, L.;
Workflow Handbook 2003; Future Strategies Inc. and Book Division, Lighthouse
Point, Florida, 2003.

[222] M. R. Quillian. *Semantic Memory.* In: Minsky, M.; Semantic Information Processing; Cambridge (MA), 1968.

[223] Telesko R., Karagiannis D., and Woitsch R. Knowledge Management Concepts
and Tools: The PROMOTE Project. *In Gronau N. Wissensmanagement Systeme-
Anwendungen-Technologien, Shaker Verlag, p. 95-112, 2001.*

[224] E. Rahm and G. (Eds.) Vossen. *Web and Datenbanken - Konzepte, Architekturen
und Anwendungen.* dpunkt.verlag Heidelberg, 2003.

[225] Elaine Rich. *Artificial Intelligence.* McGraw-Hill, 1983.

[226] M. Richter. *Prinzipien der künstlichen Intelligenz.* Teubner, 2. überarbeitete Auflage, Stuttgart, 1998.

[227] Shelley Robbins. The Evolution of the Learning Content Management System.
http://www.learningcircuits.org/2002/apr2002/robbins.html, 2003/Jan/15th.

[228] Robby Robson. Metadata, Schmetadata.
http://www.elearningmag.com/elearning/article/articleDetail.jsp?id=18574,
2002/May/25th.

[229] Marc J. Rosenberg. *E-Learning: Strategies for delivering Knowledge in the Digital
Age.* McGraw-Hill, 2001.

[230] A. Rossett and K. Sheldon. *How can we use Knowledge Management.* in The ASTD
E-Learning Handbook; McGraw-Hill, USA, 2002.

[231] S. Russell and P. Norvig. *Artificial Intelligence. A modern approach.* Prentice Hall,
New Jersey, 1995.

[232] R. T. Rust and P. K. Kannan. E-Service: A new Paradigm for Business In the
Electronic Environment. *In: Communications of ACM; Volume 46, Number 6,
June; ACM press,* 2003.

[233] Saba. Saba Learning - Enterprise Edition.
http://www.saba.com/english/products/pdf/Saba_Learning_Ent.pdf,
2002/May/25th.

[234] A.-W. Scheer. *ARIS, Vom Geschäftsprozeß zum Anwendungssystem.* Springer,
Heidelberg, 1999.

[235] A.-W. Scheer. *ARIS, Modellierungsmethoden, Metamodelle, Anwendungen.*
Springer, 4th edition, 2001.

[236] A.-W. Scheer and F. Habermann. Making ERP a success. *In: Communications of
the ACM April 2000/Vol. 43, No. 4, pp. 57-61,* 2000.

[237] P. Schefe. *Informatik und Philosophie - eine Einführung.* In: Schefe, P, Hastedt, H.
and Dittrich, Y. and Keil, G;Informatik und Philosophie; BI Wissenschaftsverlag,
1993.

[238] H. Schmidt. *Philosophische Wörterbuch.* Alfred Kröner Verlag Stuttgart, 1991.

[239] W. Schneiders. *G. W. Leibniz: Das Reich der Vernunft.* In: Speck, J.; Grundprobleme der großen Philosophen - Philosophie der Neuzeit I; UTB Vandenhoeck,
1979.

[240] D. Schober. Ontologien in den Biowissenschaften.
http://www.bioinf.mdc-berlin.de/~schober/bio-ontologien.htm, 2003/Jul/4th.

[241] U. Schöning. *Logik für Informatiker.* BI Wissenschaftsverlag, 1989.

[242] Petra Schubert. *Einführung in die E-Business Begriffswelt.* Hanser, 2000.

[243] R. Schulmeister. *Lernplattformen für das virtuelle Lernen. Evaluation und Didaktik.*
Oldenbourg, 2003.

[244] Rolf Schulmeister. *Grundlagen hypermedialer Lernsysteme.* Addison-Wesley Publishing Company, 1996.

[245] Rolf Schulmeister. *Virtuelle Universität - virtuelles Lernen.* Oldenbourg Wissenschaftsverlag GmbH, 2001.

[246] R. Schütte. Subjektivitätsmanagement bei Informationsmodellen.
http://sunsite.informatik.rwth-aachen.de/Publications/CEUR-WS/Vol-
9/schuette.ps, 2003/Jul/4th.

[247] S. Seufert and D. Euler. Nachhaltigkeit von eLearning-Innovationen Ergebnisse einer Delphi-Studie. http://www.scil.ch/publications/docs/2004-01-seufert-euler-nachhaltigkeit-elearning.pdf, 2004/Jul/14th.

[248] Sabine Seufert, Back Andreas, and Martin Häusler. *E-Learning: Weiterbildung im Internet - Das Plato-Cookbook für internetbasiertes Lernen.* SmartBooks Publishing, 2001.

[249] Sabine Seufert and Peter Mayr. *Fachlexikon e-le@rning.* managerSeminare Gergard May Verlags GmbH, 2002.

[250] sgi. SGI - Services and Support: Standard Template Library Programmer's Guide. http://www.sgi.com/tech/stl/, 2003/Jan/3rd.

[251] Ruimin Shen, Peng Han, Fan Yang, Qiang Yang, and Joshua Zhexue Huang. An Open Framework for Smart and Personalized Distance Learning. *Proceedings of ICWL 2002*, pages 19–30, 2002.

[252] Allan Silverman. Plato's Middle Period Metaphysics and Epistemology, In: The Stanford Encyclopedia of Philosophy (Summer 2003 Edition), Edward N. Zalta (Ed.). http://plato.stanford.edu/archives/sum2003/entries/plato-metaphysics/, 2003/Jun/22nd.

[253] Bernd Simon. *E-Learning an Hochschulen - Gestaltungsräume und Erfolgsfaktoren von Wissensmedien.* E-Learning; Band 1; Herausgegeben von Prof. Dr. Dietrich Seibt, Köln, Prof. Dr. Freimut Bodendorf, Nürnberg, Prof. Dr. Dieter Euler, St. Gallen, und Prof. Dr. Udo Winand, Kassel, 2001.

[254] S. W. M. Siqueira, M. H. L. Baptista Braz, and R. N. Melo. E-Learning Environment Based on Framework Composition. *Proceedings of the The 3rd IEEE International Conference on Advanced Learning Technologies (ICALT03)*, 2003.

[255] Robin Smith. Aristotle's Logic, In: The Stanford Encyclopedia of Philosophy (Winter 2000 Edition), Edward N. Zalta (Ed.). http://plato.stanford.edu/archives/win2000/entries/aristotle-logic/, 2003/Jun/22nd.

[256] SonyEricsson. Sony Ericsson J2ME SDK.
http://www.ericsson.com/mobilityworld/sub/open/technologies/java/tools/j2m
e_sdk/, 2003/Aug/19th.

[257] J. F. Sowa. *Knowledge Representation. Logical, Philosophical and Computational Foundations.* Brooks/Cole. Thomson Learning, 2000.

[258] J. (Ed.) Speck. *Handbuch wissenschaftstheoretischer Begriffe.* UTB Vandenhoeck, Göttingen, 1980.

[259] Peter Sprenger. *Zur Bedeutung von web-basierten Inhalten in virtuellen Lernar-chitektiren.* Gabler Verlag, 2001.

[260] T. F. Stafford. E-Services. *In: Communications of ACM; Volume 46, Number 6, June; ACM press*, 2003.

[261] O. Stiemerling. Web-Services als Basis für evolvierbare Softwaresysteme. *In: WirtschaftsInformatik, 44. Jahrgang, Heft 5/2002*, 2002.

[262] W. Stier. *Empirische Forschungsmethoden.* Springer, 1996.

[263] S. Strahringer. *Metamodellierung als Instrument des Methodenvergleichs.* Shaker Verlag, 1996.

[264] Christian Suess. Introduction.
http://daisy.fmi.uni-passau.de/pakmas/lmml/11/doc/en/html/allgemeines.xml,
2002/May/25th.

[265] Christian Suess. The General Structure of a LMML-Document.
http://daisy.fmi.uni-passau.de/pakmas/lmml/11/doc/en/html/aufbau.xml,
2002/May/25th.

[266] Sun. *eLearning operability standards.* White Paper - Sun Microsystems, Inc., 2002.

[267] Sun. Sun Enterprise Learning Platform.
http://suned.sun.com/US/images/ELP_Data_SheetFinal.pdf, 2002/May/25th.

[268] Sun. J2ME Web Services.
http://developer.java.sun.com/developer/community/chat/JavaLive/2003/jl0325.h
tml, 2003/Aug/19th.

[269] Sun. Java 2 Platform, Micro Edition (J2ME).
http://java.sun.com/j2me/, 2003/Aug/19th.

[270] Sun. JSR-000172 J2METM Web Services Specification.
http://jcp.org/aboutJava/communityprocess/review/jsr172/index.html,
2003/Aug/19th.

[271] Sun. JavaTM Technology and Web Services.
http://java.sun.com/webservices/, 2003/Jan/10th.

[272] Sun. Suntm ONE Overview DART Model.
http://wwws.sun.com/software/sunone/overview/dart/index.html,
2003/Jan/10th.

[273] Sun. E-Learning Framework - Technical Whitepaper.
http://www.sun.com/products-n-solutions/edu/whitepapers/pdf/framework.pdf,
2004/July/10th.

[274] Y. Sure and R. Studer. *A Methodology for Ontology-based Knowledge Management.*
In: Davies, J. and Fensel, D. and van Harmelen, F.; Towards the Semantic Web -
Ontology-Driven Knowledge Management; John Wiley and Sons Ltd., 2003.

[275] A. Swartz. RDF Site Summary (RSS) 1.0.
http://web.resource.org/rss/1.0/, 2004/Jul/13rd.

[276] C. Swertz. Web-Didaktik.
http://www.lerndorf.uni-bielefeld.de/cswertz/vortraege/webdidaktik_wien/index.h
tml, 2004/Jul/13rd.

[277] S. L. Tanimoto. *KI: Die Grundlagen.* Oldenbourg. München Wien, 1990.

[278] ebXML Business Process Project Team. ebXML Business Process Specification
Schema Version 1.01.
http://www.ebxml.org/specs/ebBPSS.pdf, 2003/Jan/7th.

[279] ebXML Registry Project Team. Using UDDI to Find ebXML Reg/Reps.
http://www.ebxml.org/specs/rrUDDI.pdf, 2003/Jan/7th.

[280] SHOE team. SHOE.
http://www.cs.umd.edu/projects/plus/SHOE/, 2003/Jul/4th.

[281] E. Tegtmeier. *Einleitung.* In: Tegtmeier, E.; Ontologie; Alber-Texte Philosophie,
2000.

[282] P. Timmers. *Electronic Commerce.* John Wiley and Sons Ltd., 1999.

[283] B. Tuohy. Creating a Knowledge Society (Keynote address held at E-Learning Results 2004).
http://www.elearningresults.com/ppt/OPENING%20PLENARY/Brendan%20Tuo hy/Presentation%20to%20eLearning%20Results%20Conference%20(BT)%20v6.ppt, 2004/May/24th.

[284] M. Turner, D. Budgen, and P. Brereton. Turning Software Into a Service. *IEEE Computer.org, October 2003 (Vol. 36, No. 10)*, 2003.

[285] UDDI.org. UDDI.org.
http://www.uddi.org, 2002/Nov/3rd.

[286] UDDI.org. UDDI.org.
http://www.uddi.org/about.html, 2003/Jan/3rd.

[287] UDDI.org. UDDI Version 3 Features List.
http://www.uddi.org/pubs/uddi_v3_features.htm, 2003/Jan/4th.

[288] UDDI.org. UDDI Version 3.0 - Published Specification, 19 July 2002.
http://uddi.org/pubs/uddi-v3.00-published-20020719.pdf, 2003/Jan/4th.

[289] UDDI.org. UDDI.org.
http://www.uddi.org/about.html, 2003/Jan/4th.

[290] S. Vinoski. Web services and dynamic discovery.
http://www.webservices.org/index.php/article/articleview/66/, 2003/Jan/4th.

[291] E. Vollrath. *Aristoteles: Das Problem der Substanz*. In: Speck, J.; Grundprobleme der großen Philosophen - Philosophie des Altertums und des Mittelalters; UTB Vandenhoeck, 2nd edition, 1978.

[292] W3C. Web Services Architecture.
http://www.w3.org/TR/2002/WD-ws-arch-20021114/#whatisws, 2002/Dec/17th.

[293] W3C. Web Services Architecture.
http://www.w3.org/TR/2002/WD-ws-arch-20021114/#stacks, 2002/Dec/24th.

[294] W3C. About the World Wide Web Consortium (W3C).
http://www.w3.org/Consortium/, 2002/May/25th.

[295] W3C. Metadata Activity Statement.
http://www.w3.org/Metadata/Activity.html, 2002/May/25th.

[296] W3C. Semantic Web.
http://www.w3.org/2001/sw/, 2002/Nov/3rd.

[297] W3C. OwlAndRdf.
http://esw.w3.org/topic/OwlAndRdf, 2003/Aug/19th.

[298] W3C. RDF Query and Rules: A Framework and Survey.
http://www.w3.org/2001/11/13-RDF-Query-Rules/, 2003/Aug/19th.

[299] W3C. RDF Validation Service.
http://www.w3.org/RDF/Validator/, 2003/Aug/19th.

[300] W3C. RDF/XML Syntax Specification (Revised).
http://www.w3.org/TR/rdf-syntax-grammar/, 2003/Aug/19th.

[301] W3C. Recording Query Results.
http://www.w3.org/2003/03/rdfqr-tests/recording-query-results.html,
2003/Aug/19th.

[302] W3C. Web Services Description Language (WSDL) Version 1.2.
http://www.w3.org/TR/wsdl12/, 2003/Jan/4th.

[303] W3C. Web Naming and Addressing Overview (URIs, URLs, ...).
http://www.w3.org/Addressing/, 2003/Jul/30th.

[304] W3C. Extensible Markup Language (XML).
http://www.w3.org/XML/, 2003/Jul/4th.

[305] W3C. OWL Web Ontology Language - Overview.
http://www.w3.org/TR/owl-features/, 2003/Jul/4th.

[306] W3C. Representing vCard Objects in RDF/XML.
http://www.w3.org/TR/vcard-rdf, 2003/Jul/4th.

[307] W3C. Resource Description Framework (RDF) Model and Syntax Specification.
http://www.w3.org/TR/1999/REC-rdf-syntax-19990222/, 2003/Jul/4th.

[308] W3C. W3C Semantic Web Activity.
http://www.w3.org/2001/12/semweb-fin/w3csw, 2003/Jul/4th.

[309] W3C. Web Services Architecture.
http://www.w3.org/TR/2002/WD-ws-arch-20021114/#whatisws, 2003/Jul/4th.

[310] W3C. DAML+OIL (March 2001) Reference Description.
http://www.w3.org/TR/daml+oil-reference, 2003/Jul/9th.

[311] W3C. OWL Web Ontology Language Overview.
http://www.w3.org/TR/owl-features/, 2003/Jul/9th.

[312] W3C. Resource Description Framework (RDF) Schema Specification 1.0.
http://www.w3.org/TR/2000/CR-rdf-schema-20000327/, 2003/Jul/9th.

[313] W3C. Web-Ontology (WebOnt) Working Group.
http://www.w3.org/2001/sw/WebOnt/, 2003/Jul/9th.

[314] W. Wahlster. Semantisches Web und Wissensmanagement. *Universität des Saar-landes, FR 6.2 Informatik, Vorlesung WS 2001/2002*, 2001.

[315] E. E. Watson and H. Schneider. Using ERP systems In education. *In: Communi-cations of AIS Volume 1, Article 9*, 1999.

[316] R. Weber. *Ontological Foundations of Information Systems*. Coopers and Lybrand, 1997.

[317] WebServices.org. WebServices.Org - The Web Services Community Portal - Why Web Services?
http://www.webservices.org/index.php/article/articleview/75/1/61/, 2002/Dec/17th.

[318] WebServices.org. WebServices.Org - The Web Services Community Portal - Stan-dards.
http://www.webservices.org/index.php/article/archive/3/, 2002/Dec/24th.

[319] WebServices.org. WebServices.org.
http://www.webservices.org/, 2002/Nov/3rd.

[320] WebServices.org. WebServices.org.
http://www.webservices.org/, 2003/Jul/4th.

[321] S. A. White. *XPDL and BPMN*. In: Fischer, L.; Workflow Handbook 2003; Future Strategies Inc. and Book Division, Lighthouse Point, Florida, 2003.

[322] R. Widhalm and T. Mück. *Topic Maps*. Springer, 2002.

[323] J. Wielemaker, G. Schreiber, and B. Wielinga. Prolog-based Infrastructure for RDF: Scalability and Performance.
http://www.swi.psy.uva.nl/projects/SWI-Prolog//articles/iswc-03.pdf, 2003/Jul/9th.

[324] D. A Wiley. Connecting learning objects to instructional design theory: A definition, a metaphor, and a taxonomy.
In D. A. Wiley (Ed.), The Instructional Use of Learning Objects: Online Version; http://reusability.org/read/chapters/wiley.doc, 2003/Jan/13rd.

[325] J. Williams. The Web-Services debate. *In: Communications of ACM; Volume 46, Number 6, June; ACM press*, 2003.

[326] Katrin Winkler and Heinz Mandl. *Knowledge Master: Wissensmanagement-Weiterbildung mit WBT*. Oldenbourg, 2002.

[327] P. H. Winston. *Künstliche Intelligenz*. Addison-Wesley Publishing Company, 1987.

[328] D. Woelk. e-Learning, Semantic Web Services and Competency Ontologies.
http://www.elasticknowledge.com/SemanticWebandOntologies.pdf, 2002/Nov/3rd.

[329] WSI. WS-I Overview.
http://www.ws-i.org/docs/20030115.wsi.introduction.pdf, 2003/Jul/28th.

[330] XTM. XML Topic Maps (XTM) 1.0.
http://www.topicmaps.org/xtm/index.html, 2003/Jul/9th.

[331] XTM. XML Topic Maps (XTM) Processing Model 1.0.
http://www.topicmaps.org/xtm/1.0/xtmp1.html, 2003/Jul/9th.

[332] J. A. Zachmann. A framework for information systems architecture. *IBM Systems Journal*, 26(3):276–293, 1987.

[333] D. Zschocke. *Modellbildung in der Ökonomie*. Verlag Franz Vahlen, München, 1995.

www.ingramcontent.com/pod-product-compliance
Lightning Source LLC
LaVergne TN
LVHW022303060326
832902LV00020B/3240